"Professor Terri Watson's new book, *Developing Clinicians of Character: A Christian Integrative Approach to Clinical Supervision*, is a delight and just what the doctor ordered! It is well written and researched, very engaging and practical, and highlights the critically important and mostly neglected topic of character and ethical formation among clinical supervisors in mental health fields from a uniquely Christian perspective. Certainly this is a must read for any clinical supervisor who embraces the Christian tradition, but it likely would be of interest and value to those of other faith traditions as well. This is a winner for sure and will surely help generations of supervisors and trainees alike."

Thomas G. Plante, clinical adjunct professor in psychiatry at Stanford University, director of the Spirituality and Health Institute at Santa Clara University

"This fantastic new textbook on supervision is a huge, transforming step forward in supervisory practice. Going beyond core competencies in counseling, care for the client, and conscientious monitoring of counseling, Terri Watson adds character formation to the supervision mix. The result is a thoughtful, scholarly, creative, innovative, practical, and completely Christian integrative model of virtues in counseling. If you supervise or teach psychotherapy or MFT, read this book and catch the transformation of the field."

Everett L. Worthington Jr., coauthor of *Couple Therapy: A New Hope-Focused Approach*

"There is now a wealth of research showing that psychotherapy is generally very effective, but now we need to understand how to develop mature, virtuous therapists who relate well, care about justice and diversity, and embody transformative forms of hope and courage over the long haul. In *Developing Clinicians of Character*, Dr. Terri Watson offers us an integrative and holistic model of clinical supervision that charts pathways toward this goal. She has worked for many years providing training and studying the processes of trainee character formation to generate the approach described in this book. Those of us in clinical practice and clinical training know the core challenge involves developing the character necessary for the deep exposure to suffering that accumulates over a clinical career, and Watson is our wisest integrative voice on this topic for Christian training communities."

Steven J. Sandage, Boston University

"This scholarly book goes far beyond the mere teaching of theory, research, and practice of supervision and training by focusing on Christian virtue and character as essential elements in the development and formation of professional clinicians. Teaching supervision in the school of psychology graduate school at Fuller for years, this text would have been extremely useful to me for the rich content, organization and thoroughness of the material, practical application, helpful charts, supervision forms, and contracts. I endorse and highly recommend this book as a groundbreaking Christian integrative approach to supervision."

Judith Balswick, senior professor at Fuller Theological Seminary, school of psychology

"Brilliant! Every clinical supervisor needs this treasure-trove of information. Terri Watson has given all of us an incredible gift with this immensely practical book."

Les Parrott, founder of the SYMBIS Assessment

"Terri Watson's *Developing Clinicians of Character* is a well written and substantial work on a Christian integrative approach to clinical supervision. It comprehensively and clearly covers faith, hope, love, practical wisdom, justice, temperance, courage, and personal and spiritual formation in counseling, psychology, and MFT education. I highly recommend it as essential reading in Christian clinical supervision."

Siang-Yang Tan, professor of psychology at Fuller Theological Seminary, and author of *Counseling and Psychotherapy: A Christian Perspective*

"I've read a lot of books on clinical supervision and this one is unique, original, practical, accessible, and even encouraging—which I've never found in a book on supervision. It integrates a valuable overview of psychological theories, research-based outcomes, and clinical practice in the context of a solid biblical, theological and spiritually formative foundation. It's clinically relevant, intellectually rigorous, and spiritually engaging. The suggestions for specific spiritual practices for the formation of virtues add significant value to this unique resource. This is a book that you will learn and grow from both personally and professionally, and I guarantee that it's one that you'll read more than once."

Gary J. Oliver, clinical psychologist, professor of psychology and practical theology at John Brown University

"Dr. Terri Watson's *Developing Clinicians of Character* will be used in my doctoral level supervision classes. Supervision is to provide clarity for clinicians who work in the obscured environs of intense human suffering. Her contribution to this process is to advocate for the integrity found in Christian virtue as a vital aspect of the process. I am grateful for this valuable resource to prepare effective supervisors."

James N. Sells, assistant dean of psychology and counseling, Regent University

"*Developing Clinicians of Character* is an essential read for both practitioners and students who approach their clinical work from a core foundation of integrative practice. Dr. Watson draws from a theological framework and her extensive experience as a clinician, educator, and clinical supervisor to illustrate a thoughtful and intentionally collaborative structure for supervision. She highlights the necessity of moving beyond the basic application of theory and method to include character, values, and virtue development for the emerging therapist. Dr. Watson provides practical insight for addressing transformative growth in both the supervisee and supervisor through intentional commitment to spiritual discipline, reflective and contemplative practice, social justice advocacy, and what she terms, 'clinical humility,' the cornerstone for competent clinical practice. This text is a vital resource for any professional in the field who plays an influential role in the development of next generation therapists."

Deborah Gorton, clinical mental health counseling at Moody Theological Seminary

DEVELOPING CLINICIANS OF CHARACTER

A CHRISTIAN
INTEGRATIVE
APPROACH
TO CLINICAL
SUPERVISION

TERRI S. WATSON

IVP Academic

An imprint of InterVarsity Press
Downers Grove, Illinois

InterVarsity Press
P.O. Box 1400, Downers Grove, IL 60515-1426
ivpress.com
email@ivpress.com

InterVarsity Press® is the book-publishing division of InterVarsity Christian Fellowship/USA®, a movement of students and faculty active on campus at hundreds of universities, colleges, and schools of nursing in the United States of America, and a member movement of the International Fellowship of Evangelical Students. For information about local and regional activities, visit intervarsity.org.

All Scripture quotations, unless otherwise indicated, are taken from The Holy Bible, New International Version®, NIV®. Copyright © 1973, 1978, 1984, 2011 by Biblica, Inc.™ Used by permission of Zondervan. All rights reserved worldwide. www.zondervan.com The "NIV" and "New International Version" are trademarks registered in the United States Patent and Trademark Office by Biblica, Inc.™

While any stories in this book are true, some names and identifying information may have been changed to protect the privacy of individuals.

Cover design: David Fassett
Interior design: Daniel van Loon
Images: willow branch: © Guasor / iStock / Getty Images Plus
  pattern of dots and lines: © liuzishan / iStock / Getty Images Plus

ISBN 978-0-8308-2863-0 (print)
ISBN 978-0-8308-8528-2 (digital)

Printed in the United States of America ♾

InterVarsity Press is committed to ecological stewardship and to the conservation of natural resources in all our operations. This book was printed using sustainably sourced paper.

Library of Congress Cataloging-in-Publication Data

A catalog record for this book is available from the Library of Congress.

P 30 29 28 27 26 25 24 23 22 21 20 19 18 17 16 15 14 13 12 11 10 9 8 7 6 5 4 3 2 1

Y 44 43 42 41 40 39 38 37 36 35 34 33 32 31 30 29 28 27 26 25 24 23 22 21 20 19 18

To Bob, Alec, and Elise—my faithful, hopeful, and loving family.

And to the wonderful students and supervisees I have had

the joy to know—you are the inspiration for this book.

CONTENTS

PREFACE

WHAT ARE THE qualities, characteristics, and competencies of effective clinical supervisors? This question has been a driving force in my professional journey over the past thirty-five years as a clinician, educator, supervisor, and consultant. The quest to become an effective supervisor has led me through the professional credentialing process of three distinct mental health disciplines, and I have valued the opportunity to discover the unique contributions of counseling, psychology, and marriage and family therapy (MFT) to the supervision process. During a recent sabbatical, I had the opportunity to dig deep into the clinical supervision scholarship on counseling, psychology, and MFT and was encouraged by the growing depth, breadth, and diversity of the theory and research. However, it seemed evident to me that something was missing regarding the important role of clinical supervisors in the formation of personal and professional character. This led me through the interdisciplinary literature on virtue ethics and character development in theology, philosophy, psychology, and spiritual formation. I believe that there are riches in this literature that the supervision enterprise has yet to mine, and the current project is the integrative outcome of this endeavor.

The longer I supervise, the more I recognize the incredibly important role supervisors play in the formation of personal and professional habits and spiritual practices that set a trajectory for the professional lives of our supervisees. While God is ultimately responsible for the formation of their souls, we as teachers and mentors carry a great responsibility to be thoughtful about how we are influencing the character formation of our supervisees. This book offers a virtue-oriented framework for clinical supervision from a distinctively Christian perspective that aims to develop clinicians of character in maturity and Christlikeness for service to God's kingdom. Grounded in contemporary clinical supervision theory and research, and guided by best practices, this framework offers both aspirational professional goals and practical supervision interventions for the provision of competent and effective clinical supervision.

OVERVIEW

The current text provides an overview of clinical supervision models, methods, best practices, and credentialing processes in counseling, psychology, and MFT within a virtue framework. It is intended for students, supervisees, supervisors in training, educators, and experienced supervisors who want to reevaluate their models and methods. As a Christian framework, it can be incorporated into any existing model of supervision that is being utilized. Ideally, students, educators, supervisors, and supervisees will read this book together to provide a common language and shared practices for developing the character strengths necessary for long-term professional flourishing.

Chapter one provides an overview of clinical supervision models, methods, and credentialing in counseling, psychology, and MFT and then explores the literature on spiritual and religious issues in supervision. An introduction to the interdisciplinary study of character virtue is provided and linked to our contemporary ethical codes, and the merits of a virtue-oriented approach to supervision are explored. Chapter two provides an overview of a Christian integrative framework for clinical supervision with specific principles and guidelines for application. Chapters three through nine introduce the core virtues through reviewing theological and psychological perspectives, relevant supervision models and interventions, and spiritual formation practices. Chapter ten considers the optimal qualities of institutions and educational settings for facilitating character development. Considering clinical supervision as an advanced form of discipleship is offered as a concluding challenge for future exploration.

While the theoretical and empirical foundations for a Christian integrative framework for clinical supervision are described in some detail, it is also my intention to provide an immanently practical resource for supervision through an emphasis on interventions, techniques, and practices. My hope is that this practical focus sparks experiential learning opportunities that reinvigorate the practice of clinical supervision in educational and clinical contexts.

ACKNOWLEDGMENTS

I am exceedingly grateful to have been a part of the professional development of clinicians in training through teaching and clinical supervision. It is to my students and supervisees that I owe a debt of gratitude for what I have learned about clinical supervision.

To the family, friends, colleagues, and students who have made this book possible by their support and by embodying Christian virtue in their life and vocation—thank you. To my family I owe the deepest gratitude: my husband Bob for his enduring love and patience, my daughter Elise for her practical wisdom evidenced in exceedingly competent research assistance, and my son Alec, who is an inspiration in creative courage. This project would not have been possible without the generous support of Wheaton College, who granted a sabbatical from my administration and teaching duties during the fall of 2015, and the Wheaton Alumni Association, who funded two months of study in Cambridge, UK, at Tyndale House Library. I am grateful to the community of scholars at Tyndale who welcomed a psychologist into their midst who was seeking a deeper understanding of Christian virtue ethics and moral theology. To my current and past mentors and colleagues at Wheaton who image Christ in such vibrant ways, I owe a debt of gratitude for your formative impact on my life and work, particularly Fran White, Stan Jones, Rich Butman, Marjory Mead, Dot Chappell, Cynthia Neal Kimball, Barret McRay, Michael Mangis, Sally Schwer Canning, Darlene Hannah, Derek McNeil, Jamie Aten, and Ted Kahn. To the PsyD students in my spring 2017 Supervision class, thank for your feedback on the initial draft of this book; future students who read this book will thank you for your input and edits that made this text so much more readable. The external reviewers of the text provided excellent suggestions, and I am appreciative of their thoughtful review. Finally, to my writing accountability partner, the Reverend Claudia Nalven: this project would not have been completed without your faithful friendship, wise guidance, and unwavering support over countless breakfasts at Egg Harbor.

AN IMPORTANT DISCLAIMER

This project can be understood as a deep desire for my own character to be transformed toward a more virtuous personal and professional life, and not from any illusion that I have mastered the virtues (as my family, colleagues, and supervisees can well attest!). The adage "We teach best what we need to learn most" is certainly true in my case as I write about character strengths, because the literature contains the wisdom and practices that I most need to learn. This humbling truth was brought home to me over and over again in the writing of the book in both large and small ways (for example, the moment of profound irony when I realized that I had eaten my way through a large bag of peanut M&M's as I was working on the temperance chapter). One of the greatest challenges of my personal and professional life continues to be the formation of my own soul and character, and I am grateful for all that I learned toward this end in the writing of this book. While God is a gentle and persistent teacher, I am slow to learn and often come back to the same character flaws over and over again. I trust that past, present, and future supervisees will forgive me for the large and small ways I fail to live up to the aspirations in this book.

CHAPTER 1

CONTEMPORARY CLINICAL SUPERVISION

An Overview

THIS BOOK GROWS OUT of a professional journey of over thirty years as a clinical supervisor that has left me with a lingering question, and perhaps an existential crisis. The quest to become an effective supervisor has been a joyful and meaningful journey, and I remain passionate about the practice of clinical supervision. My sweet spot as a clinician is that place where psychological theory and clinical practice meet, and where as a person of Christian faith I can integrate theological understandings and spiritual practices into the work of therapy. I especially enjoy the moments in clinical supervision when theory comes alive for supervisees and we discern just the right intervention to facilitate growth and healing for a hurting family. Also deeply satisfying are those Spirit-led moments in group supervision (for example, where we veer from the agenda and practice a meditative prayer together that leads to a much-needed experience of connection with God, each other, and our deepest selves). I am convinced that the most important responsibility in the career of a mental health professional is the joy and honor of mentoring clinicians in training through this intensive, interpersonally mediated process we call supervision.

Over the years, however, a lingering question has remained. At the end of each academic year when these individual and group supervision experiences are drawing to a close, I have a moment of existential crisis and doubt. I find myself asking: "Was it enough? Did I do the best job of utilizing those valuable hours of clinical supervision to prepare supervisees for the challenges of life as a mental health professional? Have I done everything in my power to help them become their best professional selves?" I am fairly confident that students are prepared to be competent and ethical clinicians who will serve their clients well, so in that sense supervision has been successful in meeting its educational outcome. However, I fear that as a supervisor I have not adequately prepared my supervisees to navigate the inevitable challenges of mental health work such as vicarious trauma, moral and ethical failure, staying committed to lifelong learning in an ever-changing field, and remaining hopeful and compassionate when dealing with human suffering day after day. Have I done my best to encourage long-term faithfulness to God and meaningful service to Christ's kingdom as mental health professionals? I am afraid the conclusion for me is often "I have not done enough—there has to be more!" I am left with the lingering question: *Is there more to clinical supervision than our current theories and methods can provide?*

While it may be inescapable that each supervision experience feels somewhat incomplete, I do think that we often fail to help our students develop the personal and professional character and habits that will lead to long-term flourishing. We miss out on key moments in supervision because we do not know where we are going. We have lost a vision for the role of clinical supervision in forming professional character that will lead to long-term competence and effectiveness. Because our goals and aspirations for supervision are too low, I fear we are sending our students out into the professional world without the most essential tools and lessons they need for survival. We are not making the most of supervision as an opportunity for personal, professional, and spiritual formation.

Clinical supervision is inevitably formative. Students learn lessons from supervisors about thinking, living, and working as a mental health professional during the most influential stages of development. They are looking to supervisors to model how to live a vibrant and effective professional life. Our work has a long-term impact as students will internalize both our strengths and weaknesses.

If you are a supervisor or educator reading this book, take a moment to think about the clinical supervisors who have been formative in your own professional life, your professional "family of origin," if you will. No doubt you have carried your relational experience and their words of advice, challenge, and support with you throughout your own professional journey. Their influence has contributed to the formation of your professional character and fostered the development of your habits, practices, and values. Likely, you can remember pivotal moments when the supervision experience had a deep impact on your emerging sense of personal and professional identity. Reflecting on our own supervision experience can help us be purposeful about the type of supervisor we want to become, or we run the risk of simply supervising the way we were supervised and passing along the good with the bad experiences. Many of us may have been thrust into the role of clinical supervisor before we felt we were adequately prepared and with very little in the way of supervision education and experience. My hope is that this book provides an opportunity for you to consider and enhance your supervision philosophy and practices.

If you are reading this book as a student or supervisee, you are most likely experiencing the joys and challenges of clinical supervision right now. As one of the most important training experiences of your graduate experience, you may have already experienced meaningful and formative moments in supervision where you felt affirmed in your choice of profession, as well as discouraging moments where you wondered if you had made a mistake in pursuing a mental health degree. I would encourage you to use this book to reflect on your supervision experience with the hope that it may inform the kind of supervisor you will become.

Clinical supervision is the capstone educational experience for mental health professionals and has become a discipline in its own right with a growing body of research, theory, and innovative methods. However, our current models fall short of providing trainees with the formative experiences they need to prepare them to face the personal and professional challenges for long-term flourishing in mental health practice. I propose that clinical supervision at its best can be understood as an educational experience that forms the character of supervisees to help them withstand the challenges of contemporary clinical practice. By integrating the interdisciplinary literature on virtue and character strengths with clinical supervision methods and spiritual formation practices, a Christian integrative approach to clinical supervision aims to develop clinicians of faith, hope, and love who serve Christ's kingdom with wisdom, justice, temperance, and courage.

The interdisciplinary study of virtue and character formation is a virtually untapped resource for the development of clinicians through the clinical supervision process. Recent advances in positive psychology have highlighted human character strengths as an important area of empirical research, and the contribution of virtue to personal and professional flourishing has been well supported. Integrating the contemporary study of virtue in psychology with foundational theological and biblical teaching on character formation provides a rich soil from which a Christian framework for supervision can be developed.

Specifically, this book will integrate scholarship from the best of contemporary supervision literature with the interdisciplinary scholarship on virtue—including theological, philosophical, and psychological perspectives—to provide a Christian integrative framework to guide the practice of clinical supervision. Chapter one provides an introduction to clinical supervision in counseling, psychology, and marriage and family therapy (MFT) and offers a rationale for a virtue-oriented approach to clinical supervision. Chapter two introduces

a Christian integrative supervision framework through describing four integrated areas: core virtues, ethical principles, supervision models and methods, and spiritual formation practices. Chapters three through nine will each focus on a core character virtue and corresponding professional ethical aspiration and will provide character-forming supervision methods and spiritual disciplines. Finally, chapter ten will examine the characteristics and practices of institutions and training programs that effectively facilitate the character development of clinicians in training.

A core premise of the proposed framework is that supervision at its best is an integrative endeavor on many levels. Effective supervision integrates wisdom and best practices across the mental health disciplines from diverse models and methods of supervision. Holistic supervision integrates theory and research with experiential learning and self-reflection to promote formative experiences for the heart, mind, and soul of the supervisee. A Christian integrative approach considers clinical supervision from a Christian worldview and incorporates biblical teaching and spiritual practices into the supervision process.

We begin in this first chapter by examining the three distinct but related bodies of literature that provide the foundation for a Christian framework for clinical supervision. First, we review the contemporary theory and practice of clinical supervision in counseling, psychology, and marriage and family therapy. Second, we look at the literature on religious and spiritual issues in clinical supervision. Third, we explore the interdisciplinary study of virtue ethics to identify philosophical, psychological, and theological resources that will guide the character-formative aspect of clinical supervision.

OVERVIEW OF CLINICAL SUPERVISION BY DISCIPLINE: COMMONALITIES AND DISTINCT CONTRIBUTIONS

Clinical supervision is at the heart of the development, education, and training of mental health professionals. Across countries, disciplines, and contexts, clinical supervision facilitates the application of theory to practice, teaches ethical decision making, and protects the public by ensuring the continuity of professional values, standards, and best practices. According to experts, clinical supervision is described as the "signature pedagogy" (Bernard & Goodyear, 2014, p. 2) and the "cornerstone in education and training" (Falender & Shafranske, 2004, p. 3) for mental health professionals. It is a significant component of all clinically oriented graduate programs in mental health as most graduate students in counseling, psychology, and marriage and family therapy (MFT) will spend at least 100 hours per year in individual or group clinical supervision. It is highly likely that all mental health professionals will assume the role of clinical supervisor at some point during their careers. Ideally, mental health professionals will continue to be both consumers and providers of clinical supervision throughout their lives. Tremendous resources are devoted to clinical supervision in graduate education, during post-graduation toward professional licensure, and throughout the career of a mental health professional. Clinical supervision has become a respected discipline with a growing body of literature, theoretical models, and research support.

Clinical supervision is the intensive interpersonal and educational process that facilitates the application of knowledge learned in the classroom to competent intervention in the real lives of suffering individuals, couples, families, and communities. It aims to form trainees into mental health professionals who demonstrate lifelong competence, effectiveness, ethical integrity, and professional vibrancy through facilitating effective and healthy professional habits of thinking, decision making, and action. This is no small task, indeed!

A recent survey of the international literature on clinical supervision concluded that clinical supervision is "truly international and interdisciplinary" with important research and theory development occurring across the globe and across mental health disciplines (Inman et al., 2014, p. 87). Most professionals would agree that approaches to clinical supervision are more alike than different. For example, two of the most popular clinical supervision textbooks are widely used by both counselors and psychologists (Falender & Shafranske, 2004; Bernard & Goodyear, 2014). However, each mental health discipline also relies on its own models, methods, ethical guidelines, and credentialing processes. There is tremendous benefit to utilizing supervision theory and practices across mental health disciplines, as each makes a unique contribution to the best practice of clinical supervision. This section reviews the contemporary landscape of clinical supervision in counseling, psychology, and MFT and suggests the unique contributions of each discipline to the theory and practice of supervision. Building on contemporary theory and practice of supervision across disciplines, we begin to consider the question "What is missing?"

Supervision in Professional Counseling and Counselor Education

Definition and goals. Bernard and Goodyear (2014) offer a definition of supervision applicable to counselors and psychologists: "an intervention provided by a more senior member of a profession to a more junior colleague or colleagues who typically (but not always) are members of that same profession" (p. 9). The purposes of supervision are threefold: professional development of the supervisee toward competency, monitoring the quality of services provided by the supervisee to protect the welfare of the clients, and finally, gatekeeping for the profession. Professional competency includes the development of three kinds of knowledge: theoretical and research knowledge, principles and techniques of practices, and finally, supervisee self-knowledge. Supervision is the process where these various types of knowledge are integrated and applied. As articulated by Borders et al. (2014), "supervision is a *proactive, planned, purposeful, goal-oriented, and intentional* activity" (p. 157).

Models and methods. The counseling supervision literature emphasizes a number of models of supervision. *Developmental* models of supervision (Stoltenberg, McNeill, & Delworth, 1998; Stoltenberg & McNeill, 2010) consider developmental needs and training level of supervisees and then match supervisor goals and tasks with each level. For example, a beginning supervisee will likely need a more supportive, structured supervision approach focusing on skill development, while a more experienced trainee will benefit from a supervision style that facilitates autonomy and self-awareness and encourages exploration and experimentation. *Psychotherapy* models of supervision utilize the theory and techniques from a particular theoretical orientation to facilitate the didactic and experiential learning of the model and the application to clinical work. For example, a systemically minded supervisor teaches relationally oriented change

strategies to supervisees for the benefit of clients and implements these strategies in the supervision relationship by focusing on isomorphic processes. *Process-oriented* models of supervision focus on the goals, dynamics, and relational processes of the supervision experience. One widely used process model is Bernard's Discrimination Model (1997), which proposes that the supervision process involves supervisor activities around three areas of focus (intervention, conceptualization, personalization) and three roles (teacher, counselor, consultant) for any given supervision session, with the goal of balancing time and attention to each. *Integrative* approaches to supervision are contemporary models of supervision that include a combination of developmental, psychotherapy, and process models (Bernard & Goodyear, 2014). For example, the *common factors* approach to supervision uses psychotherapy outcome research to identify the therapist (and supervisor) qualities that are most effective in establishing rapport and promoting change (Hill, 2014b).

Methods of delivery in counseling supervision include individual and group sessions utilizing self-report, review of video or audiotape recordings, process notes, and live observation to assess clinical material. Triadic supervision, where one supervisor meets with two supervisees who share the supervision time, has become an increasingly popular approach over the past fifteen years as it provides the benefits of an individual focus with the opportunity to observe and learn from a peer's experience in supervision. Best practices in counseling supervision require supervisors to provide informed consent, clear goals and expectations, and evaluation procedures through use of a professional disclosure statement and supervision contract (Association for Counselor Education and

Supervision [ACES], 2011). In addition, supervisors need to maintain documentation and record keeping for supervision, provide regular feedback in verbal and written formats, and introduce diversity issues and culturally competent interventions (ACES, 2011).

Credentials and standards. The profession of counseling has a well-developed and systematic approach to training supervisors at the doctoral level. In fact, most PhD programs in Counselor Education and Supervision emphasize coursework and practicum experiences toward the development of supervision, teaching, consultation, and research skills. Masters-level students receive some exposure to clinical supervision theory as part of the curriculum of programs accredited by the Council for Accreditation of Counseling & Related Educational Programs (CACREP), and some states require continuing education in supervision as a requirement for renewal of professional counselor licensure. The Center for Credentialing and Education (CCE) has established credentials for the Approved Clinical Supervisor (ACS) designation, which includes a five-year minimum of clinical experience, 100 hours of experience in clinical supervision (supervised), 45 hours of graduate coursework in clinical supervision, and 20 hours of continuing education in clinical supervision every five years (CCE, 2015). The American Counseling Association (ACA) also has a professional division dedicated to clinical supervision, designated the Association for Counselor Education and Supervision (ACES). ACES provides excellent professional resources for clinical supervisors including best practice supervision guidelines (ACES, 2011), a quarterly journal, biannual conferences, and online resources for members (acesonline.net).

Distinctive contributions. The counseling profession provides exceptional education, training, and ongoing support for clinical supervisors. The PhD model focuses on the preparation of educators and supervisors, that is, counselor educators. Additionally, one of the unique and important contributions of the counseling supervision literature has been the emphasis on developmental models for both supervisees and supervisors. Consistent with the developmental emphasis of the counseling profession in general, these models provide a normative approach to the training of counselors that encourages clinical supervisors to provide optimal challenge and support to their supervisees at all levels of training.

Supervision Practices in Psychology

Definition and goals. Falender and Shafranske (2004) define supervision as

> a distinct professional activity in which education and training aimed at developing science-informed practice are facilitated through a collaborative interpersonal process. . . . Supervision ensures that clinical consultation is conducted in a competent manner in which ethical standards, legal prescriptions, and professional practices are used to promote and protect the welfare of the client, the profession, and society at large. (p. 3)

The intended outcome of the supervision process is the development of competent psychologists and colleagues who can use their skills to benefit both the community and the larger profession of psychology.

Falender and Shafranske (2004) identify four superordinate values integral to the process of supervision. First, integrity in relationships underscores the importance of establishing a good working alliance between supervisor and supervisee that is morally incorrupt and maintains commitment to responsibilities, similar to the client-therapist relationship. Ethical values-based practice acknowledges that psychology is not a value-free endeavor and that the role of the supervisor is to model and explore the role of personal and professional values in professional responsibilities and ethical clinical practice. Appreciation of diversity is a third value and includes the supervisory responsibility of increasing self-awareness of one's own identity, ensuring respect for individual and cultural differences, and promoting diversity competence. Finally, supervision facilitates science-informed practice through engagement with the scientific literature, involvement in applied research, and modeling an approach to clinical practice that brings a scientist's curiosity and "questioning attitude" (Falender & Shafranske, 2004, p. 34).

Models and methods. In addition to the models of supervision discussed above, the supervision literature in psychology proposes a *competency-based approach* to clinical supervision where specific clinical competencies are drawn from science-informed practice and identified as specific and measurable outcomes for supervision. Competency goals are established on the basis of standards for education and training as determined by the American Psychological Association (APA, 2016). Supervisors consider individual abilities and developmental level of supervisees and set specific goals with measurable outcomes for attainment of clinical competencies, which becomes the focus of supervision.

Methods of supervision for psychologists in training include primarily individual and group supervision, though significant attention is given in recent publications to guidelines for the provision of remote supervision and telepsychology (Association of State and Provincial Psychology Boards [ASPPB], 2015). Best practice guidelines for psychology supervision include use of a supervision contract to establish goals, competencies, and informed consent; structured methods of formative and summative evaluation; appropriate documentation of supervision; live observation or video and audiotape review of supervisees' clinical work, promoting diversity competence and monitoring ethical compliance (APA, 2014; ASPPB, 2015).

Training and credentialing of supervisors. Despite excellent theory and research in clinical supervision, the profession of psychology has been slow to develop specific guidelines and competencies for supervisors. Professional licensure is the primary credential required for supervisors in clinical psychology, and many supervising psychologists have not had a formal course in clinical supervision. For many years, the ASPPB guidelines designed to guide state and provincial licensing boards in establishing requirements for licensure have governed the clinical supervision of practicum, doctoral, and postdoctoral trainees. ASPPB guidelines were revised in 2015 and currently provide standards for supervisor competency that include coursework in clinical supervision and supervision mentoring for a minimum of six months. Recent efforts have improved the state of clinical supervision in psychology considerably, including APA's published standards for competency-based supervision in health service psychology, which outline the knowledge, skills, and attitudes necessary to be a competent supervisor of clinical, counseling, and school psychologists (APA, 2014). Ethically, psychologist supervisors are bound by the APA code of ethics, particularly Standard 7, which outlines codes of conduct related to education and training (APA, 2010).

Unique contribution. One of the unique emphases of the supervision literature in psychology is the centrality of science-informed practice in education and training. While all the mental health disciplines promote the utilization of evidence-based practices, supervision in psychology in particular facilitates scientifically informed decision making, clinical interventions, and outcome assessment as integral to competent practices. This emphasis is evident in the science-practitioner and practitioner-science models of doctoral education of psychologists, where integrating science with practice is the primary focus. A good example of this approach is the common practice of using a "hypothesis testing" approach to psychological and neuropsychological assessment where clinicians view, administer, and interpret psychological tests as a way of ruling out various explanations for symptoms before arriving at a final diagnosis and case formulation.

Supervision Practices in Marriage and Family Therapy

Definition and goals. The supervision values and goals in MFT share much in common with other mental health disciplines and view supervision as a professional relationship where a more experienced clinician fosters the clinical competencies and professional development of the supervisee, while protecting the welfare of clients. One important difference with systemically oriented supervision is the explicit emphasis on systemic and relational change processes. Storm and Todd (2014a) propose four foundational supervision processes

that are recursive and interactive. *Contextualization* of supervision occurs as supervisors consider multiple and intersecting contextual factors affecting the client and supervision system. *Systemic foundations* of supervision view the change process in therapy (and in supervision) as relational and systemic in nature. *Supervisor accountability* refers to the need to consider the supervisee's developmental needs, the supervisory relationship needs, and also the client's needs in clinical decision making. Finally, *relational responsiveness* considers the "complex web of intersecting therapeutic, professional, and personal relationships" (p. 4) and encourages attention to the supervisory alliance by a supervisor who is self-reflective about power and diversity in the relationships.

Models and methods. Many models of systemic supervision can be considered *psychotherapy models*, as supervisees learn the particular theory as they are experiencing it in supervision. Todd and Storm's (2014) supervision text includes chapters on various models of supervision, including *classic supervision models*, which utilize the principles and techniques of structural, strategic, and solution-focused theories. *Transgenerational models* of supervision facilitate supervisee reflections on their own family of origin and the impact of their sociocultural and relational experiences on their understandings of the families they work with. *Postmodern models* of supervision encourage a nonhierarchical and collaborative process in supervision where multiple perspectives are encouraged and considered. Todd (2014) also focuses on the development of *self-supervision* and self-monitoring capabilities of the supervisee as lifelong qualities that will lead to effective practice. An example of a self-supervision technique is to encourage supervisees to review and critique their own videotaped sessions and bring this self-evaluation to supervision. Models of supervision that emphasize evidence-based practices in family therapy are also growing in popularity and encourage supervisees to both utilize and participate in clinical research and to learn empirically supported treatments (Breunlin, Lebow, & Buckley, 2014).

Traditional and contemporary approaches to systemic supervision place a high value on "raw data" and "live" supervision as a critical component of the supervision process, where supervisors can directly observe their supervisees' clinical work. Supervision guidelines recommend that 20 percent of the time in supervision be spent reviewing supervisees' actual clinical work through video, audiotapes, or direct observation (American Association for Marriage and Family Therapy [AAMFT], 2014, p. 14). "Live" sessions have been a hallmark of MFT supervision and can include the use of reflection teams who observe the session and provide the therapist (or clients) with feedback, or use of a "bug in the ear" to provide the therapist with ongoing coaching during the session while the supervisor is able to watch via video feed. Arguably, systemically oriented supervision has contributed some of the most creative and experiential approaches to the process of supervision that exist today.

Credentialing and training of supervisors. One of the first credentialing processes for clinical supervisors was established by the AAMFT and remains today as a credential with rigorous requirements for supervision. The Approved Supervisor designation requires a 30-hour course on the fundamentals of supervision, 180 hours of supervised supervision experience, and 36 hours of supervision mentoring (AAMFT, 2014). Candidates must also submit a "philosophy of supervision" paper overviewing their supervision approach, values, and practices. Once the Approved Supervisor designation is achieved, supervisors are required to attend a five-hour refresher course for renewal of the designation every five years. PhD students in marriage and family studies receive coursework, experience, and supervised supervision as part of their graduate coursework, whereas master's-level practitioners pursue this designation post-degree. The *Approved Supervision Designation* handbook (AAMFT, 2014) provides clear, detailed guidelines for supervisors, including supervisor responsibilities and requirements and practical tools such as sample supervision contracts and forms. Supervisors are also expected to adhere to the AAMFT Code of Ethics, particularly Standard IV, which outlines specific responsibilities to supervisees and students (AAMFT, 2015).

Distinctive contributions. The MFT emphasis on relational competencies and systemic principles is a unique and important contribution to the effective practice of supervision. Relational, systemic, and contextual variables are considered at all levels, including the supervisor-supervisee relationship, client system, agency, community, and larger sociocultural systems. Attention to isomorphic processes, or dynamics that occur with clients and are repeated in the supervision process, is an integral component of the supervision experience and helps supervisees learn systemic principles and dynamics in an experiential way as they occur in supervision. Good MFT supervision fosters relational competencies and a systemic orientation in case conceptualization and clinical practice.

The rigorous guidelines for systemic supervisor credentials ensure continuity with the unique systemic and relational emphases of family therapy in practice.

Concluding Thoughts on Contemporary Supervision

Clinical supervision across cultural contexts and mental health disciplines has become a subdiscipline in its own right with a growing body of research, diverse theoretical models, ethical guidelines, and credentialing processes. This review of contemporary supervision in counseling, psychology, and MFT reveals both commonalities and distinct contributions. All mental health professionals view clinical supervision as a process where a more experienced professional provides regular oversight of a junior colleague's clinical work with the goal of encouraging the development of competent and ethical practice. Supervisors engage in multiple roles, including teaching, modeling, evaluating, and guiding explorations of the self of the therapist. Supervisors have the dual responsibility to ensure supervisee professional development and safeguard client welfare, and in this role we protect the public and provide a gatekeeping function for the profession. Unique contributions include the normative and developmental supervision models of the counseling profession, the science-informed and competency-based model from psychology, and the relational and systemic supervision emphases of MFTs. And while there are more similarities than differences across mental health disciplines, each supervision model and professional discipline offers an important and complementary contribution to the development of professional competence and expertise. Yet for many Christian supervisors, there is still the sense that something is missing.

RELIGIOUS AND SPIRITUAL ISSUES IN CLINICAL SUPERVISION: A REVIEW OF THE LITERATURE

A recent review of the international supervision literature concluded that religion and spirituality are neglected topics in clinical supervision, despite the importance of religion for clinical training and practice (Inman et al., 2014). A distinction is made between the terms *spirituality* and *religion*: "The consensus in the scholarly literature is that spirituality is viewed as those inner processes that create meaning in an individual's life, whereas religion emerges as the more structured, organized, and formalized expression of spiritual rituals and observances" (Garner, Webb, Chaffin, & Byars, 2017, p. 24). This body of existing literature can be organized into three broad categories. First, the clinical supervision literature addresses the need to foster supervisee awareness, knowledge, and skills pertaining to clients' religion and spirituality as an aspect of diversity competence. A second area of scholarship explores the use of clinical supervision to foster Christian integration in all aspects of theory and practice. A third category relevant to Christian integration in clinical supervision provides ethical guidelines and codes of conduct to direct professionals in their attention to religious and spiritual issues in supervision and clinical practice (Christian Association for Psychological Studies [CAPS], 2005; American Association of Christian Counselors, 2014; Association for Spiritual, Ethical and Religious Values in Counseling

[ASERVIC], 2016; American Association of Pastoral Counselors [AAPC], 2012). This review will provide us with a "state of the art" of the integration of religious and spiritual issues in clinical supervision.

Developing Spiritual and Religious Competencies in Supervision

The body of literature on religious and spiritual issues in supervision describes theory, research, and practices for development of supervisee competencies in addressing religious and spiritual issues in clinical practice. Polanski (2003) asserts that supervisors have a responsibility to ensure that clients are receiving holistic treatment through providing supervisees with the knowledge and skills to address religious and spiritual issues in therapy. Clinical supervision enhances the supervisee's professional functioning by encouraging self-exploration of personal values and beliefs, and their impact on clinical practice. Similarly, Miller, Korinek, and Ivey (2006) advocate for explicit attention to religious and spiritual issues in marriage and family therapy. Their research examined the prevalence and types of spiritual themes discussed in supervision and found four primary dimensions where spiritual discussions occurred: the client-therapist relationship, the supervisor-supervisee relationship, the diversity lens through which the therapist views the client and themselves, and the lens of meaning and values themes in therapy and supervision. The same data set (students from accredited MA and doctoral MFT programs) was also used to examine the relationship between gender, supervisory style, and discussion of spiritual themes in supervision (Miller & Ivey, 2006). Supervisors who were rated by supervisees as affiliative and self-disclosing were found to raise spiritual issues

in supervision with greater frequency than other supervisors. Same-gender supervision pairs were also found to discuss spiritual issues with more frequency. The authors conclude that "exploring spirituality as a facet of supervision is a viable practice" (p. 334).

Bienenfeld and Yager (2007) identify five training goals for clinical supervisors to address religion and spirituality in the supervision process: (1) defining important terms (i.e., the difference between client spirituality as personal beliefs and experiences, and religion as a system of beliefs and practices); (2) providing a systematic approach to assessment of patient spirituality and religiosity; (3) incorporating theories of faith and spiritual development; (4) fostering exploration of the relationship between the patient's symptoms/psychopathology and spiritual/religious beliefs; and (5) encouraging self-awareness of the supervisee's own religious and spiritual history and how this may affect countertransference with the patient. Supervision research has identified benefits to supervisees from addressing religious and spiritual issues in the supervision process. Garner, Webb, Chaffin, and Byars (2017) found a positive relationship between the frequency of discussion of spiritual issues in supervision, as perceived by supervisees, and the supervisee's sense of life purpose and meaning.

How should supervisors incorporate spiritual and religious issues into the supervision process? Several clinical supervision models for facilitating competency with religious issues in mental health practice have been proposed. Aten and Hernandez (2004) highlighted eight domains where supervisors can incorporate religion into the supervision process, including assessment, clinical intervention, case conceptualization, theoretical orientation, and formulation of treatment goals. Similarly, Ripley and colleagues proposed a developmental model for improving supervisee competence in addressing religious and spiritual issues in psychotherapy that considers supervisee faith and moral development (Ripley, Jackson, Tatum, & Davis, 2007). Ross, Suprina, and Brack (2013) conducted a grounded theory meta-analysis of literature on supervision and spirituality toward the development of a "Spirituality in Supervision" model to facilitate attentiveness to spirituality during clinical supervision. The SACRED model suggests a progressive approach to spirituality in supervision that integrates spiritual considerations into all aspects of the clinical process. And in a recent contribution to the counseling supervision literature, Hull, Suarez, and Hartman (2016) provide practical suggestions for supervisors to facilitate religious and spiritual competencies in supervision that are consistent with competencies recommended by the Association for Spiritual, Ethical, and Religious Values in Counseling (ASERVIC), a division of the American Counseling Association.

A comprehensive resource for supervisors and supervisees is offered by Shafranske (2014), who advocates for attention to religion and spirituality as an important component of multicultural competence in clinical supervision. He asserts that clinicians and supervisors have an "ethical imperative" (p. 182) to promote consideration of and respect for the client's religious and spiritual values. Consistent with a competency-based approach, supervisors should provide knowledge, skills, and values for their supervisees to competently incorporate spiritual and religious considerations into the treatment process. For example, supervisors have a responsibility to make trainees aware of the important literature on religion and coping and to help them apply this knowledge in assessment, case conceptualization, and formulating interventions. Supervisors can facilitate assessment and intervention skills relevant to religious and spiritual issues by incorporating role-playing, modeling, self-assessment, and monitoring to ensure multicultural sensitivity and competence.

Christian Integration in Clinical Supervision

A special issue of the *Journal of Psychology and Christianity* in 2007 focused on clinical supervision provides a valuable resource for Christian integration in supervision. Aten, Boyer, and Tucker (2007) conducted qualitative interviews with leaders in Christian integration and, from interview themes, proposed a conceptual framework that incorporates supervisor indicators, conceptualizations, roles, and actions. The authors found that Christian integration in supervision occurs through consideration of supervisee indicators (e.g., inquiring about supervisee's religiosity and spiritual development), fostering integrative case conceptualization (e.g., integrating spiritual and religious themes in diagnosis and treatment planning), Christian integrative supervisor roles (e.g., modeling and teaching integration), and supervisor actions (e.g., explicit use of prayer and Scripture in supervision).

Other articles in this special issue provide specific guidelines for a Christian integrative approach to the formation of the supervisee's worldview, spiritual development, and character through the clinical supervision process. Bufford (2007) provides a framework for the way Christian worldview and beliefs affect the focus, methods, and interventions of clinical supervision. Tan (2007) proposes the use of spiritual disciplines (Scripture reading, prayer, silence, etc.) in clinical supervision as a means of fostering supervisee growth and development, and as a way of modeling that would enable the supervisee to utilize spiritual disciplines with clients. Tan emphasizes the importance of informed consent from the supervisee and use of the disciplines in a way that is consistent with historical spiritual practices (i.e., reliance on the Holy Spirit for transformation and change). Butman and Kruse (2007) assert that effective clinical supervision should focus holistically and developmentally on character formation. They write: "As Christian practitioners we should be more compelled than most to employ this approach to supervision given its holistic focus on the person of the supervisee (personally, spiritually and professionally) and focus on maturation in all spheres of life. In this way, we aspire to 'disciple' the next generation of practitioners with integrity and intentionality" (pp. 311-12). Butman and Kruse caution that this more mentoring-oriented approach to supervision requires greater flexibility, informed consent, and respect for clear boundaries.

An important advocate for Christian integrative approaches to clinical supervision, Tan asserts that supervision is a crucial pedagogy for teaching students integration skills (Tan, 2009). He encourages supervisors to employ Christian integrative models, skills, and ethics, and to consider the research on how students acquire integration skills. Tan writes:

> Christian clinical supervision should be seen as a core competency area in the training of all Christian clinical practitioners or therapists. Training in Christian clinical supervision that integrates Christian faith or spirituality and clinical supervision . . . should

therefore be included in the clinical training curriculum of every Christian graduate program or school. (Tan, 2009, pp. 56-57)

Ethical Guidelines for Christian Integrative Practice

Several professional organizations offer ethical codes for their members that provide guidance for a religious and spiritual approach to clinical practice and supervision. While adherence to these codes is essentially voluntary yet strongly encouraged, these ethics are considered the ideals and standards for professional practice as an expression of religious commitment. Thus, the ethical codes provide an important resource for Christian integrative supervision and are well worth our careful consideration. In this section, we overview the ethical codes and particularly the guidelines they provide for supervision and training.

The Christian Association for Psychological Studies Ethical Statement (CAPS, 2005) exhorts members to practice ethical professional behaviors as an expression of their covenantal relationship with God. A doctrinal statement is provided as the foundation on which ethical principles rest. The first ethical principle, commitment to Christ, involves seeking God's wisdom in all professional life and viewing one's vocation as a calling. The subsequent ethical standards are consistent with the APA code of conduct and address competency, confidentiality, and specific guidelines for psychotherapy, assessment, education, and training. The CAPS code offers several guidelines specifically for the practice of clinical supervision, also parallel to APA's guidelines for education and training, which include the provision of timely feedback, refraining from requiring student personal disclosures, and an admonition against sexual relationships with students or supervisees.

The American Association of Christian Counselors (AACC) revised its code of ethics in 2014. Similar to those of CAPS, the ethical principles are predicated on biblical and doctrinal foundations as well as ethical professional and legal standards. Nine standards incorporate biblical and professional values to provide ethical guidelines for professional practice. The first principle, for example, offers a Judeo-Christian perspective on beneficence and highlights the biblical mandate to "do good" in one's professional life. Non-maleficence, or refraining from practices that cause harm, is tied to the biblical principles of compassion and servanthood. The AACC ethics offer a blend of professional and Christian values that guides the practice of Christian counseling. The AACC code provides a good deal of specificity for ethical supervision practices that are an expression of the call to "collegiality" with colleagues, students, and supervisees. Specific ethical guidelines are provided for Christian counselor education and supervisor training programs consistent with collegial values.

The code of ethics for the American Association of Pastoral Counselors (AAPC) is currently undergoing review and revision by the association. Pastoral counselors and students are expected to abide by ten interim ethical guidelines, which include a commitment to being both "spiritually grounded and psychologically informed," maintaining association with a "faith group," and adhering to state licensing laws and ecclesiastical codes to govern all counseling activities (AAPC, 2012). No specific guidelines for pastoral counseling supervision are included in the ethical code.

ASERVIC, a division of ACA mentioned above, has developed fourteen "Spiritual Competencies" for counselors to promote the need to address spiritual and religious issues in counseling (ASERVIC, 2016). Complementary to the ACA Code of Ethics, the Spiritual Competencies provide principles and guidelines for assessment and treatment practices that respect and incorporate the client's religious and spiritual beliefs (Cashwell & Watts, 2011). ASERVIC provides ongoing resources for counselors interested in religious and spiritual issues through the journal *Counseling and Values*. While the competencies do not provide specific guidelines for spiritual and religious issues in supervision, subsequent scholarship has articulated supervision goals and practices for education and training in the competencies through the supervision process (Hull et al., 2016).

The ethical guidelines provided by these professional organizations effectively advocate for their members to develop knowledge, skills, and attitudes that facilitate competent clinical practice with religious and spiritual issues consistent with the ethical requirements of professional guilds. Minimal explicit attention is given, however, to proposing guidelines for a distinctively Christian supervision and educational process.

Concluding Comments on Religious and Spiritual Issues in Supervision

A review of the literature on spiritual and religious issues in clinical supervision suggests that Christian integrative aims of clinical supervision include developing spiritual and religious competencies, fostering Christian integration in all aspects of clinical work (including the holistic personal and professional development of the supervisee), and promoting adherence to ethics and values of Christian mental health practice. While this is an excellent and growing literature, it is surprising that there is very little in the way of comprehensive models or frameworks for Christian integration in clinical supervision, particularly given the central role that clinical supervision plays in the training and development of mental health professionals. As it stands, our supervision efforts are left without a foundational theological framework and guiding pedagogy.

CHARACTER FORMATION AND VIRTUE: IMPLICATIONS FOR EDUCATION AND SUPERVISION

What has happened to the role of character formation in education and society? Journalist David Brooks, in his recent book *The Road to Character*, laments the "Big Me" culture of contemporary society that values "résumé virtues" detailing skills and accomplishments over "eulogy virtues," which pertain to what kind of person you are at the core (virtues that will be expounded on at one's funeral). He writes: "We are morally inarticulate. . . . We've lost the understanding of how character is built" (Brooks, 2015, p. 15). Leaving moral traditions behind, he asserts, has led to "a certain superficiality to modern culture, especially in the moral sphere" (p. 15). Brooks concludes that the character virtues lauded in contemporary society are in stark contrast to the virtues of intellectual and personal humility that lead to true wisdom.

As Christian clinical supervisors, we need little persuading to agree wholeheartedly with Brooks that *maturity of character matters*, particularly in the mental health professions, where we are trusted by the public to care for people at their most vulnerable moments. And because clinical supervision is inevitably formational for supervisees—both personally and professionally—it befits us to be purposeful and thoughtful about the importance of virtue in the development of clinicians.

In this next section, we draw from the rich resources on character formation in philosophy, theology, psychology, and education

to inform the development of a Christian integrative framework for clinical supervision that aims to form supervisees in the likeness of Christ for competent and effective service to his kingdom.

Philosophical and Theological Foundations

From ancient times, philosophers, theologians, and scientists have deeply considered what it means for human beings to develop and flourish. Plato's *Republic* proposed that the virtues of wisdom, courage, temperance, and justice, when pursued by citizens of the state, would lead to a well-ordered person and society. Plato's student, Aristotle, is widely considered the father of "virtue theory." Aristotle's important work on virtue, *Nicomachian Ethics*, described a systematic theory of virtue and moral behavior. The early Greek philosophers identified *eudaimonia*, or the pursuit of happiness, as the highest good or essence of human life. Aristotle described the happy person as one who acts in accordance with both intellectual virtues and character virtues (Polansky, 2014). Classical philosophy defines moral virtue as a habit or repeated practice that becomes part of one's very nature. Character is formed when virtuous action becomes a consistent practice "characteristic" of a person that flows out of their very being. Contemporary virtue ethicists emphasize the role of social goals and outcomes, rather than individual happiness and self-fulfillment, as the highest aims of the character formation process (MacIntyre, 1984).

Greek philosophy provided an important foundation for early Christian writers, particularly Thomas Aquinas. Aquinas's *Summa Theologica* has provided an important theological foundation for a Christian virtue ethics. In the *Summa*, Aquinas distinguished between the theological or *infused* virtues of faith, hope, and love that are given as gifts from God to the believer so we may know and love Him, and the moral or *acquired* virtues of prudence, courage, temperance, and justice. According to Aquinas, the cardinal or moral virtues are developed through habits of the will and intellect that eventually predispose one to act in a way that leads to the ultimate end of human flourishing, which is knowing and loving God. To act in a morally virtuous way is to reflect God's very image (Farley, 1995). Aquinas differs from Aristotle and the early Greek philosophers with his emphasis on the *infused* virtues, which provide a hopeful vision of human beings who, upon receiving God's gift of grace, are transformed in their very nature. "Aquinas describes grace as a habitus that effects the very essence of the soul, so that man's very nature is altered. As part of this alteration, men receive new dispositions, dispositions which render him capable of a qualitatively different kind of action" (McKay, 2004, p. 28). The indwelling of the Holy Spirit through the gift of grace enables human beings to walk in the "light of grace" in faith, hope, and love (p. 34).

Summaries of historic biblical and theological teaching on Christian virtue can be found in the *Catechism of the Catholic Church*. It is invaluable for our understanding of moral virtue and character formation to consider this comprehensive definition provided in the *Catechism*:

A virtue is a habitual and firm disposition to do the good. It allows the person not only to perform good acts, but to give the best of himself. The virtuous person tends toward the good with all his sensory and spiritual powers; he pursues the good and chooses it in concrete actions. The goal of a virtuous life is to become like God.

Human virtues are firm attitudes, stable dispositions, habitual perfections of intellect and will that govern our actions, order our passions, and guide our conduct according to reason and faith. They make possible ease, self-mastery, and joy in leading a morally good life. The virtuous man is he who freely practices the good.

This first section of the *Catechism* on virtue describes the purpose of human virtue (to conform ourselves to God's image) and provides a definition of virtue. A holistic perspective on virtue is offered as a combination of attitude, dispositions, and habits of the mind and will that guide action—practiced freely and with joy. The *Catechism* then describes how the various virtues are developed and outlines the specific moral (cardinal) virtues:

The moral virtues are acquired by human effort. They are the fruit and seed of morally good acts; they dispose all the powers of the human being for communion with divine love.

Four virtues play a pivotal role and accordingly are called "cardinal"; all the others are grouped around them. They are: prudence, justice, fortitude, and temperance. "If anyone loves righteousness, [Wisdom's] labors are virtues; for she teaches temperance and prudence, justice, and courage." These virtues are praised under other names in many passages of Scripture.

While many virtues are extolled in Scripture, this section of the *Catechism* identifies four primary moral virtues that encompass virtues praised "under other names" in Scripture. The moral virtues are developed through our own efforts as expressions of God's love. The *Catechism* then describes the origin and purpose of the theological virtues for human beings:

> The human virtues are rooted in the theological virtues, which adapt man's faculties for participation in the divine nature: for the theological virtues relate directly to God. They dispose Christians to live in a relationship with the Holy Trinity. They have the One and Triune God for their origin, motive, and object.
>
> The theological virtues are the foundation of Christian moral activity; they animate it and give it its special character. They inform and give life to all the moral virtues. They are infused by God into the souls of the faithful to make them capable of acting as his children and of meriting eternal life. They are the pledge of the presence and action of the Holy Spirit in the faculties of the human being. There are three theological virtues: faith, hope, and charity. (*Catechism of the Catholic Church*, 2003, para. 1803-5, 1812-13)

The hopeful vision of humanity described in the *Catechism* is foundational to a Christian understanding of virtue and distinguishes Christian virtue ethics from positive psychology perspectives. Christian teaching asserts that faith, hope, and love are "infused by God into the souls of the faithful" through the Holy Spirit. The infused virtues are the foundation of all virtuous activity as they animate, "inform and give life" to the moral virtues. The theological virtues are a gift from God that allow us, as God's children, to live in relationship with the Father, Son, and Holy Spirit as our "origin, motive, and object." God does not call us to the virtuous life without equipping us with the faith, hope, and love we

need to live a life of justice, temperance, wisdom, and courage.

While the *Catechism* speaks of virtue as enabling Christians to "merit" eternal life, Protestant theological writings seek to understand virtue in the context of God's gift of eternal life. Early Protestant reformers were cautious about emphasizing a strong theology of virtue ethics because of the reformers' emphasis on grace alone as the foundation of the believer's salvation and sanctification (Farley, 1995). However, there has been a resurgence of interest in virtue ethics among Protestant theologians of the last century. Contemporary Protestant theologians provide a way of thinking about character formation and virtue in the context of justification, sanctification, and restorative justice (Gushee & Stassen, 2016; Hauerwas & Wells, 2011ab; Wright, 2010; Farley, 1995). Protestant virtue ethicists understand the character formation of the believer as part of the process of sanctification that occurs as God draws the believer to himself in grace and love through the sacrifice of Christ's death and his resurrection. In other words, we are justified through faith and trust in Christ, and not through good works or virtuous actions. God is active through the Holy Spirit in sanctifying us into Christlikeness through the gifts of faith, hope, and love as we seek to develop into wise, courageous, just, and self-controlled believers who seek first the kingdom of Christ. Christian ethics rightly understood is this: "God's Holy Spirit gives God's people the resources they need to live in God's presence" (Hauerwas & Wells, 2011b, p. 13).

In a thoughtful and accessible contemporary exposition on Christian virtue, N. T. Wright (2010) asserts that the primary focus of the Christian life is the development of Christlike character as we prepare in hope for

Christ's kingdom. Virtue is defined by Wright as a restoration of all persons to what it means to be truly human, to be remade in the image of God through practicing individual and corporate habits of heart, mind, and action. Like the rich young ruler in the New Testament narrative, Jesus teaches that our longing for eternal life, for "something more," can only be met by not simply obeying commandments but by giving all we have and transforming our lives to follow him. This, according to Wright, is what virtue is all about: "The call to holiness comes precisely because it is as genuine human beings that we will be able to sum up the praises of creation, and as genuine human beings that we will be able to bring God's justice, freedom, beauty, peace, and above all rescuing love to the world" (p. 557). Wright proposes that this development of virtue happens in Christian community through what he calls the elements of a "virtuous circle": Scripture, stories, examples, community, and practices. As we grow in Christlikeness, we grow in our ability to engage in kingdom work and restorative justice, which Wright asserts "must happen in us so it can happen through us" (p. 563).

Far from an individualized process, the formation of Christian character and virtue happens through both individual and community practices where the end goal is not the development of individual virtue but the love of God and neighbor. To quote Hauerwas and Wells (2011a):

> The liturgy offers ethics a series of ordered practices that shape the character and assumptions of Christians, and suggest habits and models that inform every aspect of corporate life—meeting people, acknowledging fault and failure, celebrating, thanking, reading, speaking with authority, reflecting

on wisdom, naming truth, registering need, bringing about reconciliation, sharing food, renewing purpose. This is the basic staple of corporate Christian life—not simply for clergy, or for those in religious orders, but for lay Christians, week in, week out. It is the most regular way in which most Christians remind themselves and others that they are Christians. It is the most significant way in which Christianity takes flesh, evolving from a set of ideas and convictions to a set of practices and a way of life. (p. 7)

Historical and contemporary theological perspectives on virtue provide an essential foundation for the development of a distinctly Christian approach to clinical supervision. Our longing for "something more" in the way we prepare Christian mental health professionals for their vocation must include helping them become more Christlike, more fully human in the way that God has intended them to be. A biblically and theologically grounded virtue framework provides us with a roadmap for what these essential habits of heart and mind should look like.

Which Virtues Are Important?

Catalogues of the Christian virtues tend to follow Aquinas in his identification of faith, hope, and love as the theological or infused virtues that are gifts from God, and prudence, temperance, justice, and courage as the moral or cardinal virtues that are both infused and acquired through human effort and practice (Kaczor & Sherman, 2009). However, descriptions of Christian moral character qualities also draw from Jesus' teaching in the Sermon on the Mount, Paul's description of the fruit of the Spirit in Galatians 5, and other biblical texts. Gushee and Stassen (2016) make a strong case for examining the teachings of Jesus as a foundation for determining which virtues are essential to discipleship. They suggest that the Beatitudes and Paul's list of virtues show significant resonance as they include humility, righteousness, mercy, purity of heart, peacemaking, endurance, and joy (p. 37). D. C. Jones proposes that the virtues should be considered as forms of love. From Jesus' teaching, he suggests that justice, mercy, and faithfulness are the "primary forms of obedient love" that "constitute the fundamental and irreducible moral norms that are always and everywhere to be maintained in practice" (Jones, 1994, p. 79). Jones suggests that to maintain these interpersonal expressions of love, the cardinal personal virtues of discernment, courage, self-discipline, and humility are required (p. 95). Farley (1995) describes the philosophical and ethical practice of categorizing virtues as "self-regarding" and "other-regarding" (p. 160). Virtues important for one's own moral and character growth include such traits as faith, freedom, wisdom, discernment, repentance, courage, peace, and joy. Character virtues that are "other-regarding" pertain to love of neighbor and prepare us to live out our love for God in ethical actions such as justice, beneficence, respect, truthfulness, kindness, and gratitude (p. 168).

Westberg (2015) makes a case for retaining the classical categories of theological and moral virtues proposed by Aquinas, as the other biblical virtues can be seen as subcategories. An excellent biblical example of this approach can be seen in Paul's comprehensive definition of love in 1 Corinthians 13, as he includes patience and kindness as essential aspects. It is important to keep in mind that we model our character after the person of Jesus, rather than any system or model of distinct character traits: "But in contrast to Plato or Aristotle, or Confucianism, or any other system of virtues, the Christian life has an exemplar who is not merely a model, but is actually drawing us to be conformed to his image" (Westberg, 2015, p. 142). Our categories or lists of virtues are less important, as they are in a sense artificial since the virtues are interdependent. For example, we cannot be just without also demonstrating wisdom to guide our just actions.

Counseling, Psychology, and Virtue

In the field of counseling and psychology, the study of human virtue is most evident in the positive psychology movement of the last fifteen years. Martin Seligman's introduction to a special issue of the *American Psychologist* in 2000 proposed a new direction for a psychology focused on positive human traits and civic virtues that lead to human resilience, flourishing, and the "good life" (Seligman & Csikszentmihalyi, 2000). In a landmark and ambitious project, Peterson and Seligman (2004) reviewed historic and contemporary resources on character and virtue and developed a classification system identifying 6 core virtues and 24 corresponding traits. Very similar to the classic moral virtues, the core character strengths identified in their virtues project include wisdom, courage, humanity, justice, temperance, and a virtue the researchers call "transcendence," which is similar to the theological virtues of faith and hope. Peterson and Seligman aimed to develop a virtues classification that is universal, and they have found general agreement across cultures for many of the core virtues. This project has stimulated much ongoing research in the areas that have been described as the three pillars of positive psychology research: the study of well-being, character strengths, and positive communities (Sperry & Sperry, 2012, p. 150). Positive psychology approaches to clinical practice that have grown out of this movement focus on the development of positive traits and character qualities of clients that lead to resilience and flourishing. Christian psychologists have found both resonance and areas of incompatibility with positive psychology (Kaczor, 2015; Charry, 2011; Tan, 2006; Hackney, 2007).

Virtue ethics has also been applied to the training of psychologists. In *Virtue and Psychology*, Fowers (2005) proposes a model of psychology and virtue that focuses on the development of prudence, or practical wisdom, in clinical practice and ethical decision making, making a case for virtue ethics as a more integral component of the training and supervision of clinicians. Fowers has also published widely on psychology and virtue, including applications of virtue ethics to marital therapy (2001), multiculturalism (Fowers & Davidov, 2006), and therapist virtues (Fowers & Winakur, 2014).

Character-Virtue Development

A recent resurgence of interest in character virtue has given rise to the interdisciplinary study of the development of virtue integrating philosophy, psychology, neurobiology, education, and ethics. Contemporary virtue ethicists consider the embodied nature of the acquisition of virtue, incorporating findings from contemporary neuroscience to inform how we think about moral development. For example, contemporary research in cognition suggests that in the critical moments in life (particularly crisis situations) our decisions and behaviors are determined more by ingrained, automatic, and largely unconscious cognitive processes; this underscores the importance of habits of moral thought and action (schemas, if you will)

that are developed over time, are consistently practiced, and become a part of our neural pathways (Van Slyk, 2015; Edwards, 2015). Equally important for the process of supervision, research on "mirror neurons" and the role of imitation and simulation in the development of moral behaviors suggests that moral exemplars are integral to facilitating moral thinking and behavior (Van Slyk, 2015). *Virtue development studies* (Annas, Narvaez, & Snow, 2016) has been proposed as a descriptor for the interdisciplinary study of moral virtue development. Virtue developmentalists consider the influence of early infant-caregiver relationships, for example, in the development of empathic and relational capacities that form the foundation for future moral behaviors (Narvaez, 2014). The value of religious communities for modeling and reinforcing virtuous habits is also supported by cognitive neuroscience (see Edman, 2015, for a good summary).

Contemporary neuroscience perspectives encourage us to think about virtue in a holistic way. While historically the treatment of virtue often categorizes moral character as an expression of one aspect of personhood—for example, faith as an intellectual virtue, hope as a virtue of the will, and love as an emotional virtue—we know from neuroscience that these aspects of personhood are integrated and inseparable. This body of research makes a strong case for the importance of virtue in ethical decision making in crisis situations, for example, and for the significance of role models and mentors in the formation of virtuous habits, lending support to a virtue-oriented approach to clinical supervision.

Professional Ethics and Virtue

The virtues and values of the mental health professions are most visible in the ethical codes of conduct that govern the professional behaviors of all counselors, psychologists, and marriage and family therapists. The ethical codes represent the normative thinking in each profession about shared values that guide expectations for professional conduct. However, it is important to keep in mind that "the word *ethics* could refer either to the legal or mandatory floor adopted by the profession or to the aspirational ceiling of voluntary efforts to live out high moral ideals" (Knapp, Vandecreek, & Fingerhut, 2017, p. 4). In most ethical codes, the preamble sections of the documents summarize the highest aspirational goals of the profession (the ethical "ceiling") and are followed by the codes of conduct detailing specific behavioral expectations (the ethical "floor") and ethical guidelines (ACA, 2014; APA, 2010; AAMFT, 2015).

A review of the preamble sections and codes of conduct across mental health professions reveals a strong consistency of aspirational professional values that, interestingly, correspond to the classical virtues (more about this later). Thomas (2014) reviewed ethical codes across countries and mental health professions and found that commonly espoused principles include a commitment to seek human and societal welfare, safeguard human dignity and rights, promote social justice, and maintain professional competence. While it is common for professionals and students alike to skim over the preamble and focus on the "rules" that govern professional behavior, a review of the guiding principles provides clinical supervisors with a clear description of professional values that are both aspirational and inspirational for the profession and that guide clinical training and supervision. Shared aspirational values across mental health professions include the following:

- Beneficence—engaging in one's profession to benefit the public and society through working for good and promoting human health and well-being

- Nonmaleficence—"doing no harm" by practicing humility, self-regulation, and self-reflection

- Fidelity and responsibility—upholding public trust and acting responsibly and with integrity in all professional relationships by honoring one's commitments, fulfilling one's responsibilities, and upholding standards of professional conduct

- Integrity—maintaining accuracy, honesty, and truthfulness in professional relationships, clinical practice, research, and education

- Justice and fairness—promoting equality and treating individuals and groups equally; being aware of one's own biases and acting to minimize them

- Respect for the dignity and worth of all people—respecting differences, reducing biases, respecting individual rights for self-determination, maintaining privacy and confidentiality

- Competency—applying accurate knowledge, skills, and values to practice; upholding standards and practices of the profession

Integral to the clinical supervision process is a deep familiarity with the professional values and virtues that govern our profession. These values provide clear goals and expectations for professional conduct and behaviors (Grus & Kaslow, 2014). Supervisors bring these superordinate values to bear on all aspects of the supervision process and encourage the development of professional habits of thought and action that lead to good ethical decision making throughout one's career.

While graduate education largely focuses on teaching students to apply ethical principles in clinical situations, some scholars have raised the relative value of *principle ethics* versus *virtue ethics* (Jordan & Meara, 1990; Bersoff, 1996). Principle ethics involve learning to apply broad ethical principles to situations or dilemmas and focuses on the question "What should I do?," while virtue ethics views the character development of the practitioner as the foundation for ethical judgment, focusing on "Who shall I be?" (Jordan & Meara, 1990). Positive psychologists, as discussed above, make a strong case for an increased emphasis on virtue ethics in fostering ethical decision making and behaviors (Fowers, 2005).

Education, Virtue, and Clinical Supervision

The importance of character formation in higher education, along with the role of faculty educators in this process, has been persuasively articulated by a host of important educators (Newman, 1996; Holmes, 1987; Palmer, Zajonc, & Scribner, 2010). A recent example is Wong, Baker, and Franz's (2015) appeal to reclaim the character formation aims of business education. Drawing from recent and historical scholarship on virtue theory, the authors challenge the prevailing education-as-*information* model in Christian higher education today. They advocate for an education-as-*formation* approach to business education that focuses on the development of virtue in Christian community as the most effective way to produce businesspersons for faithful service.

Certainly, an education-as-formation approach to the training of mental health professionals seems obvious and compelling. It is surprising that a review of the literature revealed scant published material on virtue-informed approaches to graduate education in counseling, psychology, or marriage and family therapy. Two sources propose a model of supervision that is virtue-based: existential therapy supervision and the pastoral care supervision literature. Let us review each to consider contributions to a virtue-informed Christian integrative model of supervision.

The work of existential therapists van Deurzen and Young (2009) proposes existentially oriented clinical supervision as the application of philosophical thinking about human existence to clinical supervision and clinical practice. As existential therapy is more of an attitude or orientation than a specific set of techniques or dogmatic theory, the authors propose that existential supervision can be an add-on perspective combined with other models of supervision. Existential supervision has the purpose of encouraging the supervisee to reflect on larger issues of existence for the client and seeing current problems in the context of an overall approach to living. The authors write:

> Specifically trained existential supervisors act as philosophical guides, who provide a clear space for re-thinking and re-experiencing what has happened in sessions and in the life of the client. Existential supervision is a time to take stock and elucidate our usually all too vague understanding of the complexities of human existence. This means the supervisors will ask many questions of their supervisees so as to inspire them to explore, amplify and clarify their understandings of their client's reality. (van Deurzen & Young, 2009, p. 6)

Examples of existential approaches to clinical supervision include Macaro's (2009) application of virtue theory to the development of practical wisdom in supervisees through use of Socratic reasoning and Aristotle's doctrine of the mean. Likewise, Moja-Strasser (2009) relies on the writings of Kierkegaard to provide an approach to supervision based on the virtue of love. We examine both supervision methods in greater detail later in the text.

A special 2012 issue of *Reflective Practice: Formation and Supervision in Ministry*—a journal for theological educators, pastoral counselors, and spiritual directors—focused on the importance of virtue ethics for pastoral and theological education. This collection of articles explored the importance of a virtue-oriented approach to education and supervision of ministry candidates. What Christian leaders need, asserts Anderson (2012) in the editorial comments, is not only training in knowledge, strategies, and marketing but the formation of "robust character." Fleischer (2012) suggests that the theological and classical virtues provide an important foundation for the character-formative goals of pastoral education. She critiques contemporary models of pastoral education: "The theory-to-practice paradigm incorporates knowledge and skills into the educational process but tends to relegate virtue 'formation' to extra-curricular activities such as retreats, spiritual events, and a personal integration left up to the student" (p. 173). The solution, suggests Fleisher, is a more praxis-oriented approach to graduate education in ministry where practical theology is learned by individual and corporate practices in community with the goal of transformation in Christ. She suggests the key questions for the graduate student are essentially questions about virtue development: "Who am I becoming? How am I (or we) being transformed in Christ" (p. 175).

Christian educators in psychology identify the spiritual formation of students as an explicit goal of a distinctively Christian education. A special issue of the *Journal of Psychology and Christianity* in 2013 examined the spiritual formation of students in Christian doctoral psychology programs. Articles from the various Christian programs articulated a commitment to student spiritual formation as an explicit aim and described the various ways spiritual growth opportunities are integrated into the curriculum, including courses in Christian integration, theology coursework, spiritual formation classes, practicum seminar supervision, and Christian community. A survey of doctoral students across explicitly Christian programs found an overall decline in students' faith commitments and involvement in faith communities during their doctoral work in psychology (Fisk et al., 2013). The authors suggest that factors affecting student spiritual formation include motivation, fatigue, and exposure to contemporary psychology's naturalistic assumptions. An explicit focus on spiritual formation in graduate education is recommended as a "protective factor" for students facing the rigors of graduate school.

Concluding Thoughts on Character Formation

The virtue ethics literature in philosophy, theology, psychology, and education is highly relevant for the practice of a Christian integrative clinical supervision. In fact, this integrative literature indeed provides "something more" for the supervision process through offering a guiding framework for virtue that has been developed throughout human history, is interwoven into the theology and practices of the Christian faith, and is currently emerging as a contemporary topic of research in psychology. Best of all, a virtue-oriented approach to clinical supervision provides a vision for the kind of professionals we most hope to become: clinicians of faith, hope, and love who serve Christ's kingdom with wisdom, courage, justice, and temperance.

CONCLUSION

Thus far, we have considered the contemporary landscape of the distinct professional activity known as clinical supervision. We have found it to be a subdiscipline with vibrant professional organizations, a thoughtful and growing literature, diverse models and methods of practice, and a small but excellent literature on Christian integrative approaches. We have identified the need for a clinical supervision approach that aims to form mental health professionals of character who can navigate the challenges of long-term mental health practice and maintain their own spiritual health. From the historic and contemporary literature on character-virtue formation, we have articu-lated a theological and biblical foundation for the formation of character and moral virtue. From the professional ethical codes, we have also identified common "professional values" that represent the aspirational aims of mental health professionals and thus desired outcomes for the supervision process. Finally, we examined the important role of individual and community spiritual disciplines for educational experiences oriented toward personal formation as a valued component of the educational process. The next chapter brings these threads together to propose a Christian integrative framework for the supervision process.

CHAPTER 2

A CHRISTIAN INTEGRATIVE FRAMEWORK FOR CLINICAL SUPERVISION

We are apt to mistake our vocation by looking out of the way for occasions to exercise great and rare virtues, and by stepping over those ordinary ones which lie directly in the road before us.

HANNAH MORE

For this very reason, make every effort to add to your faith goodness; and to goodness, knowledge; and to knowledge, self-control; and to self-control, perseverance; and to perseverance, godliness; and to godliness, mutual affection; and to mutual affection, love. For if you possess these qualities in increasing measure, they will keep you from being ineffective and unproductive in your knowledge of our Lord Jesus Christ.

2 PETER 1:5-8

A CHRISTIAN INTEGRATIVE approach to clinical supervision invites supervisors and supervisees to discover what is missing in contemporary clinical supervision and to look to the interdisciplinary literature on virtue and character formation for direction. It is based on the premise that supervision ought to inspire trainees by offering a hopeful vision of the kind of person and professional that we can become, through God's transforming work. In supervision we have the opportunity to focus our attention on God's great work of forming us as human beings in Christ's likeness. This theologically informed vision is one that can sustain counselors, psychologists, and MFTs through the rigors and challenges of clinical practice.

A virtues-oriented framework brings a holistic theological and psychological understanding of how character is formed to the practice of clinical supervision. The formative nature of supervision has always been implicit, and this approach provides something more for the supervision process through integrating an explicit focus on character formation with supervision models and best practices. By theologically grounding the process of clinical supervision in ancient and contemporary Christian virtue ethics, we find a road map for developing clinicians of character who will aspire to professional excellence as they grow in faith, hope, and love, and whose professional conduct will be marked by wisdom, justice, self-control, and courage. We draw from the rich resources of philosophical, theological, and biblical understandings of human formation and flourishing to frame the supervision process with these larger goals in mind.

As followers of Christ, we can look to Scripture, theological insights, and Christian tradition to provide depth and direction for our theory and practice of clinical supervision. We think of the model of our Lord Jesus Christ, who invested a majority of his precious ministry time on earth discipling a small number of men and women whom he empowered to establish his church on earth. We draw from his model of discipleship as servant leadership as we seek to wash the feet of those entrusted to our care. Christian teaching informs a framework for supervision that prioritizes the development of mental health professionals to be conformed to the likeness of Christ as faithful, hopeful, and loving practitioners who seek above all to serve Christ's kingdom. As supervisors facing the daunting task of professionally imprinting trainees with skills and attitudes they will carry with them their whole professional lives, we can rest assured knowing that ultimately it is our Lord who shapes their souls and guides their steps. We can participate through the formation of Christian learning communities where cultivating professional competency and encouraging Christian character formation go hand in hand.

As clinical professionals, we can also look to the literature in counseling, psychology, and marriage and family therapy for resources on virtue formation in clinical supervision. The positive psychology movement has focused our discipline's attention on character strengths and positive human characteristics that lead to flourishing (Seligman, 2011), and several authors have explored implications of positive psychology for the goals and practices of clinical supervision (Howard, 2008; Wade & Jones, 2015). Our ethical codes provide aspirational professional values that offer a vision of optimal professional virtues and habits that benefit society. The growing contemporary supervision literature has much to offer in terms of models, methods, and best practices for promoting supervisee development. While organized around the character virtues, this framework will provide an introduction to contemporary supervision models, draw empirically formed supervision practices from supervision research, and offer practical tools for competent clinical supervision.

In this chapter, we consider a Christian integrative approach to clinical supervision that serves as a guide for the priorities, goals, and practices of clinical supervision. Conceptually, it locates the practice of clinical supervision within the larger context of moral character formation. Specifically, a virtue-oriented clinical supervision framework envisions clinical supervision as an educational experience that forms the professional and personal character of the supervisee for long-term competence, effectiveness, and service to God's kingdom.

FOUR COMPONENTS OF A CHRISTIAN INTEGRATIVE FRAMEWORK

A Christian integrative framework integrates four complementary priorities. First, the theological and moral virtues provide the overarching vision for aspirational character strengths for the clinician. Second, professional ethical principles tie these virtues to the aspirational values of our professions. Third, supervision models, methods, and best practice guidelines foster development of competence and effectiveness. And fourth, individual and community Christian practices are integrated with the framework to foster the formation of our character in Christlikeness. Together, these four priorities provide a roadmap for the supervision process that provides "something more" than any one category alone. Let us examine each of these areas.

Virtue / Character Strengths

The first priority of a Christian integrative framework establishes virtue development and character formation as an explicit aim of the supervision process with the goal of professional competence, effectiveness, and flourishing. As discussed in chapter one, effective educational approaches provide opportunities for *formation* as well as *information*, and clinical supervision, as the signature pedagogy for the education of clinicians, should be no exception. Supervisors have the opportunity to focus trainees' attention to the larger question: What kind of counselor, psychologist, or MFT do I want to be?

Drawing from theological and biblical literature, the three theological virtues (faith, hope, and love) and the four moral or cardinal virtues (wisdom, justice, temperance, and courage) are identified as lifelong personal and professional character formation goals that can be encouraged and fostered through the clinical supervision process. Virtues are defined as habits of thought and action that, when practiced consistently, become "characteristic" of our personal and professional lives. The development of a character virtue is not an end in itself, but rather forms us for the love of God and neighbor. Supervisors encourage the development of

personal and professional practices and habits that promote long-term competency and flourishing. The supervisor is a part of God's overall work in the life of the supervisee, as they are both being formed by the Holy Spirit into Christlikeness. A virtue-informed approach recognizes that personal and professional development are inseparable, and that the most impactful supervision helps supervisees develop the habits and character that will prepare them to face the challenges of long-term mental health practice. An interdisciplinary understanding of virtue values perspectives from philosophy, theology, psychology, and cognitive neuroscience. The Christian framework provided later in the chapter provides a brief description of each virtue.

Professional Ethical Principles and Values

A second supervision priority is the cultivation of professional values and aspirations that provide the foundation for ethical guidelines and behaviors. All the mental health disciplines emphasize the responsibility of clinical supervisors to facilitate supervisees' understanding of the professional values and guidelines articulated by ethical codes and standards. Professional ethical principles and codes of conduct provide the standards by which competent professional practice is measured. Supervisors can practice both *principle ethics* and *virtue ethics* in supervision to help supervisees become clinicians of character who act ethically in a characteristic and consistent way throughout their professional careers.

Integral to the supervision process is a deep familiarity with the ethical principles of the profession and the ethical decision-making processes that guide clinical practice. Comparisons of the core ethical principles across mental health professions demonstrate consistency (see table 1). The proposed framework connects aspirational ethical principles with a corresponding character virtue as complementary goals of clinical supervision. For example, nonmaleficence, or doing no harm, is linked to the character virtue of temperance, which involves cultivating habits of self-control, restraint, and humility.

Table 1. Ethical principles in counseling, psychology, and MFT

ACA foundational professional values (ACA, 2014)	APA general principles (APA, 2010)	AAMFT aspirational core values (AAMFT, 2015)
Autonomy		• Innovation and advancement of systemic and relational therapies
Beneficence and nonmaleficence	Beneficence and nonmaleficence	• Honoring public trust • Commitment to service, advocacy, and public participation (preamble)
Justice	Justice	• Diversity, equity, and excellence in clinical practice, research, education, and administration • Acceptance, appreciation, and inclusion of diverse membership
Fidelity	Fidelity and responsibility	• Responsiveness and excellence in service to members
Veracity	Integrity	• Integrity and high threshold of ethical and honest behavior
		• Distinctiveness and excellence in training of MFTs

SUPERVISION MODELS AND METHODS

The third category in our Christian integrative framework connects supervision models and methods with specific supervision techniques aimed to foster the development of professional values and character virtues. An integrative approach to clinical supervision utilizes multiple supervision theories and models with consideration for the domain of expertise of each model. Clinical supervision best practices and evidence-based techniques are incorporated throughout the framework (see table 2 for a comparison of best practices in clinical supervision by discipline). Supervision methods to foster Christian integration and competency with religious and spiritual issues are also incorporated into this component of the framework.

Consider the example above of the relationship between temperance and doing no harm. A supervisor could use a person-of-the-therapist approach to supervision, which is especially suited to the development of self-reflective habits and practices. As supervisees develop their reflective-practice skills, they learn to pay attention to their emotional reactions to clinical situations, developing greater awareness of their impact on clients. Consequently, they are less likely to do harm.

Table 2. Supervision best practices in counseling, psychology, and MFT

Best practices in counseling supervision (Borders et al., 2014)	Guidelines for clinical supervision in health service psychology (APA, 2014)	AAMFT Approved Supervisor Guidelines (AAMFT, 2014).
Initiating supervision: informed consent, structure, and process		
Goal setting		• Purpose and goals of supervision
Giving feedback		
Implementing supervision	Supervision competence	• Various supervisory approaches and practices and how they connect with various therapy approaches and practices • Systemic MFT thinking as applied in therapy, supervision, mentoring, and the isomorphic dynamics among different levels of the training system • Articulation of a systemic personal philosophy or approach to supervision and how it integrates with therapy approaches • Integration of couple and family therapy literature, both seminal and recent
Supervisory relationship	Supervisory relationship	• Supervisory roles and relationships, including attention to management of multiple relationships
Diversity and advocacy considerations	Diversity	
Ethical considerations	Ethical, legal, and regulatory considerations	• Processes for supervising within applicable legal requirements for licensure or certification or obtaining various levels of membership in AAMFT • Jurisdictional legal factors such as duties to report or warn, working with minors in therapy, recordkeeping, and so forth • Processes for attending to ethical factors in therapy and supervision • Current thinking, literature, ethics, requirements, and challenges of the use of technology in therapy and supervision

Best practices in counseling supervision (Borders et al., 2014)	Guidelines for clinical supervision in health service psychology (APA, 2014)	AAMFT Approved Supervisor Guidelines (AAMFT, 2014).
Maintaining documentation		
Evaluation	Assessment, evaluation, feedback	• Supervisory processes for screening, contracting with, and evaluating trainees
Supervision format		• Structure of supervision, problem solving, and implementation of a variety of supervisory practices • Modalities for supervising including group/ individual and case consultation/audio recording/ video recording
Supervisor competency		• Mentoring factors such as contracting, relationship, responsibilities, and processes
Supervisor preparation, training, and supervision of supervision		• The supervision mentoring process as described in the Approved Supervisor Guidelines

Spiritual Formation

The fourth component of a Christian integrative framework identifies individual and community spiritual formation practices that can be incorporated into the supervision process. Clinicians are invited to utilize spiritual disciplines and engage in community practices as opportunities for growth in character and Christlikeness toward a holistic formation of professional and personal character. The Christian integrative literature on clinical supervision encourages the use of the spiritual disciplines as an important component of a distinctively Christian supervision process (Tan, 2007; Bufford, 2007; Campbell, 2007; Fisk et al., 2013). Not only is this practice spiritually formative for the supervisor and supervisee, but it also demonstrates the use of explicit spiritual practices in a clinical setting.

To continue our example above, to cultivate reflective practice skills, a supervisor could introduce a trainee to the spiritual discipline of self-examination, which involves setting aside regular time for a prayerful examen of conscience. This spiritual practice cultivates spiritual self-awareness and contributes to reflective practice in a professional context. Spiritual self-examination and person-of-the-therapist supervision can work in an integrated way to help the supervisee develop practices and habits that cultivate self-control, nonmaleficence, and temperance.

Together, the four complementary priorities provide an overarching framework and roadmap to guide the process of clinical supervision, as summarized in table 3.

Table 3. A Christian integrative framework for clinical supervision

Character virtue	Professional ethical principles and values	Clinical supervision best practices, models, and techniques	Spiritual formation: individual and community practices
Faith: trust, belief, and obedience to God; intellect and will assenting to God's truth.	**Fidelity** and **responsibility** to individuals, community, and public; establishing trust, upholding standards of conduct, honoring commitments, fulfilling one's responsibilities	• Establishing supervision alliance and frame • Attachment-based models • Christian integrative supervision, attachment, and Christian worldview	• Contemplative prayer • Christian community, liturgy and the sacraments
Hope: expectation and trust in God as our meaning and purpose; pursuing Christ's kingdom as our desire	**Beneficence:** benefit to others, working for good, promoting health and well-being in society	• Providing vocational mentoring • Developmental models • Positive psychology • Existential supervision • Christian integrative supervision, the Holy Spirit, and eschatology	• Sabbath • Worship
Love: agape/caritas, love of God and neighbor, mercy	**Relational competencies** and **respect** for dignity and rights: respect worth of all people; respect privacy, autonomy, confidentiality, and self determination	• Fostering relational competence • Humanistic-experiential • Transgenerational Family Systems supervision • Psychodynamic approaches • Existential supervision • Christian integrative supervision and incarnational, trinitarian love	• Interpersonal spiritual disciplines • Intercessory prayer
Wisdom: practical wisdom and good judgment	**Competence** and **ethical decision making**	• Competency-based models • CBT supervision • Existential supervision • Ethical decision-making models • Competence in applied Christian integration	• Scripture study and meditation • Discernment

Character virtue	Professional ethical principles and values	Clinical supervision best practices, models, and techniques	Spiritual formation: individual and community practices
Justice: wanting what is fair and good for others	**Justice:** fairness, equality, eliminating biases, treating individuals equally, respect for diversity and individual differences	• Prioritizing diversity competence and advocacy skills • Multicultural models • Advocacy-based models • Christian integrative supervision and diversity competence	• Attentiveness • Hospitality • Service
Temperance: self-control, restraint, and humility	**Nonmaleficence:** do no harm, awareness of own health in practice, self-regulation, and humility	• Evaluation in supervision • Person-of-the-therapist models • CBT supervision • Psychodynamic supervision • Christian integrative supervision and self-examination/transformation • Encouraging reflective practice	• Self-examination • Fasting
Courage: fortitude, endurance, resilience, commitment, confidence, and magnanimity	**Integrity:** accuracy, honesty, and veracity in clinical and research practices	• Fostering professional wellness and resilience • Wellness-oriented models • Trauma-informed supervision • Self-compassion • Meaning, purpose, and theodicy in Christian integrative supervision	• Stories and examples • Rule of life • Silence • Solitude

PRINCIPLES OF APPLICATION

The Christian integrative framework provides a supplemental resource for the clinical supervision process. Supervisors working from any supervision philosophy or model can benefit from considering this roadmap for the development of character virtue as an explicit goal of the supervision process. To achieve this goal, it is imperative that supervisors operate within the best practices and ethical guidelines of our respective professions. In this section we examine four foundational principles that provide parameters for the application of the framework.

Supervision Best Practices

A Christian integrative approach to clinical supervision incorporates best practices consistent with supervision research, ethics, and standards across mental health disciplines. Borders et al. (2014) suggest that supervision competencies and best practices are both important and complement each other:

> Competencies outline required declarative knowledge, or what a competent supervisor needs to know; best practices provide the basis for procedural knowledge, describe when and how declarative knowledge is applied, or what a supervisor does during supervision. Best practices provide evidence-based guidelines for implementing or applying competencies (as well as ethical codes). (p. 152)

Descriptions of supervision best practices are informed by supervision research, theory, ethics, and desired competencies, and these guide the practice of supervision in educational and clinical training settings. The Association of Counselor Education and Supervision (ACES) has developed a list of twelve categories of best practices for clinical supervisors in the counseling profession that are applicable for supervisors from all mental health disciplines (Borders et al., 2014). Similarly, APA provides guidelines in seven domains in its *Guidelines for Clinical Supervisors in Health Service Psychology* (2014). For marriage and family therapists, the *Approved Supervision Designation Standards* handbook (AAMFT, 2014) provides nine learning objectives and a description of supervisor responsibilities and guidelines. See table 2 for a comparison of best practices in clinical supervision across these disciplines.

Developing supervision habits and practices that reflect competency and effectiveness is at the heart of the virtue-oriented approach to clinical supervision proposed in this text. Consequently, supervision best practices and evidenced-based supervision interventions are incorporated throughout the following chapters.

Supervisor Roles and Responsibilities

Supervision as a professional activity is distinct from personal therapy and spiritual formation, as it holds the *professional* formation of supervisees as the primary goal. A Christian integrative framework, with its focus on character formation in the context of clinical supervision, operates with these responsibilities in mind. The gatekeeper role of clinical supervisors requires regular evaluation of supervisees, which inevitably establishes hierarchy and a power differential in the relationship. While transparent supervision practices such as a supervision contract can foster the establishment of collaboration and trust within this power differential (as we will discuss in chap. 3), the reality is that the evaluative process distinguishes clinical supervision from other types of professional relationships such as mentoring or consultation. Let us briefly review the relevant guidelines on supervisor roles and responsibilities.

It is widely recognized that supervisors adopt a variety of roles, and supervision best practices require supervisors to provide explicit clarification of roles at the outset as part of establishing the supervision alliance and introducing the process of supervision: "The supervisor describes his/her role as supervisor, including teacher, counselor, consultant, mentor, and evaluator" (Borders et al., 2014, p. 33). At the same time, a supervisor "clearly defines the boundaries of the supervision relationship and avoids multiple roles or dual relationships with the supervisee that may negatively impact the supervisee or the supervision relationship" (p. 37). The ACES supervision guidelines provide this example of the use of supervision to address personal issues that affect clinical work:

The supervisor explains to the supervisee the appropriate parameters of addressing the supervisee's personal issues in supervision (identifies the issue, helps the supervisee see the clinical implications, works to minimize the detrimental effects in the supervisee's clinical work, contributes to a plan for resolution that does not directly involve the supervisor) and acts accordingly. (Borders et al., 2014, p. 39)

Similarly, the APA's *Guidelines for Clinical Supervision in Health Service Psychology* (2014) states that "supervision is . . . distinct from consultation, personal psychotherapy, and mentoring" (p. 11). The subsequent footnote in the document provides helpful clarification of how these roles are differentiated: "Supervision is distinguished from these other professional activities by 1) professional responsibility and liability, 2) the purpose of the activity, 3) the relative power of the parties involved, and 4) the presence or absence of evaluation" (p. 11).

Goodyear and Rodolfo provide a balanced and nuanced discussion of supervisor roles and responsibilities in the *APA Handbook of Ethics* (2012). According to the authors, supervision inevitably includes a substantial component of teaching, use of therapeutic skills, and the fostering of supervisee development, including discussion of the personal and interpersonal issues that affect their work with clients. They note that it is common for supervisors to experience tensions between their evaluative and professional development roles. However, the welfare of the public and profession must always take precedence for the supervisor, and in a situation where the client welfare is at stake, supervisors must operate in the evaluative role even when it is hurtful to the supervision alliance (Goodyear & Rodolfo, 2012, p. 269).

Supervisee personal and professional development is an integral part of the supervision process and in many ways inseparable from its educational and clinical objectives. As supervisors, we manage these multiple roles by keeping in mind our primary responsibilities to the public, the profession, and the clinical training of the supervisee. We are also mindful of the power differential that our gatekeeping and evaluation roles require and the more vulnerable position this places our supervisees in. Supervision ethics provides important protections for supervisees in the context of this power differential. A virtue-oriented framework for supervision fosters the professional and personal development of supervisees while operating within professionally defined roles and boundaries.

Supervision Ethics for Incorporating Religious and Spiritual Issues

In chapter one, we reviewed the literature on religious and spiritual issues and the supervision process. Holistic care of the client involves attention to religious and spiritual issues and incorporating these issues into the treatment process, particularly if they are important to the client. Likewise, for supervisees with religious or spiritual commitments, incorporating Christian integrative supervision practices and spiritual disciplines into the supervision process provides the opportunity to develop integration skills and foster holistic growth and formation (Tan, 2009).

What are the ethical considerations to keep in mind when incorporating religion and spirituality into the supervision process? Fortunately, we can look to the literature on ethics for religious and spiritual issues in clinical practice for guidance. While the literature on religious and spiritual issues in clinical supervision is quite limited, we can also adapt the ethical guidelines for spiritual and religious interventions with clients for the supervision relationship (these resources are indicated by italics). The following is a summary of ethical guidelines for integrating religion and spirituality into the supervision process:

- Supervisee informed consent is essential. Supervisors assess supervisee interest in religious and spiritual issues and provide a clear professional disclosure of how spiritual issues might be incorporated into the supervision process. The supervision contract provides documentation of this disclosure and supervisee consent and also provides clarification of roles, responsibilities, and evaluation procedures (Tan, 2007; *Hathaway & Ripley, 2009*).

- Supervisors respect the religious and spiritual values and beliefs of supervisees and only incorporate them into the supervision process with the supervisee's interest and consent (Plante, 2009; *Hathaway, 2011*).

- Incorporation of religious and spiritual issues into supervision should be consistent with the overall supervision and professional formation goals for the supervisee, developed collaboratively. Supervisors keep in mind that the primary focus of supervision is professional and clinical (Miller, Korinek, & Ivey, 2006).

- Supervisors clearly communicate and operate within their role and should not overstep their role, usurp the role of a pastor/spiritual leader, or take inappropriate spiritual authority with a supervisee (Miller et al., 2006; *Hathaway, 2011*).

- Supervisors need to recognize their own limits and develop competencies with

spiritual and religious interventions in supervision. Competency can be obtained through education, training, supervision of supervision, and seeking regular consultation (*Plante, 2009; Hathaway, 2011; Vieten et al., 2013*).

- Spiritual and religious practices should be used with a clear rationale and purpose and in a way that is consistent with religious teaching and tradition (Tan, 2007; *Hathaway & Ripley, 2009*).

- Spiritual and religious practices should not be used exclusively in place of evidence-based supervision interventions with known effectiveness (*Hathaway & Ripley, 2009*).

- Supervisors should check back with supervisees and process their level of comfort and perceived benefit of incorporating religious and spiritual issues in supervision.

Approaching religious and spiritual issues ethically, respectfully, and competently in clinical supervision is of critical importance as it will likely affect how supervisees handle these issues with clients. Through our respect for supervisees' autonomy and attention to their welfare as a primary consideration, supervisors model respectful and ethical practice with religious and spiritual issues and increase the likelihood that these issues will be handled ethically and competently by supervisees with their clients.

Person of the Supervisor

As supervisors, our own character strengths and failings are an inevitable and important part of the supervision process, affecting our supervisees directly. God is also forming our character through our supervisees, which requires our attentiveness, humility, integrity, and courage. Supervisees will benefit from our authenticity and appropriate disclosure of our own spiritual and character formation journey. And as we will see in the next chapter, the spiritual life of the supervisor has a significant impact on the development of a student's integration competencies. Note Parker Palmer's (2007) words: "The personal can never be divorced from the professional. 'We teach who we are' in times of darkness as well as light" (p. xi). This is certainly true of the clinical supervisor. May God grant us the courage to engage in our own character formation journey as supervisors.

Conclusion: Putting Together the Principles of Application

Together, the integrative framework and principles of application provide a roadmap for the development of personal and professional character through the clinical supervision process. Supervisors can incorporate this framework into their existing models of supervision to provide guiding theory and interventions for the character development aims of clinical supervision. The virtues, aspirational professional values, and clinical supervision models and methods are applicable for all supervisees. Incorporating the spiritual formation practices into clinical supervision will depend on the supervisor's assessment and the supervisee's consent, as discussed above. For supervisees who are interested in and consent

to incorporating religious and spiritual issues in clinical supervision, the spiritual formation practices described in each chapter bring the teaching and practices from Christian tradition on character development into the clinical supervision process.

Spiritual disciplines are never imposed, but rather are invitations to deepen our experience of God and his formation of our character in day-to-day life. Because of the power differential in supervision, however, even the suggestion of a spiritual discipline to a supervisee could be experienced as a mandate, even when there is informed consent. Supervisors should be wise, prudent, and sensitive about how these practices are suggested. In each chapter, you will notice the use of verbs such as "invite," "offer," and "suggest" to introduce spiritual disciplines to the supervision process. Probably the most effective way to introduce the disciplines is for supervisors to model their use and demonstrate the benefits of the disciplines for their own work as counselors, psychologists, and MFTs. Most importantly, we recognize that sanctification and formation of character are God's work in the life of the believer, not the sole responsibility of the supervisor. God is the master teacher and supervisor who forms our souls in Christlikeness. As supervisors, we have the privilege of participating in this endeavor through the supervision process. Our continual prayer should be, "Lord, how can I be a part of your formational work in this supervisee's life?"

DEVELOPING THE VIRTUES

The following chapters focus in depth on each of the core virtues and their importance for ethical and effective clinical supervision. Each chapter provides a theological perspective on

the virtue, a review of psychological theory and research, and a brief discussion of the corresponding ethical principle. Then each chapter outlines relevant clinical supervision models, methods, and specific interventions for developing professional and personal habits and practices. Lastly, individual and community spiritual formation practices are provided in each chapter, representing time-tested approaches to the formation of virtue from Christian teaching and Scripture. While each of the virtues are discussed independently for the sake of clarity, we must keep in mind that the theological and moral virtues are inseparable and interdependent. As Paul reminds us in 1 Corinthians 13:2, "If I have a faith that can move mountains, but do not have love, I am nothing."

It is important to note that the theological section on each virtue provides just a taste of the rich literature on the ideals for human character. I sought to include diverse voices from Protestant, Catholic, historical, and contemporary thought. The reader will notice, however, that the perspectives of Catholic philosopher Josef Pieper and Anglican theologian N. T. Wright are included in many of the chapters along with other respected scholars. Both Pieper and Wright have been particularly influential for Christians in the development of our understanding of virtue; Pieper's scholarly work is widely cited by many virtue scholars, and Wright's practical theology of Christian character formation is also commonly referenced as a guide to Christian living. It is hoped that inclusion of their perspective in many of the virtue chapters provides a thread of continuity and an ecumenical touchpoint by highlighting Protestant and Catholic influences on Christian virtue ethics.

CONCLUSION

This chapter provides a theoretical foundation and rationale for a Christian integrative framework for clinical supervision. There *is* more to the clinical supervision process than current models and theories propose. Integrating a theological and biblical understanding of character formation with professional ethics and supervision best practices allows us to add another layer of depth and meaning to the supervision process and to participate with God in the formation of supervisees who will flourish in their clinical vocations.

Through the process of clinical supervision, we aim to develop

- faithful clinicians who are securely connected to the living God through Jesus Christ and empowered by his Holy Spirit to form trusting and secure relationships with those they serve, and who engender "good faith" in the community through being faithful and responsible professionals;

- hopeful clinicians who maintain a vision for mental health work as benefiting individuals, families, and communities, and who see their place in serving Christ's kingdom through promoting health and hope;

- loving clinicians who have a deep sense of respect for the dignity and worth of all as created in the image of God, and who demonstrate empathy, positive regard, and respect for the rights of those they serve by honoring confidentiality and privacy;

- wise clinicians who are lifelong learners, curious, and able to tolerate complexities; who value God's Word and science-informed practice; who are competent and ethical, able to apply knowledge and make good clinical judgments with practical wisdom and discernment;

- justice-oriented clinicians who prioritize service and advocacy for "the least of these" and practice diversity competence for the sake of Christ's kingdom, so that there is fair access to mental health services for all;

- self-controlled clinicians who do no harm and can self-regulate and self-supervise, who in all humility are aware of strengths and limitations, and who are other-centered; and

- courageous clinicians who demonstrate integrity, fortitude, honesty, commitment, and veracity; who can demonstrate resilience and engagement in the profession for the long haul; and who can act on ethical principles and contribute to the profession and larger society with confidence and humility.

CHAPTER 3

FAITH

Belief and Trust

Now faith is confidence in what we hope for and assurance about what we do not see. This is what the ancients were commended for. By faith we understand that the universe was formed at God's command, so that what is seen was not made out of what was visible.

HEBREWS 11:1-3

DESPITE OUR BEST INTENTIONS and efforts, sometimes one of the regrettable outcomes of graduate education in psychology, counseling, or marriage and family therapy is the diminishment, dampening, or deconstruction of a student's faith. Consider the following scenario. A student begins graduate studies in clinical psychology at a faith-based institution. She has been actively involved in ministry but also feels a call from God to develop her counseling knowledge and skills in order to be more effective in her service to the kingdom. While in her graduate program, she is immersed in the scientific study of psychology. She learns about professional ethics and is taught to "bracket" her Christian values and beliefs in her clinical work with clients. She takes theology classes and begins to develop a more intellectually rigorous theological and biblical knowledge, but her study of theology also challenges her personal faith as some of her deeply held assumptions are deconstructed. With the time

demands of her classes, clinical practicum, and part-time job, she finds it difficult to locate and get involved with a church. Often God feels very distant from her studies, and she is not sure how to integrate her spiritual experiences with her work in the counseling office. She finishes her graduate program well prepared for her vocational work as a psychologist, but with many questions and conflicts about how her Christian faith identity fits with her professional work.

Imagine a different scenario where her faculty, supervisors, and peers model and encourage individual and community practices that nurture a robust Christian worldview and deepen personal faith. Her supervisor invites her to bring the interface of spirituality and counseling into the supervision experience, and to explore how her clinical and classroom experiences are influencing her own relationship of belief and trust in God. As she feels more trusting and secure in the supervisory relationship, she feels free to share the questions and doubts that are emerging as she studies psychology and engages in clinical practice. She is encouraged to find a church community and attends weekly worship where she hears God's Word, takes communion, and reaffirms her identity as a believer. She finishes graduate school with a faith that is challenged and deepened, and with professional and personal habits and practices that nurture her trust in Christ and her ability to see her profession through the lens of a Christian worldview. Maybe ideal, yes; but possible, certainly!

It is fitting that our first character strength for consideration is the virtue of faith, for belief and trust mark the beginning of our life with Christ, of which professional life is one small part. Faith, as a gift from God, allows the believer to trust in the God whom she cannot see or prove. Faith is deepened as she begins to see all of life, including psychology, through the eyes of this fundamental belief in a loving Creator who offers a real relationship of trust and love through Jesus Christ. In a parallel way, the supervision process begins when the supervisor establishes trust through offering the supervision experience as a secure base from which the supervisee can learn, explore, reveal

their successes and mistakes, and thus be formed as a professional. Christian integrative supervision aims to form faithful clinicians who are securely connected to the living God through Jesus Christ and empowered by his Holy Spirit to form trusting and secure relationships with those they serve, and who engender "good faith" in the community through being faithful and responsible professionals.

In this chapter, we examine faith from a theological perspective and find parallels in the corresponding professional value of fidelity. We explore psychological perspectives on religious belief and attachment theory that inform our understanding of the development of the virtue of faith. We identify attachment-informed supervision practices that foster a good beginning of trust, including informed consent, the supervision contract, and attention to the "frame" of supervision. We identify how Christian integrative supervision will also include attentiveness to the supervisee's attachment to God, and to approaching the practice of counseling, psychology, and MFT from a Christian worldview as we reason from a foundation of faith. Finally, we examine spiritual practices that foster faith and attachment to God and Christian community.

FAITH: BIBLICAL AND THEOLOGICAL PERSPECTIVES

Faith, the first of the three theological virtues described in 1 Corinthians and later elaborated by Aquinas, involves belief, trust, and willing obedience to God. According to the *Catechism of the Catholic Church* (2003):

> Faith is the theological virtue by which we believe in God and believe all that he has said and revealed to us, and that Holy Church proposes for our belief, because he is truth itself. By faith "man freely commits his entire

self to God." For this reason the believer seeks to know and do God's will. "The righteous shall live by faith." Living faith "work[s] through charity." (para. 1814)

Aquinas asserts that the object of faith for the believer is the "First Truth," who is God Himself, "against which all other truths are measured" (Kaczor, 2008, p. 8). Faith is more than intellectual assent, according to Aquinas, as it "involves both *believing someone* (formal aspect of the faith) and *believing something* (material aspect of the faith)" (Kaczor, 2008, p. 10). Faith is inseparable from hope and love as the "infused" theological virtues by which the believer comes to know, trust, believe, and love God.

In the biblical narrative, we see God's initiation of a relationship with his people through his covenant with Israel and later through the new covenant offered through faith in Jesus Christ and his death and resurrection. By receiving God's gift of faith, we enter into a lifelong, loving relationship with the God of the universe, characterized by a secure and abiding love from which nothing can separate us (Rom 8:38-39). Farley (1995) summarizes three aspects of historical Christian teaching on faith: faith as "a subjective response to the self-revelation of God," faith as "an intelligent and moral response to the objective events of history from Abraham through the Apostles," and faith as "a gift of God's gracious will for the human heart to entrust itself to the divine" (p. 147). German philosopher Josef Pieper (1997) emphasizes the importance of trusting in that which we cannot see as essential to faith: "Belief means to regard something as true on the testimony of someone else" (p. 15). As Jesus said to the apostle Thomas, "Blessed are those who have not seen and yet have believed" (Jn 20:29).

Historically, the theological virtue of faith has often been equated with the intellect, that is, giving intellectual assent to the truths of the gospel (Waddams, 1964). However, a number of historical and contemporary theologians also equate faith with *trust*. Swiss theologian Emil Brunner (1956) writes that faith includes belief in the historical reality of Christ's death, resurrection, and atonement of our sins, but is not simply an intellectual agreement with historical facts. Rather, Brunner calls faith "an act

of the heart" (p. 23) that is a response to God's love—a mystical, spiritual experience of becoming one with Christ. He suggests that the most parallel human experience is that of "entrusting oneself to another" (p. 28). Brunner is quick to caution us of the risks of trusting in fallible human beings, who are not able to be completely selfless in loving another.

> But it is different with God, who is all-powerful and whose nature is love. God alone is absolutely trustworthy, not being frail but all-powerful, not being selfish but love itself. It is that God whose infinite love is revealed in Jesus Christ, who makes it possible for us to entrust ourselves completely and without reserve, because he has revealed himself without reserve as unconditional love. It is to him and only him who is holy Love as revealed in the cross of Christ, that we *can*, that we *dare* to give ourselves completely. (Brunner, 1956, p. 29)

N. T. Wright also equates faith with belief and trust. In his historical introduction to faith, *Simply Christian*, he writes, "Faith is the settled, unwavering trust in the one true God whom we have come to know in Jesus Christ" (Wright, 2006, p. 203). Further, Wright provides a historical context for the early Christian understandings of faith reflected in the New Testament:

> What the early Christians meant by "belief" included both believing *that* God had done certain things and believing *in* the God who had done them. This is not belief that God exists, though clearly that is involved, too, but loving, grateful *trust* [emphasis added]. When things "make sense" in that way, you are left knowing that it isn't so much a matter of you figuring it all out and deciding to take a step, or a stand. It's a matter of Someone calling you, calling with a voice you dimly recognize, calling with a message

that is simultaneously an invitation of love and a summons to obedience. The call to faith is both of these. It is the call to believe that the true God, the world's creator, has loved the whole world so much, you and me included, that he has come himself in the person of his Son and has died and risen again to exhaust the power of evil and create a new world in which everything will be put to rights and joy will replace sorrow. (Wright, 2006, p. 207)

The virtue of faith in practice can be evidenced by acts of fidelity and trustworthiness toward one's community. Christian ethicist D. C. Jones writes that Christians are called to faithfulness as a form of love, along with justice and mercy. Faithfulness as an essential attribute of God is represented in Scripture by God as our rock, symbolizing the immutability of God as trustworthy, stable, reliable, and unchanging in his very nature and character (Jones, 1994, p. 93). In the same way, Christians are called to honesty, trustworthiness, and fidelity as character traits. Farley also makes the connection between the Christian virtue of faithfulness and the universal human virtue of fidelity. Just as believers respond to God's faithfulness expressed in covenant love to the people of Israel first and then through Christ, so Christians should practice faithfulness and fidelity as a human virtue as evidenced by trustworthiness, honesty, and responsibility (Farley, 1995, p. 137).

Is the experience of doubt antithetical to faith? Spiritual writers suggest that doubt is actually an essential aspect of resilient faith. Frederick Buechner (1973) calls doubt the "ants in your pants" that keeps faith awake, alive, and thriving. Similarly, Paul Tillich (1975) describes doubt as an existential aspect of faith that is not in opposition to true faith:

The affirmation that Jesus is the Christ is an act of faith and consequently of daring courage. It is not an arbitrary leap into darkness but a decision in which elements of immediate participation and therefore certitude are mixed with elements of strangeness and therefore incertitude and doubt. But doubt is not the opposite of faith; it is an element of faith. Therefore, there is no faith without risk. (pp. 116-17)

Contemporary theologian and spiritual writer Fr. Ron Rolheiser (2001) asserts that doubt in God's existence is not the opposite of faith; rather, the *anxiety* that God cannot be trusted is in opposition to faith. Rolheiser points us to the example of Jesus, who in the darkness of Gethsemane prayed in trust to his Father. So we, too, should have faith in God's goodness and care for us and "fear not," as Scripture admonishes. Rolheiser writes:

What is faith? Faith doesn't have you believe that you will have no worries, or that you will not make mistakes or betray, or that you and your loved ones won't sometimes too fall victim to accident, sickness, and suicide. What faith gives you is the assurance that God is good, that God can be trusted, that God won't forget you, and that, despite any indication to the contrary, God is still solidly in charge of this universe. (Rolheiser, 2001, p. 1)

In summary, biblical and theological perspectives contribute to our understanding of the virtue of faith as both the intellectual and willful assent to the truth of the gospel message and an experiential trust in and relationship with the Author of this message. The gift of faith in Christ, as an infused virtue, marks the beginning of our relationship with God when by grace we trust in his covenant love. As Christians, we are called to practice the virtue of faithfulness in our communities as manifested by fidelity, trustworthiness, and responsibility. A Christian integrative approach to clinical supervision will include attentiveness to belief, trust, and doubt as essential elements of faith and encourage the development of faithful practices and habits.

FAITH: PSYCHOLOGICAL PERSPECTIVES

Important for our virtue-oriented approach to supervision is an understanding of virtue from a psychological perspective. How do we understand the character strength of faith from psychological theory and research? How do individuals develop belief and trust? Does faith as a character strength contribute to human health and flourishing? In this section, we delve deeper into our understanding of the virtue of faith through exploring belief and trust as psychological constructs.

Positive psychologists Peterson and Seligman (2004) include the virtue of faith as one of the character strengths of "transcendence," or the human traits that provide meaning to one's life through connecting individuals to something outside themselves. Transcendence incorporates characteristic traits such as spirituality, gratitude, humor, hope, and appreciation of beauty. Spirituality and religiosity are defined as "beliefs and practices that are grounded in the conviction that there is a transcendent (nonphysical) dimension of life. These beliefs are persuasive, pervasive, and stable. They inform the kinds of attributions people make, the meanings they construct, and the ways they conduct relationships" (Peterson & Seligman, 2004, p. 600). From a positive psychology perspective, people with the character strength of spirituality have a strong sense of coherence, fulfillment, and purpose in their life that is often nurtured through practicing rituals and traditions.

Psychology of Religious Belief

From its very earliest days, the discipline of psychology has examined the psychological processes involved in religious belief and behavior. Students of the psychology of religion will recognize the name of William James, author of one of the first treatments of religiosity from a psychological perspective (James & Marty, 1982). Many of the important early theorists incorporated an understanding of religion into their models of personality (Freud, Strachey, & Gay, 1989; Jung, 1933; Allport, 1950). The psychology of religion has evolved as a major subdiscipline within the field, with many outlets for collaborative research, including APA's Division 36 and the division's journal, *The Psychology of Religion and Spirituality*. A common distinction is made in the literature between the terms *religion* and *spirituality*—"Spirituality involves a person's beliefs, values, and behavior, while religiousness denotes the person's involvement with a religious tradition and institution" (Hood, Hill, & Spilka, 2009, p. 9—while at times the terms are used interchangeably in the literature, with spirituality as the more general category. Currently, the psychology of religion can be understood as the study of human beings' search for meaning, which includes cognitive, motivational, and social facets (Hood, Hill, & Spilka, 2009). Although a survey of this literature is beyond the scope of this book, it is important for our understanding of the virtue of faith to explore psychology of religion's contributions to understanding religious belief.

Important for the study of religion and personality has been Allport's conception and measurement of intrinsic versus extrinsic religious orientation (Allport & Ross, 1967). According to Allport, intrinsically oriented religious individuals "live" their religiosity, whereas extrinsically oriented people utilize religious beliefs and practices toward an instrumental goal or end. A meta-analysis of early research on this topic found associations between extrinsic religious orientation and greater psychological distress, poorer coping, and even prejudice, whereas individuals with intrinsic religious motivation tend to exhibit higher levels of well-being and better coping (Worthington, Kurusu, McCollough, & Sandage, 1996). More recent research suggests that individuals who act on their religious commitments experience more life satisfaction and exhibit higher scores on a number of character strengths than people who are nonreligious or do not practice their religious affiliation (Berthold, Ruch, Von Hecker, & Rosenberg, 2014).

"Quest" is proposed as a third type of religious orientation to describe individuals who approach religion as a journey or quest (Batson, 1976). Questing individuals are characterized by an open, seeking, and growth-oriented orientation as they explore religious questions and doubts to make sense of the world. Research suggests this orientation can be associated with greater anxiety and depression but also spiritual reward (Batson, Schoenrade, & Ventis, 1993). A recent project explored the impact of the quest orientation on the well-being, religiosity, and identity of a large sample of religious emerging adults (Cook, Kimball, Leonard, & Boyatzis, 2014). The research found that a high questing orientation, when combined with intrinsic religious motivation, was positively related to strong religious identity and coping. In contrast, a high questing orientation alone was associated with lower religiosity. The authors conclude, "For intrinsics, quest may engender a distinctive developmental trajectory, a path of existential searching by which emerging adults successfully manage the demands of contemporary culture while developing a more mature faith" (Cook et al., 2014, p. 87). This research supports the assertion that religious questioning and doubt can play a key role in the development of secure and mature faith, particularly during emerging adulthood.

How do individuals develop religious belief? The vast literature on the development of religious and spiritual beliefs in childhood, adolescence, and adulthood has explored the individual, interpersonal, contextual, and interactive factors that contribute to religious belief and practice. Scholars are moving away from stage theories of religious and moral development (Piaget, 1948; Kohlberg, 1984; Fowler, 1981) toward identifying the interactive influence of social-ecological context on religious development, particularly the influence of family and social environment (Boyatzis, 2012). Contemporary research on religious and spiritual development has particularly focused on three areas: socialization and the impact of the family, the impact of attachment relationships, and the development of a God concept (Nelson, 2009).

A contemporary advance in the psychology of religion has been the interdisciplinary study of the cognitive and information-processing systems that explain religious belief and practice. Described as the cognitive science of religion (CSR) (Barrett, 2011), this discipline explores neuropsychological and developmental understandings of religious phenomena and experience that are observed across different religions and cultures. For example, research in this area has identified a "teleological bias" in children manifested by a cognitive tendency to view natural occurrence as having a purposeful or teleological design (Kelemen, 2004; Casler & Kelemen, 2007). Barrett describes the implications of this line of research as follows:

> These intriguing findings . . . suggest one possible cognitive reason for the culturally widespread existence of religious beliefs in deities that either order or create the natural world: such ideas resonate with an early developing and persistent intuition that the natural world looks purposefully designed. Positing a designer (or designers) fits with our intuitions. (Barrett & Burdett, 2011, p. 253)

The cognitive study of religious belief includes psychological theory that seeks to explain the cognitions and behaviors that contribute to the development and maintenance of religious belief, and the implications of religious belief on human functioning (Barrett, 2011).

Psychological studies of religious belief contribute to our understanding of the neurological processes underlying the development and maintenance of religious belief and practices. As a field of study, CSR can contribute to our understanding of optimal educational and environmental practices for nurturing belief and fostering Christian formational practices. Edman (2015) describes the challenges of sustaining counterintuitive theological beliefs due to our dual-system mind. Theological errors occur when our intuitive mind quickly defaults to assumptions about God and others based on our human relational experiences, which may conflict with the reflective mind's more conscious theological positions and deliberations. The solution is active engagement

in communities of faith that can provide the "cultural scaffolding" (Barrett, 2011) required to override these "intuitive cognitive defaults." Edman (2015) writes, "Beliefs that are massively counterintuitive, such as God's radical and complete grace, can come to 'feel' right to people with consistent memorable instruction, repeated ritual, and the influence of a nurturing church community full of people who support and reinforce the belief in question" (p. 245). Developmental perspectives on religious belief provide important considerations for the development and maintenance of faith. Research in the cognitive science of religion, in particular, underscores the importance of community practices to develop and sustain the virtue of faith. Let us further examine the role of attachment in faith development.

The Psychology of Trust, Attachment, and Religious Development

One of the earliest theorists to propose the development of trust (versus mistrust) as an essential task in childhood was Erik Erickson. He proposed that trust lays the foundation for future social relationships including the capacity to trust in a "supernatural provider" through organized religion (Erickson, 1963). However, it was John Bowlby's theory and research on attachment that accelerated our understanding of the importance of trust and connection with early caregivers on children's development (Bowlby, 1969). Bowlby proposed that human beings enter the world with the basic need for connection and attachment that is essential for our very survival. Responsive, consistent, and attentive caregiving provides an essential emotional foundation, a "secure base" from which the infant can explore the world. To the extent that secure attachment is facilitated, human beings develop an internalized working model of self and others that forms the basis for subsequent relationships. Research by Ainsworth and colleagues found that early relational experiences result in the development of different types of relational patterns, including secure, anxious, avoidant, and traumatized/reactive attachment styles (Ainsworth, Blehar, Waters, & Wall, 1978). Subsequent research has established that secure attachment with caregivers contributes to the achievement of developmental milestones and fosters a host of markers of psychological health, including empathy and good emotional regulation (Colin, 1996). Clinical applications seek to promote psychological health by fostering secure attachment in parent-child and adult relationships and include empirically supported models such as Parent-Child Interaction Therapy (Eyberg et al., 2001), Emotionally Focused Couple Therapy (Johnson, 2004), and Attachment-Based Family Therapy (Diamond, Diamond, & Levy, 2014).

Psychology of religion research has also examined the impact of early attachment relationships on the development of religious and moral behaviors (Kirkpatrick, 2005). Kirkpatrick (2005) proposed that "beliefs about what God or gods are like, and one's ability to have a personal relationship with God, appear to be consistent with one's experience in human relationships with attachment figures" (pp. 125-26). Kirkpatrick proposed two hypotheses to explain this relationship. First, the *correspondence hypothesis* predicts that individuals' early attachment experiences and resultant internal working model can predict their beliefs and experiences of God. A securely attached adult, for example, would likely have a high level of trust in God as consistent, caring, and responsive. The *compensation hypothesis* proposes that individuals with inadequate early attachment experiences are motivated to seek a relationship with God as a substitute attachment experience. Research supports the predictive value of early attachment experiences for adult religiosity and attachment to God (Rose & Exline, 2012; Kirkpatrick & Shaver, 1990; Granqvist, 1998).

Attachment theory underscores the importance of trust as a basic human need and a foundation for all relationships that is fostered through responsiveness, attentiveness, and consistency. As Bowlby (1988) eloquently stated, "All of us, from cradle to grave, are happiest when life is organized as a series of excursions, long or short, from the secure base provided by our attachment figure(s)" (p. 62). The development of faith and trust in all our relationships are likely affected by our early attachment experiences. This area of psychological inquiry has important implications for our understanding of the significance of the supervisory relationship as a "secure base" for the development of mature faith that leads to faithful practice as a clinician. Importantly, research supports the exploration of questions and doubts as a pathway to mature faith development. We will explore these implications further as we consider professional ethics and supervision practices relevant to the virtue of faith.

PROFESSIONAL ETHICS AND VALUES: FIDELITY AND RESPONSIBILITY

A more robust understanding of the virtue of faithfulness from theological and psychological perspectives provides deeper meaning for the professional ethical principle of fidelity. As clinicians of character, we strive to foster trusting relationships with colleagues and clients that reflect God's faithfulness to us. We recognize the importance of our truthfulness and fidelity in fostering secure working relationships marked by trust and safety. We acknowledge that the optimal context for teaching, research, and clinical practice, including the formative process of supervision, takes place in connection. We uphold the ethical principle of fidelity—not only because we have to, but because it has become an essential part of our personal and professional character, guiding our attitudes, activities, and relationships.

A professional expression of the virtue of faith involves a commitment to fidelity, responsibility, and honoring the public trust. Fidelity is defined as "honoring commitments and keeping promises, including fulfilling one's responsibilities of trust in professional relationships" (American Counseling Association [ACA], 2014). The APA, ACA, and AAMFT ethical codes articulate the importance of fidelity and responsibility as a foundational professional value (American Psychological Association [APA], 2010; ACA, 2014; American Association for Marriage and Family Therapy [AAMFT], 2015). This professional aspiration is evident in a number of ways. First, mental health professionals are responsible for safeguarding public trust through accurate representation of the profession, including compliance with ethical standards. Second, responsibility to the public is also maintained through engaging in activities in the public sphere in a way that enhances public welfare, including dedicating a portion of professional activities to pro bono work. As stated in the AAMFT code of ethics, "Marriage and family therapists embody these aspirations by participating in activities that contribute to a better community and society, including devoting a portion of their professional activity to services for which there is little or no financial return" (AAMFT, 2015). A third aspect of fidelity pertains to veracity in our communications with the public, with colleagues, and with students. Mental health professionals "aspire to open, honest, and accurate communication" (ACA, 2014). Finally, mental health professionals are expected to honor commitments and fulfill responsibilities in their professional and educational responsibilities. As stated in the APA code of ethics, "Psychologists establish relationships of trust with those with whom they work" (APA, 2010). Applying an ethic of "faith" and "trustworthiness" to our work requires the development of characteristic habits and practices of honesty, integrity, and reliability in our professional lives and ethical decision making.

The ethical codes also provide specific guidelines for the responsibilities and commitments of supervisors to their trainees. These responsibilities are outlined in the APA Ethics Standard 7: Education and Training; ACA Section F: Supervising, Training, and Teaching; and AAMFT Code of Ethics Standard IV: Responsibilities to Students and Supervisees. There is a high degree of consistency across ethical codes regarding supervisor responsibilities, and a summary is provided here. Supervisors demonstrate "good faith" and fidelity through the following practices:

- establishing informed consent at the beginning of supervision, including disclosure of a structured process for feedback and evaluation, supervisor expectations, supervision processes, handling of emergencies, and due process for complaints about supervision

- meeting regularly with supervisees to monitor client welfare, clinical performance of supervisee, and supervisee professional development

- recognizing our position of influence and taking care not to exploit the trust of supervisees

- avoiding multiple relationships that could be harmful to the supervisee and protecting the boundaries of the supervision relationship

- refraining from engaging in sexual relationships with supervisees

- refraining from the provision of psychotherapy or counseling to supervisees or supervisee family members

- protecting the confidentiality of supervisees unless informed consent is given

- refraining from requiring supervisees to share personal information about their histories unless there is informed consent to reveal personal historical information necessary for the clinical supervision process

- using technology competently for supervision and ensuring privacy of information transmitted electronically

For faithful supervisors, maintaining ethical commitments to supervisees is an essential value and is foundational to the establishment of trust and constancy. Supervisors keep their promises by providing ethical, competent, and reliable supervision practices.

FAITH AND TRUST IN CLINICAL SUPERVISION

Clinical supervision research supports the central importance of a secure, trusting supervisory relationship as the foundation for all supervision activities. A review by Watkins (2014a) of the last 50 years of theory and research on the supervision alliance concluded: "If there is a common, integrative factor in psychotherapy supervision of supreme significance, then the supervisory alliance would be it" (p. 159). Research suggests that a stronger supervision alliance contributes to increased supervisee honesty and self-disclosure (Webb & Wheeler, 2008; Mehr, Ladany, & Caske, 2010), predicts stronger supervisee alliances with clients (Patton & Kivlighan, 1997), and contributes to job satisfaction, well-being, and decreased burnout (Livni, Crowe, & Gonsalvez, 2012). In a survey of effective and ineffective supervision behaviors, the supervision relationship emerged as a significant factor that impacts the education and training of supervisees (Ladany, Mori, & Mehr, 2013). According to supervisees surveyed in this study, effective supervisors utilize empathy, encouragement, and empowerment to facilitate a supervision alliance that fosters learning and self-efficacy. While parallels are drawn between the theory and research on therapeutic alliance with clients and the supervisory alliance, important differences exist, including the educational aims and evaluative components that must be navigated in the supervision relationship (Watkins, 2014a&b).

Important research on the supervisory relationship comes out of the United Kingdom, specifically the Oxford Institute for Clinical Psychology Training Supervision Research Group, where both qualitative and quantitative research has been conducted to determine the necessary components of an effective supervisory relationship. Key findings from the Oxford group include the importance of establishing a "safe base" at the outset of supervision, defined as an emotional bond between supervisor and supervisee that includes elements of safety, openness, honesty, and trustworthiness (Clohessy, 2008; Pearce, Beinart, Clohessy, & Cooper, 2013). "Beginning well" is important for effective clinical supervision, as supervision research suggests that a good beginning in the first month predicts continued interpersonal openness and collaboration, while a poor beginning with unmet and unexpressed expectations is difficult to recover from (Frost, 2004). Also essential to the supervision process is the provision of a "boundaried" supervisory relationship where the supervisor provides consistent structure, organization, regular uninterrupted space and time, professional boundaries, emotional safety, and containment (Beinart, 2014).

The importance of the supervision relationship is emphasized in all the major textbooks on clinical supervision models and practices. Falender and Shafranske (2004) propose "integrity in relationship" as a superordinate value in clinical supervision. They emphasize that supervisors need to exhibit a high degree of responsibility for ensuring that the supervision experience is both complete and morally incorrupt through paying careful attention to professional responsibilities and boundaries. Characteristics of effective supervisors who practice supervision with integrity include flexibility, humor, self-evaluative capacities, support and encouragement, the ability to foster appropriate autonomy, and a willingness to address conflict (Falender & Shafranske, 2004, p. 58).

Bernard and Goodyear (2014) recommend a supervision model that takes into account the factors affecting supervisee engagement as well as the supervisor factors that affect the quality of the relationship. Based on a review of the supervision research, their model suggests that supervisees' level of engagement is influenced by six primary supervisee characteristics: level of resistance, attachment style, shame, anxiety, competence concerns, and transference. Supervisors also are affected by three primary factors: their attachment style, use of power in the relationship, and countertransference issues. Supervisors can minimize the impact of these factors on the supervision alliance by directly addressing and normalizing the role of attachment and relational dynamics in the supervision alliance. As deeper trust develops and supervisees experience the relationship as a secure base, they are able to engage more fully and authentically in the supervision process.

An MFT perspective encourages an understanding of the supervisory relationship as embedded in a larger systemic "web of interrelated relationship" (Todd & Storm, 2014, p. 9). Psychodynamic models of MFT supervision emphasize the importance of the frame in both clinical supervision and family therapy to provide a consistent and secure holding environment (Reiner, 2014). The supervisory frame provides definition, protection, and clarification of "the space in which teaching and modeling can occur" (Reiner, 2014, p. 171). Important components of the supervision frame include consistency of meeting location, time, and frequency and commitment to addressing any ruptures in the supervision alliance that may occur. A strong supervision alliance with a clear and consistent frame allows the supervisor to address supervisee transference, countertransference, and parallel process issues that arise in the context of clinical work. From a psychodynamic, systemic supervision perspective, personal issues of the supervisee can be raised and addressed in supervision as they pertain to the educational and training goals, but should be referred to the supervisee's own individual therapy if treatment is necessary.

It is clear from a review of the supervision research and theory that prioritizing the establishment of a strong supervision alliance characterized by trust, fidelity, and responsibility on the part of the supervisor is essential for effective supervision to occur. We can assume that the development of character strengths of faith and trust in supervisees begins with a responsible and trustworthy supervisor's ability to establish a strong alliance and supervisory frame. We now turn our attention to specific models and practices that guide the process of beginning well in supervision.

Attachment-Based Models of Supervision

Psychodynamic models of supervision in general, and attachment models in particular, provide a theoretical foundation for the development of a secure base in supervision through establishment of a supervision alliance based on trust and secure attachment. These models emphasize the primary importance of establishing the frame in supervision through appropriate structure and supervisor consistency and responsiveness. The secure supervisory relationship, then, provides the optimal holding environment for supervisee development and growth, and can even provide a "corrective emotional experience" (Alexander & French, 1946) for mediating the effects of the supervisee's own historical attachment experiences.

Pistole and Watkins (1995) were among the first to apply Bowlby's attachment theory to the clinical supervision process. They propose three areas of supervision where attachment theory may be most relevant and helpful. First, like human development, supervisee professional growth can also be viewed through a developmental lens with a greater need for support, dependence on the supervisor, and close monitoring at the beginning of supervision, moving toward greater autonomy as supervision progresses. Second, the supervision relationship should provide a "secure base," defined as a supervisor-supervisee relationship that serves to ground or hold the supervisee in a secure fashion (Pistole and Watkins, 1995, p. 13). This secure base provides support, resources, close monitoring, and a place of safety from which the supervisee can venture to try out new skills and theories, trusting the supervisor to provide guidance. The authors suggest that the secure base is facilitated through the provision of structure, goal agreement, consistent availability of the supervisor, and regularity of meeting place and time. Third, Pistole and Watkins suggest that attachment theory is useful in making sense of supervisee attachment styles that can pose a hindrance to the supervision process, such as supervisees who are overly independent (compulsive, self-reliant supervisees), overly dependent (anxiously attached supervisees), or overly solicitous of the supervisor and their clients (compulsive caregivers). Through exploring these attachment styles and history, supervision impasses can be addressed and supervision can ideally provide a corrective emotional experience for reworking internalized models of self and other.

Over ten years later, Bennett (2008) reviewed the small but significant literature on attachment theory and clinical supervision and concluded that there is now a clear evidence base to support the importance of secure attachment to the development of the supervisory alliance. Bennet theorizes that in the inevitable stressors of the supervision experience, the attachment needs of supervisees are activated, and it is natural to seek security and safety in the supervisory relationship. Bennett also introduces the importance of "parallel process" in clinical supervision: what happens in the supervisory relationship is often repeated in the supervisee's relationship with their clients. Citing neurological research on "mirror neurons," Bennett suggests that supervisees "mirror" their supervisor's relational style in their relationship with clients. For example, supervisors who are effective in providing a calming response to supervisee anxiety will increase the likelihood that supervisees will be able to provide a similar calming response to client anxieties. Bennett also emphasizes the importance of supervisor attunement and responsiveness to supervisee professional needs and concerns as essential to the fostering of a secure attachment relationship. Educating supervisors on attachment theory concepts, the importance of a secure base, parallel process, dealing with alliance ruptures, and the termination process is recommended as a means of fostering stronger supervision alliances (Bennett, 2008).

Supervision Best Practice: The Supervision Contract

An essential practice for beginning well and establishing a secure base is the development of a supervision agreement at the outset of supervision (see appendix A for a sample supervision contract). Initiated by the supervisor, this written contract provides an ongoing structure for supervision by identifying supervision goals, expectations, procedures, evaluation processes, and resolution of differences, and it can be consulted as difficulties arise. As an ethical requirement, the supervision agreement provides informed consent for the supervisee by providing information about the supervision experience that is also critical for the establishment of trust (Thomas, 2007). Through establishment of a supervision agreement, supervisors demonstrate to supervisees that they are committed to their professional and personal growth, development, and well-being. The supervision contract can be considered a "living agreement" that is developed collaboratively, regularly consulted, and revised and adjusted as needed (Storm & Todd, 2014b). As the agreement is collaboratively developed, it promotes shared responsibility for the learning experience. Although supervision agreements may differ across mental health professions, clinical settings, and supervision approaches, the following section describes the important elements of a comprehensive supervision contract.

Supervisor's philosophy of supervision and professional background. Many supervisors include a brief overview of their supervision philosophy to introduce the supervisee to their style of supervision, theoretical underpinnings, and supervision process and interventions. Completion of a supervision philosophy is a required component of supervision training for AAMFT Approved Supervisors (AAMFT, 2014). Approved Clinical Supervisors in the counseling profession complete a professional disclosure statement that provides information to supervisees about the supervisor's educational and clinical background (CCE, 2015). A brief introduction of the "person of the supervisor" promotes the establishment of informed consent and models authenticity and transparency. A philosophy statement instills confidence and trust through letting the supervisee know that the supervisor is approaching the experience with intentionality and purpose, with their education and training in mind. It can also help the supervisee understand the focus of the supervision sessions. For example, a supervisor with a relational psychodynamic focus will want the supervisee to discuss reactions to the client in supervision and consider transference, countertransference, and parallel process issues in supervision.

Purpose of supervision and roles/responsibilities of supervisor. The supervision contract describes the purpose of supervision and desired outcomes, and clarifies the roles and responsibilities of the supervisor. This is an important opportunity for explicit discussion of supervisee expectations. Purposes of supervision might include training and education, supervision toward professional licensure, or professional consultation to assist an experienced clinician in continued professional development. The supervision contract should clearly state that supervisors are responsible for ensuring the welfare of the client as well as the training and educational needs of the supervisee, and for ensuring ethical compliance.

Supervisors may adopt any number of roles during the supervision experience related to the primary purpose of supervision. Morgan and Sprenkle (2007) have proposed a "common factors" approach to supervision that identifies supervisor roles, responsibilities, and approaches that are common to all models of supervision. Supervisors tend to adopt four overlapping but distinct roles in effective supervision. As *coaches*, supervisors focus on a more directive approach to facilitating compe-

tency in clinical skill development. As *teachers*, supervisors provide the knowledge and theoretical models that inform application of clinical skills. In the *mentor* role, supervisors attend to the supervisee's personal and professional development, including use of self in therapy and development of professional identity, confidence, and efficacy. *Administratively*, supervisors socialize supervisees to the profession, ensuring adherence to ethics and providing structured evaluation and feedback. Clarification of the roles and responsibilities of the supervisor can inform supervisee expectations for the supervision experience.

Responsibilities of supervisees. The supervision agreement also describes the expectations of supervisees. Responsibilities include but are not limited to maintaining liability insurance, adhering to agency record-keeping guidelines, videotaping or audiotaping therapy sessions, documenting hours, informing clients of supervisee status, and following necessary procedures in the event of a crisis or emergency (Bernard & Goodyear, 2014). Supervision contracts can also advise supervisees that their "person of the therapist" issues are a necessary component of supervision discussions and may include exploration of attitudes, beliefs, values, cultural blind spots, and interpersonal issues that arise in the context of clinical practice. It can be helpful to clarify that while supervision is not therapy, it may at times require exploration of the supervisee's personal and professional development issues for the purpose of facilitating growth as a clinician (Falender & Shafranske, 2004).

Goal setting. Supervisors collaborate with supervisees in identifying specific goals for supervision. Goal setting is an important step in the supervision process and includes consideration of supervisee developmental level, perceived strengths and areas for growth, and specific competencies required by educational institution and/or placement. Use of goal setting in supervision has been found to be highly correlated with the development of a strong supervision alliance and with overall supervisee satisfaction (Lehrman-Waterman & Ladany, 2001).

Best practice guidelines for goal setting recommend a collaborative approach between supervisor and supervisee where the supervisor provides scaffolding and support to the supervisee's process of reflecting on their strengths and needs toward the development of specific and measurable goals. Gonsalvez et al. (2013) recommend a competency-based developmental plan (CDP) to guide supervision activities, methods, and evaluation procedures. Supervisors are encouraged to make sure that goals are SMART: Specific, Measurable, developmentally Appropriate, Relevant and consistent with expectations of professional guilds, and realistic within the given Timeframe for supervision (Gonsalvez et al., 2013, p. 294). Specific best practice guidelines for goal setting include the following:

- Supervisors should initiate the process several weeks before supervision begins.

- Supervisees are encouraged to consider their individual strengths, experiences, theoretical models, knowledge, and skill needs through reflective questions from the supervisor.

- Consideration is given to common domains of competencies as outlined by professional guilds (i.e., APA, ACA, AAMFT).

- Review of summative evaluation forms at the outset of supervision can help supervisees formulate goals and identify institutional expectations.

- Developmental level of supervisee is considered, and competency goals are identified.

- Supervisor and supervisee collaborate on a written plan outlining specific competencies, supervision methods, and outcome evaluation methods.

Goal setting is an integral component of the evaluation process in supervision, as the identification of specific goals and competencies in the initial contract provides the basis for future evaluation and assessment procedures (Bernard & Goodyear, 2014). Supervisors are encouraged to regularly revisit the initial goals and provide feedback on supervisee progress in an ongoing manner as a part of formative evaluation processes.

Structure of supervision. Fidelity and faithfulness to even the small things of supervision such as a regular meeting time, documentation, paperwork, and so forth, goes a long way toward establishing trust in the supervisor and supervision process. Many poor experiences of supervision occur when supervisees feel that their supervisor does not have time for them, that they are a bother for seeking consultation, and that they cannot trust that their supervisor will keep their promises to meet regularly. Neglecting the structure of supervision communicates that supervision is not a valued professional enterprise and runs the risk of supervisees repeating these neglectful patterns in their own professional lives with clients and even future supervisees.

In the supervision agreement, the supervisor provides clear guidelines and expectations regarding the basic structure and content of the supervision experience. Important details include the duration of supervision, frequency and length of supervision sessions, cancellation policies, financial arrangements, and documentation expectations. Procedures and contact information for clinical emergencies should be specified. It can also be helpful to provide an overview of supervision sessions and how the supervisee can best prepare. Discussion of expectations for reviewing the supervisee's actual clinical work is an important component of the structure of supervision. This can include clarification of procedures for recording sessions, scheduling observations or co-therapy sessions with supervisors, and of course obtaining informed consent from clients for this. Guidelines and expectations for review of the supervisee's assessment or psychotherapy documentation should be included in the supervision agreement.

Evaluation procedures. It is important at the outset of supervision to provide clarity and transparency about the feedback and evaluation processes that will be incorporated into the supervision experience. This includes review of the nature and frequency of evaluations, disclosure of forms that will be used, and clarification about who will provide input and review. Processes for appeal should be disclosed at this time. Transparency regarding evaluation procedures is a critical component of attending to the inevitable power differential in supervision and goes a long way toward establishing trust. Transparent power provides clear and accurate information about evaluation procedures, criteria for evaluations, and appeal processes. These details can be spelled out in the supervision contract.

Structured evaluation is important for supervisees, as they need to know that their supervisors will directly address areas of needed growth and development and will not allow them to "do harm" to clients. This is a matter of trust and faith. Specific evaluation procedures and guidelines will be provided in chapter eight.

Documentation of supervision. In addition to the supervision agreement, a well-organized system of documentation facilitates the fulfillment of supervisor responsibilities and contributes to the establishment of a supervision "frame" that can accomplish goals and maintain commitments (see appendix B for a sample supervision documentation form). It can be helpful to introduce supervisees to these documents at the outset of supervision as part of the supervision contract. In addition to documentation of supervision sessions, supervisors maintain the following documentation for each supervisee: a learning contract with agreement on goals (this can be part of informed consent or the supervision contract), copies of consents for taping, copies of transcripts of sessions or the supervisee's process notes, and documentation of evaluation and feedback procedures and forms.

Summary

Supervisors facilitate fidelity and trust through the establishment of the supervision frame and structure and by taking responsibility for following through on their commitments. These best practices are essential for beginning well in a way that can foster the development of the character strengths of faithfulness, responsibility, and trustworthiness in supervisees, which provide a foundation for their future relationships with clients, colleagues, and supervisees.

CHRISTIAN INTEGRATIVE SUPERVISION PRACTICES THAT NURTURE BELIEF AND TRUST

A Christian integrative approach to supervision utilizes best practices in clinical supervision to foster fidelity and responsibility, which are foundational professional and personal character traits; it also adds "something more" to the supervision experience through fostering Christian integrative thinking and practice. In a faith-based context, supervisors sometimes also serve as spiritual mentors, not only through facilitating trust in the supervision experience, but also through nurturing supervisees' faith and trust in God as an essential component of their development as counselors, psychologists, and MFTs. Supervisors play a key role in encouraging attachment to God as their supervisees navigate vocational and clinical challenges that may activate anxiety, doubt, and even fear. In addition, supervisors facilitate the integration of a Christian worldview with theory and practice as supervisees apply what they have learned in the classroom to real-life clinical encounters.

Trust and Attachment in Christian Integrative Supervision

The psychoanalytic psychologist Randy Sorenson has perhaps made the greatest contributions to our understanding of the role of attachment in fostering Christian integrative thinking and practice among graduate students. Sorenson conducted a series of quantitative and qualitative studies across Christian integrative graduate programs to explore student perceptions of major influences on their integrative thinking (Sorenson, 1997; Sorenson, Derflinger, Bufford, & McMinn, 2004). Results provide strong support for the importance of a student's attachment to a significant faculty mentor for the student's integration process. Specifically, this line of research found that students' access to a mentor's spiritual journey and ongoing relationship with God in the context of an emotionally transparent, open relationship was most valued by students for their own integrative journeys. Research replicating Sorenson's model with a larger sample of graduate students concluded that an attachment-based approach to Christian integrative education should be considered evidence-based (Ripley, Garzon, Hall, Mangis, & Murphy, 2009). This subsequent research also found that faculty who were considered "bulwarks" because of their firm faith commitments, well-developed Christian worldview, and ongoing relationship with God made the most contributions to students' integrative development.

Integration research supports the importance of an attachment-oriented approach to Christian integrative clinical supervision as an essential foundation for fostering clinical integration and Christian worldview. Supervisors have the opportunity to foster the development of faithful professional practices that facilitate belief and trust in God through establishing a supervisory relationship characterized by supervisor emotional presence, transparency, and openness about the supervisor's own relationship with God. When working with supervisees who share Christian faith commitments, supervisors can incorporate Christian integrative supervision philosophy and practices into all components of the initial supervision contract, including philosophy of supervision, roles and expectations, goals, supervision structure, and even evaluation processes. This begins with informed consent and explicit disclosure that Christian integrative thinking and practices will be incorporated into the supervision experience. As part of informed consent, supervisors describe the spiritual mentoring component of clinical supervision and inform supervisees that they will be invited to consider spiritual disciplines and practices as part of the personal and professional formation process. Christian integrative supervisors facilitate faithfulness and trust in clinical supervision through the following practices:

- As supervisors, we strive to be trustworthy and keep our promises to our trainees by upholding ethical principles and best practices for supervision. Through modeling and practicing faithfulness, we seek to foster secure attachment and trust as a foundation for the supervision working alliance. We consider the supervisee's attachment history, prior supervision experience (what has been helpful and not helpful), and developmental stage as we foster the supervision alliance.

- We help our supervisees establish habits of fidelity and faithfulness that aid in the development of trusting and secure therapeutic alliances with their clients. We call them to consistency, to faithfulness, and to mind the therapeutic frame in their work as a part of a Christian ethic of care—even in the midst of the busy student life when they are tempted to put their own academic needs above those of their clients (e.g., canceling or rescheduling a client to study for a test or finish a paper).

- At the outset of supervision, we invite supervisees to describe their faith journeys, and we also share how God is at work in our own life and vocation. We consider their spiritual "growing edge" as we collaboratively formulate goals and objectives for supervision and discuss roles and expectations.

- We teach our supervisees to "mind the small things" (such as completing paperwork in a timely fashion and keeping session notes) as part of the faithful practices of ethical mental health professionals. We ensure that they honor their commitments to clients as acts of fidelity and faithfulness through returning phone calls as promised, timely completion of assessment reports, or finding the resources for clients that they have committed to doing.

- While keeping the focus on the supervisee, we offer moments of transparency regarding our own ongoing relationship with God, the ups and downs of our trust and attachment to him, and the relevance for our professional lives.

- We consider the benefits of sharing our own moments of doubt and how questioning has contributed to the development of our own faith.

- We look for opportunities to integrate professional ethics of fidelity and responsibility with Christian ethical commitments to faithfulness.

Incorporating a Christian Worldview

Clinical supervision provides the ideal opportunity for applied integration as supervisees begin to implement what they have learned in the classroom in real-life clinical situations. Christian integrative supervisors play an important role as we facilitate the development of professional habits and practices that incorporate belief in God and his Word into all areas of mental health practice. In doing so, we affirm mental health practice as a Christian vocation for supervisees and decrease the risk of professional "splitting," where supervisees feel they must keep their faith and professional lives separated. As Christians, we approach our discipline from belief and trust in God as our primary foundation, valuing contributions from science but always examining them through the lens of Scripture. Clinical supervision provides an opportunity for students to learn the practice of applied Christian integration in the trenches of clinical work.

The Christian integrative literature provides excellent resources for fostering a Christian worldview through the clinical supervision process. Bufford (2007) encourages Christian supervisors to be "conscious and intentional rather than unconscious and co-incidental" (p. 294) in seeking opportunities to incorporate a Christian worldview into the process of clinical supervision. He outlines Christian beliefs in five major philosophical domains and provides excellent examples of specific applications for the supervision process that are summarized here:

- Christian beliefs inform our metaphysics in that we believe in spiritual realities including the real presence and existence of God as Father, Son, and Holy Spirit. In supervision we can actively seek God's presence, guidance, and protection for our clinical work.

- A Christian worldview affects how we know and seek sources of truth (our epistemology). Christian supervisors encourage supervisees to study Scripture and seek biblical wisdom.

- Our worldview as Christians includes beliefs about cosmology, as we believe God is present and active in the world today. Supervisors can encourage supervisees to pray for God's healing and intervention in their own lives and the lives of their clients.

- Christian beliefs guide our ethics and morality as we look to Scripture, church tradition, and those in spiritual leadership positions for wisdom and guidance on ethical decision making. Clinical supervisors practice consultation with these sources of authority on ethical matters and encourage supervisees to do the same.

- A Christian worldview informs our theological anthropology as we view supervisees and clients as created in the image of God, worthy of love and respect. For example, supervisors can encourage the cultivation of habits of thinking and talking about clients in "humanizing" and respectful ways, as individuals who are beloved and valued by God (Bufford, 2007).

Applied integration in clinical supervision also involves bringing a Christian worldview to the examination and application of psychological theories and interventions in clinical practice. Important integrative texts on this topic include Jones and Butman (2011), Johnson (2010), and McRay, Yarhouse, and Butman (2016).

Finally, as an ongoing act of belief and faith, Christian integrative supervisors acknowledge our complete dependence on God as the foundation for all of life, of which our clinical vocation is just one small part. Campbell (2007) suggests that a Christian integrative approach to clinical supervision focuses on the reality of God's active presence and work in the life of the client, supervisee, and supervisor as an important dimension of the supervisory task. Campbell writes, "Making these relationships explicit may result in a deepening of faith for both the supervisor and supervisee, as well as for the client if this is appropriate and consistent with the client's desires" (p. 326). Considering God's active presence in clinical work may involve seeking God's help, wisdom, and perspective during sessions through prayer, or inviting clients and supervisees to consider spiritual disciplines as an explicit aspect of growth and change. As Campbell states: "This perspective promotes the idea that God is actively involved within our lives and seeks to develop deeper relationships with us. Although problems can be complex and fragmenting, God seeks to guide and help us in ways that we may not always understand at the time" (p. 325).

Faithful supervisors facilitate the development of supervisee belief and trust through fostering secure attachments, encouraging faithful practices, and regularly accessing the power and presence of God in explicit and implicit ways throughout the process of supervision. This integrative process can be tremendously enhanced by incorporating spiritual formation practices from the Christian tradition into the supervision process with the aim of holistic formation of character.

SPIRITUAL DISCIPLINES FOR CULTIVATING FAITHFULNESS: INDIVIDUAL AND COMMUNITY PRACTICES

Essential to the development of the virtue of faithfulness are individual spiritual disciplines and community practices that nurture belief and trust in our Creator. Throughout the history of the Christian faith, two practices in particular have been essential to the faithful: contemplative prayer and Christian community. Let us explore these practices further and how they can be used in a Christian integrative approach to supervision.

Contemplative Prayer

Just as a life of faith begins with an openhearted prayer of belief and trust in Christ's saving power, lifelong faith and trust in Christ are nurtured through the spiritual discipline of contemplative prayer. British preacher P. T. Forsyth (2002) observed that "prayer is for the religious life what original research is for science—by it we get direct contact with reality. The soul is brought into union with its own vaster nature—God"

(p. 90). Through regular times of entering into God's presence in prayer, we affirm our belief and trust in his presence, providence, and provision. Contemplative prayer is an experiential practice of both speaking and listening in God's presence. Henri Nouwen (1981) writes, "To pray is to descend with the mind into the heart, and there to stand before the face of the Lord, ever-present, all-seeing, within you" (p. 73).

For mental health professionals immersed in the science of psychology, developing habits of prayer is as essential as food and water for nourishing the soul and sustaining trust and belief in God during the rigors of graduate school, academic life, and professional practice. We are all vulnerable to developing professional tunnel vision as we invest a majority of our time and energy in the study of counseling, psychology, and systemic theory and therapy. While this strengthens our faith and confidence in our disciplines, it can lead to the neglect of the essential practices that solidify our faith in Christ. Through prayer, God becomes as tangible to us as our day-to-day studies of science and psychology. Prayer is an expression of humble trust in our Creator as we affirm that he is the source of all wisdom and knowledge.

Contemplative prayer is an important antidote to the cynicism, doubt, and spiritual neglect that are so characteristic of contemporary culture. Rolheiser (2004) observes that many Christians are living lives of "quiet agnosticism," in which they have little or no experience of God in their daily lives. He identifies aspects of contemporary culture that work against experiential faith: narcissism, pragmatism, and unbridled restlessness. Believers need to develop "good lungs" through the ancient practice of contemplative prayer so they are able to "breathe in" the existence of God in their daily lives. Rolheiser writes:

> To be contemplative is to be fully awake to all the dimensions within ordinary experience. And, classical spiritual writers assure us, if we are awake to all that is there within ordinary experience, if our ordinary awareness is not reduced or distorted through excessive narcissism, pragmatism, or restlessness, there will be present in it, alongside everything else that makes up experience, a sense of the infinite, the sacred, God. (p. 23)

Similarly, Foster (1992) speaks of contemplative prayer as "loving attentiveness to God" (p. 158). He quotes Thomas Merton's beautiful description of contemplation: "God loves you, is present in you, lives in you, dwells in you, calls you, saves you, and offers you, an understanding and light which are like nothing you ever found in books or heard in sermons" (Foster, 1992, p. 160). Truly, this is a wonderful

picture of secure attachment to God through prayerful attentiveness.

Integrating prayer into the supervision experience fosters greater awareness of the active presence of the living God in the work of the Christian counselor, psychologist, and MFT. Contemplative prayer can be incorporated into clinical supervision during the supervision session, and this can encourage spiritual practice on a day-to-day basis. Specific suggestions include the following:

- initiating moments of silence in supervision to invite and experience God's presence

- pausing in supervision to offer a prayer of thanksgiving and gratitude to God for good clinical outcomes, supervisee growth in meeting goals, or spiritual breakthroughs

- seeking God's comforting and healing presence during supervision as trainees experience moments of doubt, anxiety, and distress

- encouraging supervisees to be attentive to God's providence in their lives as God works through clinical challenges and clients to bring deeper understandings of self and other

- teaching contemplative prayer practices such as breath prayer and the Jesus Prayer and encouraging supervisees to practice them regularly as a means of drawing near to God when they are alone, or even to practice silently in sessions with clients

- encouraging supervisees to meditate on an image from Scripture of God's nurturing care for them that fosters secure attachment to God, such as the good shepherd, a loving parent, or our rock and shield

- prayerfully considering moments of disclosure of your own spiritual journey and dark nights of the soul

- minding the attachment in supervision as a corrective emotional experience that may open a supervisee to God's love

Through integrating contemplative prayer practices into the supervision experience, both in session and as recommended between-session practices, supervisors encourage the development of habits of the mind and heart that nurture faith and trust as an essential element of Christian vocation for counselors, psychologists, and MFTs.

Community Practices: Nurturing a Christian Identity Through Church Engagement

Prayer nurtures our faith in God and grounds our very being in the reality of his constant presence, but we cannot rely on individual practices alone. The body of Christ, the church, is an essential context for developing and nurturing Christian faith and character. As we discussed at the outset, faith is a theological virtue and a gift from God. However, a growing and vibrant faith requires acts of the will as we commit ourselves to Christian communities where the gift of faith is celebrated, affirmed, and developed. This commitment provides a foundation for all of life and work. Westberg (2015) affirms the importance of Christian community for developing the character virtue of faith:

> Regular worship and prayer and participation in the sacraments are the means not only through which our minds and hearts are reminded of the reality of God as creator, redeemer and sanctifier, but also through which we have the opportunity to realign and affirm with our whole beings this fundamental relationship. We then bring this

vision and conviction ("Go in peace to love and serve the Lord") to the framework by which we make all our decisions. Our intentions, deliberations and decisions are conducted in the light of the truth that we have about God, our acknowledgement of him as the overarching object of our love and the hope we have in God as our final happiness. (pp. 157-58)

Wright (2010) makes a strong case for the importance of church and Christian community for the development of Christian character. He proposes a "virtuous circle" of practices for the formation of character, including Scripture, stories, examples, communities, and spiritual practices, all occurring in the context of the body of Christ. Wright asserts, "One of the primary locations where, and by means of which, any of us learns the habits of the Christian heart and life is what we loosely call the church" (p. 271). Similarly, Hauerwas is a strong voice for the development of virtue in the context of the worshiping community. Like Wright, he asserts that virtues are not meant to be developed and practiced individually and in isolation; rather, they are developed *in* community and *for* community:

> The liturgy offers ethics a series of ordered practices that shape the character and assumptions of Christians, and suggests habits and models that inform every aspect of corporate life—meeting people, acknowledging fault and failure, celebrating, thanking, reading, speaking with authority, reflecting on wisdom, naming truth, registering need, bringing about reconciliation, sharing food, renewing purpose. This is the basic staple of corporate Christian life—not simply for clergy, or for those in religious orders, but for lay Christians, week in, week out. It is the most regular way in which most Christians remind themselves and others that they are Christians. It is the most significant way in which Christianity takes flesh, evolving from a set of ideas and convictions to

a set of practices and a way of life. (Hauerwas & Wells, 2011a, p. 7)

Herdt (2011) provides an additional picture of the "formative power of the liturgy" (p. 542) for the development of Christian virtue. She writes that as Christians worship, pray, sing, and read Scripture together, through grace "we are being kneaded together into a body with a shared vision of the life with God to which we are called, a good which can integrate our agency and frame all of our experience" (p. 537).

How do we affirm the importance of Christian community through the supervision process? Consider the following suggestions:

- Explore your supervisees' religious histories as part of your initial supervision assessment to get a sense of heritage, important practices, and potential attachment injuries. Encourage supervisees to engage in their faith community as part of their personal and professional identity development.

- Share how Christian community has been formative in your own faith development, including challenges and benefits.

- Schedule an educational, prevention-oriented workshop at a local church and invite your supervisees to co-teach with you. Talk about the role that Christian mental health professionals can play in advocacy and service to the church.

- If you supervise at a faith-based institution with chapel services, consider attending a service with your supervisees. For students and faculty in many Christian graduate programs, chapel services are an opportunity to affirm our shared identity in Christ.

As supervisors, we recognize our position of power and influence and take care to ensure that supervisees do not feel obligated, coerced, or required to engage in spiritual disciplines, as we discussed in chapter two. We offer spiritual formation practices as an opportunity to participate in God's transforming work on our character.

CONCLUSION

How does a Christian integrative approach to clinical supervision facilitate the development of habits of mind, heart, and behavior that lead to lifelong faithfulness and fidelity? The supervision research confirms that it is imperative that we begin well with supervisees through establishing a secure supervision alliance marked by trust, constancy, and unwavering ethical commitments. The supervision agreement is an important practice that provides structure, collaborative goal setting, informed consent, and the opportunity to clarify expectations and hopes. Attachment-informed perspectives on both clinical supervision and the integration of Christian faith with psychology provide guidance on establishing the kind of supervisory relationship that is optimal for supervisee development.

A Christian integrative supervisor adds "something more" to the supervision process through facilitating the applied integration of a Christian worldview with all aspects of professional development and practice. As supervisors, we actively look for ways to incorporate a Christian worldview into the supervision process in appraisal and application of psychological theories and encourage a faith-motivated advocacy. We don't shy away from religious questions that are raised in the application of theory to practice, but rather provide a safe space and faithful presence for the exploration of doubts. We offer spiritual practices that nurture secure attachments to God and others in Christian community. Finally, we do our best to authentically model fidelity, promise keeping, and faithfulness in our own walk with God and engagement in Christian vocation. In doing so, we have faith that God will form our supervisees into faithful clinicians who engage in mental health practices from a place of secure attachment to him through faith in Jesus Christ.

CHAPTER SUMMARY / SUPERVISION GUIDE

Virtue	• **Faith:** belief, trust, veracity, fidelity
Description	• Trustworthiness in relationships; honoring commitments and fulfilling responsibilities
Scripture	• "Now faith is confidence in what we hope for and assurance about what we do not see. . . . By faith we understand that the universe was formed at God's command, so that what is seen was not made out of what was visible" (Heb. 11:1, 3).
Ethical principles	• Fidelity and responsibility to the public and the profession • "Honoring commitments and keeping promises, including fulfilling one's responsibilities of trust in professional relationships" (ACA, 2014) • "Psychologists establish relationships of trust with those with whom they work" (APA, 2010)
Supervision best practices	• Establish trust and supervision alliance • Complete supervision contract • Agree on structure of supervision and regular meeting times • Collaboratively set developmentally appropriate goals • Foster supervisee skills in establishing trusting alliances with their clients • Establish system of documentation
Christian integration focus	• Provide informed consent about including spiritual practices and faith conversations in supervision • Invite supervisees to describe their faith tradition and journey • Establish supervision as a safe space to explore questions and doubts • Consider appropriate moments for transparency regarding your own spiritual journey • Incorporate a Christian worldview into the process of clinical supervision as relevant to clinical questions and issues • Attend to God's active presence in supervision
Spiritual practices	• Contemplative prayer • Christian community, liturgy, and the sacraments
Desired outcome	• Faithful clinicians who are securely connected to the living God through Jesus Christ and empowered by the Holy Spirit to form trusting and secure relationships with clients, and who engender "good faith" in the communities they serve through faithfulness and responsible practices

CHAPTER 4

HOPE

A Steadfast Turning

Therefore, since we have been justified through faith, we have peace with God through our Lord Jesus Christ, through whom we have gained access by faith into this grace in which we now stand. And we boast in the hope of the glory of God. Not only so, but we also glory in our sufferings, because we know that suffering produces perseverance; perseverance, character; and character, hope. And hope does not put us to shame, because God's love has been poured out into our hearts through the Holy Spirit, who has been given to us.

ROMANS 5:1-5

IF FAITH IS THE STARTING POINT of our relationship with Christ and service to him, then hope pertains to the purpose and meaning of our faith and that which we desire: the kingdom of God. Hope nourishes the Christian soul to bear daily struggles and to persevere in the formation of Christlikeness and Christian virtue, for the sake of the kingdom. Likewise, fostering hope in clinical supervision involves encouraging supervisees to maintain a sense of meaning and purpose throughout the long developmental process of becoming a clinician who can serve the public and bring benefit to society (beneficence). Christian integrative supervision brings these purposes together and aims to form hopeful clinicians who maintain a vision for mental health work as benefiting individuals, families, and communities, and who remain hopeful and resilient in the face of suffering and ultimately can see their place in building God's kingdom.

This chapter focuses on the theological virtue of hope, the corresponding professional aspiration of beneficence, and the supervision practices and spiritual disciplines that foster meaning and purpose for the supervisee. It addresses the professional challenge of disillusionment, cynicism, and acedia that can be a byproduct of mental health work in which professionals are immersed in experiences of human brokenness and suffering. Fostering meaning and purpose in clinical supervision can be an important protective factor against the disillusionment and loss of innocence that occurs when supervisees begin to deal with the enormity of human pain and suffering. Spiritual practices of keeping the Sabbath and community worship provide a "taste of eternity" to remind believers of our ultimate professional calling to build Christ's kingdom now and for the future.

HOPE: BIBLICAL AND THEOLOGICAL PERSPECTIVES

As the second of the theological virtues, hope is a gift from God through faith in Jesus Christ that allows the believer to be in the "already but not yet" position in relation to Christ's kingdom. With hope, we trust God's supernatural work in and through us. As an infused virtue, hope is a gift, but it is also nurtured in our relationship with God: "Hope is always linked to faith, since one cannot have a living faith without also having both love and hope" (Kaczor, 2008, p. 83). Hope reminds us that regardless of our own sin and the fallen world, in Christ "all shall be well, and all shall be well, and all manner of thing shall be well" (Julian of Norwich, 1901, p. 95).

The *Catechism of the Catholic Church* (2003) describes hope as "the theological virtue by which we desire the kingdom of heaven and eternal life as our happiness, placing our trust in Christ's promises and relying not on our own strength, but on the help of the grace of the Holy Spirit" (para. 1817) and as the "sure and steadfast anchor of the soul" (para. 1820). In addition, hope "affords us joy even under trial" (para. 1820). Hope is differentiated from naive or shallow optimism, as Christian hope is based on Christ's resurrection and the kingdom to come (Waddams, 1964). It is not only a personal hope for our own salvation and place in Christ's kingdom but also a hope for the world to be redeemed and restored (Brunner, 1956).

Hope in the present and future fulfillment of Christ's kingdom provides an eschatology for the formation of Christian character (Grenz, 1997; Wright, 2008). As Wright (2010) describes, virtue formation is about becoming the kind of people that God will use to build his kingdom; hope in Christ's kingdom motivates character formation through a hopeful vision of the future and a positive anticipation of what is to come. In hope, we trust in God's sanctification process as he forms us in the likeness of Christ. Three "theologians of hope" are particularly instructive for our understanding of the formation of hope in the life of the believer: Moltmann, Pieper, and Wright. We explore their writings here.

Moltmann (1967) offers an important theological treatise on Christian hope. A POW during World War II, he sought theological training after his release, and *Theology of Hope* was his first major work. Moltmann holds that eschatology is the foundation of all Christian theology, including a theology of hope. He writes:

> Christianity is eschatology, is hope, forward looking and forward moving, and therefore also revolutionizing and transforming the present. The eschatological is not one element *of* Christianity, but it is the medium of Christian faith as such, the key in which everything in it is set, the glow that suffuses everything here in the dawn of an expected new day. For Christian faith lives from the raising of the crucified Christ, and strains after the promises of the universal future of Christ. Eschatology is the passionate suffering and passionate longing kindled by the Messiah. Hence eschatology cannot really be only a part of Christian doctrine. Rather, the eschatological outlook is characteristic of all Christian proclamation, of every Christian existence and of the whole Church. (Moltmann, 1967, p. 6)

This future hope provides the source of meaning for all of life and for the work of the church, according to Moltmann. The church's discomfort in the present, then, becomes the foundation for the pursuit of change in the world.

Pieper (1997) describes the theological virtue of hope as a "steadfast turning" of human beings in the direction of their true supernatural nature through faith in Christ, a hope that is both personal and universal. For Christians, this means embracing our current condition of living "on the way" to a kingdom that is "not yet" (Pieper, 1997). Hope grants the believer a "supernatural grounded youthfulness" of vitality, strength, resilience, perseverance, and joy, and Pieper reminds us that "even though our outer man is decaying, yet our inner man is being renewed day by day" (2 Cor 4:16); we remember, "they that hope in the Lord shall renew their strength" (Is 40:31) (Pieper, 1997, pp. 111-12). The natural expression of hope is magnanimity, a confidence in what humankind can do and accomplish toward good in the world. True hope is also tempered with humility and a recognition of the distance between humans and God; Pieper reminds us that it is only through God that true accomplishments are made.

Wright (2008) offers a compelling vision for Christian vocation in light of a kingdom eschatology where our vocational work today is a part of building Christ's kingdom for the future. In hope, Wright suggests, Christians live in the "already but not yet" kingdom, becoming God's people, the royal priesthood, through cultivation of virtue and engagement in building for the kingdom:

> But what we can and must do in the present, if we are obedient to the gospel, if we are following Jesus, and if we are indwelt, energized, and directed by the Spirit, is to build for the kingdom. This brings us back to 1 Corinthians 15:58 once more: what you do in the Lord is not in vain. You are not restoring a great painting that's shortly going to be thrown on the fire. You are not planting roses in a garden that's about to be dug up for a building site. You are—strange though it may seem, almost as hard to believe as the resurrection itself—accomplishing something that will become in due course part of God's new world. Every act of love, gratitude, and kindness . . . all of this will find its way, through the resurrecting power of God, into the new creation that God will one day make. (Wright, 2008, pp. 327-28)

Wright suggests that Christian vocation involves holding the pain of the world in one hand and the love of Christ in the other. Certainly, this is an apt description for the work of psychology, counseling, and MFT, where we simultaneously join with others in their suffering and hold on to a sense of hope in the love of Christ to ultimately wipe every tear from their eyes. Wright reminds us that "what you do with your body in the present matters because God has a great future in store for it" (p. 327).

The opposite of hope, according to classical and contemporary writers, is despair or acedia. The early church father Evagrius describes acedia as the "noonday demon" that afflicts the faithful, often during prayer, when they begin to feel distraction, dissatisfaction, and even hatred of their life and work (Evagrius, 1972). Acedia is distinguished from depression in that it is a disorder of the soul related to loss of a sense of meaning and purpose in the everyday acts of life and vocation (Nelson, 2009). Pieper (1997) describes acedia as the refusal to acknowledge who we are created to be by God. It can manifest in sloth and laziness as well as overexertion to prove our significance—refusing to take a Sabbath, for example. Pieper writes: "It is a kind of anxious vertigo that befalls the human individual when he becomes aware of the height to which God has raised him. One who is trapped in acedia has neither the courage nor the will to be as great as he really is. . . . Acedia is a perverted humility" (p. 119). Others describe acedia as a "work-engendered depression" where the single-minded pursuit of vocation, industry, financial gain, and accomplishment can lead to a loss of experiences of that which makes us human, including leisure, art, creativity, values, and spiritual pursuits (Bartlett, 1990). The antidote to acedia is gentle reengagement with work, Sabbath, and individual and community Christian practices that affirm hope and faithfulness.

Biblical and theological understandings of hope provide an important foundation for a Christian integrative approach to clinical supervision. While hope is a gift from God that comes as a result of a living faith in Jesus Christ,

we can also nurture hope through a "steadfast turning" of our minds and hearts toward our eschatological hope in the kingdom to come. Through hope, we trust in God's sanctification process as he lovingly develops our character. Christian hope gives meaning and purpose to vocation in counseling, psychology, and MFT. Through fostering hope in our supervisees, we equip them to withstand the challenges of life as a mental health professional, which can include overexertion to help others, despair in the face of human suffering, and apathy. Encouraging hopeful practices that prepare supervisees for long-term service to the kingdom and allow them to be a hopeful presence to others, then, is part of our responsibility to bring "something more" to the supervision experience. We now examine contributions from psychology to the development of hopeful character strengths.

HOPE: PSYCHOLOGICAL PERSPECTIVES

Peterson and Seligman (2004) include the character strength of hope as part of the cluster of strengths of transcendence. They offer the following definition: "Hope, optimism, future-mindedness, and future orientation represent a cognitive, emotional, and motivational stance toward the future" (Peterson and Seligman, 2004, p. 570). Hopeful and optimistic people expect that desired outcomes will happen in the future, and act on these expectations with positive feelings and goal-oriented behaviors that increase the likelihood that the events will occur.

According to Peterson and Seligman (2004), development of the personality characteristics of optimism occurs in three primary ways. First, optimistic individuals possess a tendency to expect good things will happen. Second,

optimism can be understood as an explanatory style related to a person's sense of agency. Finally, models have been proposed that include both expectancy and agency as personality characteristics related to optimism. Peterson and Seligman link the character strengths of hope, optimism, and future mindedness with a number of positive mental health outcomes related to both mood and adaptive behaviors. For example, Seligman's (1991) "learned optimism" perspective proposes that individuals can link agency to achieving positive outcomes through their actions and develop a sense of themselves as efficacious rather than helpless.

Snyder (1994) has written extensively on the development of hope as a personality characteristic. His theory of hope views the construct less as an inherited personality trait and more as an ability that is learned in childhood and developed through adolescence and adulthood. Specifically, Snyder's theory proposes that hope is "a cognitive process through which individuals actively accomplish their goals. . . . Goals are hoped-for ends" (Feldman & Kubota, 2012, p. 50). Snyder's research proposes that hope is a cognitive capacity composed of two types of thinking: *pathway thinking*, in which individuals consider ways to achieve a desired outcome, and *agency thinking*, which provides the motivation to pursue these means. From the perspective of this model, religion is associated with hope and positive health outcomes because a religious framework provides a clear sense of hoped-for outcomes as well as the incentive and motivation to achieve these goals, consistent with both pathway and agency thinking (Snyder, Sigmon, & Feldman, 2003). As believers participate in religious practices including rituals, virtue development, prayer, and learning Scripture, this religious involvement provides regular motivation and social support to strengthen agency and provide a sense of achievement of subgoals along the pathway (Feldman & Kubota, 2012).

Hope theories have been applied to clinical practice through interventions designed to facilitate the development of hopeful thinking in clients (Cheavens, Feldman, Gumm, Michael, & Synder, 2006). Meta-analysis on the use of hope interventions in therapy has found a small but significant impact and suggests hope theory can enhance evidence-based interventions (Weis & Speridakos, 2011). An excellent example of hope-informed approaches is hope-focused couple counseling (Worthington, 2005; Ripley & Worthington, 2014).

Hope theory has also been applied in industrial and organizational psychology, where the beneficial impact of hope in the workplace has been identified (Youssef & Luthans, 2007). Happiness and well-being are enhanced when people feel a sense of calling, meaning, and active engagement with their vocation (Cochran, 1997; Dreher, Holloway, & Schoenfelder, 2007). Positive psychologists propose the concept of flow (Csikszentmihalyi, 1990) to describe the experience of engaging in vocation that is consistent with our own sense of our character virtues and strengths: "becoming so involved in our work that we become one with it" (Druher, 2012, p. 129).

Important to our understanding of the virtue of hope is the literature on religion and meaning. Religion contributes to hope in that it provides a belief system for purpose in life and for making meaning out of life events in a way that provides a sense of coherence, control, and comfort. Meaning can be understood as a general sense of purpose and also as an approach to coping with challenging life situations. Park (2013) describes *global meaning* as "an overarching system that provides the general framework through which people structure their lives and assign meanings to specific encounters with the environment (situational meaning)" (p. 358). Global meaning provides the worldview and schemas through which individuals view their world and the everyday experiences that provide a subjective sense of purpose for their lives. However, when life events occur that threaten or disrupt an individual's worldview, this meaning system can be questioned or challenged. *Meaning making* is the process through which individuals try to make sense of the disparity between their immediate situation and their global beliefs. This process of meaning making may involve a reevaluation of an individual's view of the situation (assimilation), or a reconsideration of one's closely held beliefs and assumptions about the world (accommo-dation), to restore a sense of order, control, and purpose (Park, 2013).

The importance of religion to both global meaning and meaning making has been well supported by research (Pargament, 1997; Park, 2005). In a review of the empirical research on psychology of religion, Pargament, Magyar-Russell, and Murray-Swank (2005) conclude that religion plays a unique role in the way people find significance, cope with difficulties, make meaning, and derive motivation. They assert that religion is distinctive in its contri-bution because of its focus on "the sacred in the search for significance" (p. 668). The authors describe the distinctive contribution in this way:

> Methods of religious coping seem to con-tribute something special to the prediction of adjustment to critical life events. What makes these methods of coping distinctive? The in-clusion of the sacred in the coping process may hold the key. In the eyes of many indi-viduals, religion may be more successful than secular systems in offering "a response to the problem of human insufficiency" (Pargament, 1997, p. 310). The language of religion—faith, hope, transcendence, surrender, forbearance, meaning—speaks to the limits of human powers. When life appears out of control, and there seems to be no rational explanation for events, beliefs and practices oriented to the sacred seem to have a special ability to provide ultimate meaning, order, and safety in place of human questions, chaos, and fear. (Pargament, Magyar-Russell, and Murray-Swank, 2005, p. 676)

Religion can have a significant influence on an individual's response to stressful events and dif-ficult life circumstances in several ways. First, it can affect an individual's initial appraisal and per-spective on a given situation as it is seen through the lens of religious beliefs; this may lead to de-creased distress as the event is understood in light of global beliefs (Baumeister, 1991; Park, 2005). Second, religious belief can directly in-fluence coping in both positive and negative ways, with the reframing of situations in a positive reli-gious perspective contributing to improved coping (Pargament, 1997). Third, religious belief can contribute to the stress-related growth that occurs for some individuals in the aftermath of difficulties (Park, 2009). Park (2013) notes, "One of the most consistent findings regarding pre-dictors of positive life change following life stressors or trauma is that religiousness . . . is a strong predictor of reports of growth" (p. 372). The role of religion in this meaning-making process is crucial to the maintenance of hope and optimism in the face of adversity.

In summary, psychological contributions to our understanding of the virtue of hope de-scribe hope as a cognitive process of agency and goal-oriented thinking that can have a positive impact on individual, relational, and vocational engagement. A contributor to hope is our ability to develop and maintain a sense of meaning for our lives, particularly in re-sponse to crises and difficult circumstances. Religion and spirituality are distinctively im-portant in this meaning-making process, as they focus on the "sacred" aspects of the search for meaning and significance. This review has important implications for cultivating hope through the supervision process and under-scores the importance of providing profes-sional, developmental "pathways" for suc-cessful growth as a clinician. In addition, hope-oriented supervisors will offer super-vision as a context for exploring the meaning and purpose of a clinical vocation, which in-cludes coping with and making meaning of professional challenges and crises.

ETHICAL PRINCIPLE OF BENEFICENCE: CONTRIBUTING TO HUMAN AND SOCIETAL GOOD

Central to a sense of calling and vocation for many clinicians is the hope and desire that we can have a positive impact on individuals, families, and communities through our work as mental health professionals. The ethical parallel to the virtue of hope is beneficence, which is the expectation that the work of the mental health professional will ultimately be beneficial for individuals and society. A virtue-informed approach to the understanding of beneficence inspires us to consider the good of individuals and society as part of our vocational calling and to remain hopeful about the potential for our professions to make a difference to the people we serve and the communities we are a part of. A positive ethical approach to beneficence invites us to think beyond the ethics "floor" by infusing our vocational efforts with a vision for what is possible in our work as an extension of our calling to serve God's kingdom.

The ethical principle of beneficence requires clinicians to consider the good of individuals and society when conducting research, clinical work, and consulting. The ACA code of ethics defines beneficence as "working for the good of the individual and society by promoting mental health and well-being" (American Counseling Association [ACA], 2014). Similarly, the AAMFT ethics includes a "commitment to service, advocacy, and public participation" (American Association for Marriage and Family Therapy, 2015). Aspirational goals for each of the ethical codes require professionals to altruistically contribute to the public good and society in their research, teaching, clinical work, and advocacy. Beneficence reminds clinicians that their professional actions have a large impact on the public

for good or for harm. Conversations about beneficence can be a hopeful inspiration to professionals to think beyond their individual work toward the good of society. Examples include pro bono services, prioritizing mental health services for those with greatest need, and committing professional time to prevention and education activities.

Beneficence provides an important ethical guide as clinical decisions and actions are considered in light of what is best for patients, their families, and the larger society. When considering beneficence, clinicians ask what decisions and actions will benefit not only their client but the most people in a given situation. Sileo and Kopala (1993) have developed the "A-B-C-D-E Worksheet" for applying the ethical principle of beneficence to ethical decision making. When considering an ethical dilemma, clinicians take the following steps:

- Assessment—carefully assess client, situation, and clinician motives and reactions.

- Benefit—consider the ethical decision that provides the most benefit.

- Consequences and consultation—examine the consequences of the decision and the potential impact on all involved; consult with supervisors, peers, and professional organizations.

- Duty—reflect on the duty or responsibility the clinician has toward the client, family, community, or profession.

- Education—access educational resources pertaining to the clinical situation or demand.

Supervisors can facilitate ethical decision-making practices that incorporate attentiveness to the issues of beneficence as a means of ensuring that future professionals will look beyond self-interest and expediency to consider the good of others and society in their professional decisions, behaviors, and priorities.

SUPERVISION MODELS AND METHODS FOR CULTIVATING HOPE AND EXPECTANCY

Hope is also understood as client expectations regarding the benefits of the therapeutic process. It is considered one of the common factors that contribute to positive outcomes in psychotherapy across theoretical models (Constantino, Glass, Arnkoff, Ametrano, & Smith, 2011). Specific factors contributing to client expectancy include therapist expressions of competence and confidence that the client will benefit from treatment, as well as therapist support and affirmation for gains made in treatment (Constantino et al., 2011). Common-factor models for supervision have also been proposed (Lampropoulos, 2002). Bernard and Goodyear (2014) summarize the common factor of supervisee expectancy in the following way: "Instillation of hope and raising of expectations, which includes not only encouragement, but also setting attainable goals and normalizing developmental challenges that supervisees face" (p. 61).

Very few references to "hope" or "optimism" can be found in reviewing the clinical supervision research or the indexes of the major textbooks on clinical supervision in psychology, counseling, and marriage and family therapy. Yet research suggests that hope and expectancy are significant variables in psychotherapy outcome research and appear to predict effectiveness across theoretical approaches. How can the clinical supervision process nurture the development of hopeful clinicians who foster positive expectancies in clients and remain hopeful and efficacious in

their vocational commitments? In this section, we will look at three models of supervision germane to these aims: developmental models, positive psychology supervision, and existential supervision.

Developmental Models of Supervision: Anticipating and Normalizing Challenges

Developmental models of supervision provide a sense of positive expectancy in the clinical training of mental health professionals as a process with defined steps, stages, and anticipated challenges. The outcome of the developmental process is the anticipated goal of greater autonomy, clinical effectiveness, and professional efficacy. For supervisees, locating themselves within this growth process normalizes current struggles and can provide positive expectancies about future performance. Especially for supervisees with high expectations for themselves, it is helpful to know that there is an anticipated progression in knowledge and skill development. As supervisees learn to sustain hope for their own progressive change process, they are better able to maintain a hopeful perspective on their client's growth through the process of counseling and psychotherapy.

Bernard and Goodyear (2014) assert that viewing the process of supervision through a developmental lens is essential. Without the hope and confidence that our supervisees will grow and change in their knowledge, skills, and effectiveness, the role of the supervisor is reduced to a gatekeeper only. Application of a developmental framework allows supervisors to match supervision goals with the supervisee developmental level. The supervisor then can tailor the interventions to encourage optimal supervisee development. Developmental models are atheoretical and can be integrated with all supervision models or types of supervision, including assessment, intervention, and advocacy.

A widely researched and utilized developmental approach to clinical supervision is the Integrative Developmental Model (IDM) (Stoltenberg & McNeill, 2010; Stoltenberg, McNeill, & Delworth, 1998). IDM draws on principles from social psychology and cognitive processing and skill development to propose three levels of supervisee development across three domains: motivation, autonomy, and self-other awareness. Supervisees can be at different developmental levels in each domain; thus a supervisee may be at level one in terms of autonomy (e.g., exhibiting a high level of need for structure and support by the supervisor) and at a level two with self-other awareness (e.g., less preoccupation with their own competence and more focus on the client's needs and experiences). Supervisors seek to match the supervision environment and interventions to the supervisee's development across domains with the goal of intrinsic motivation, greater independence, and self-reflective practice. The model provides specific supervision interventions to facilitate progressive development.

Specific recommendations for using a developmental approach to facilitate hope and positive expectancy in supervision include the following:

- Assess supervisees' developmental level across domains through direct observation of clinical work or viewing recorded sessions. Supervisees can be invited to locate themselves on the developmental framework for collaborative assessment.

- Consider that supervisees may develop differently across different domains of clinical work, and match supervision interventions accordingly.

- Utilize a developmental model for goal setting by asking the supervisee, "Where would you like to be?"

- Normalize struggles and provide a vision for the next step in the developmental process.

- Provide support and affirmation of goals accomplished.

Positive Psychology: Promoting a Meaningful and Efficacious Vocational Narrative

Positive psychology approaches to supervision adopt a strength-based approach to working with supervisees by prioritizing those human characteristics that lead to personal and professional flourishing (Wade & Jones, 2015). In contrast to approaches that emphasize problems or deficits, positive psychology assumes an inherent human motivation toward meaning, purpose, fulfillment, and human flourishing. Positive psychology has roots in Aristotelian philosophy, embracing the view that the development of facilitative habits and practices leads to human flourishing in both personal and vocational life. Applications of positive psychology to the workplace have implications for an approach to clinical supervision that can foster hope and meaning. For example, Wade and Jones (2015) apply the literature on transformational leadership to the task of clinical supervision and suggest that supervisors should inspire and encourage their supervisees to fully develop their potential through "instilling realistic feelings of self-efficacy" (p. 53) and also provide relational mentoring toward personal and professional growth so that supervisees can become their best professional selves.

Howard (2008) brings together the literature from occupational health, positive psychology, and narrative therapy to propose an approach to supervision that helps supervisees flourish in their professional lives. One of the important roles of the supervisor is to help the trainees develop and maintain a sense of well-being. Central to professional well-being, according to Howard, are concepts from positive psychology including a sense of coherence or meaning, work engagement, self-efficacy, flow, and resilience (p. 108). He suggests that supervisors use a narrative supervision approach that invites supervisees to "re-story" their clinical experience in a way that highlights areas of strength, meaning, and self-efficacy. Supervisors can use the technique of "collaborative conversation" to initiate exploration of this positive narrative, utilizing questions to promote a sense of coherence and engagement. Proposed questions include the following:

> What sense of purpose first brought you into this work?

> How has this grown and developed over time?

> How has this contributed positively to your life and how you see yourself?

> When you look back at this year's work, what are you most satisfied with?

> If we look back on your career, what are the achievements that stand out?

> (Howard, 2008, p. 110)

Positive psychology approaches to supervision utilize a strength-based approach to foster the development of personal and professional habits that can help supervisees maintain a sense of self-efficacy, strength, and resilience throughout their professional careers as they strive to reach their full potential.

Existential Supervision: Considering Vocational Meaning and Purpose

Existential approaches to clinical supervision widen the lens of supervision and clinical experiences through considering philosophical and moral perspectives on the "givens" of human existence. Supervisees are encouraged to consider the experiences of their clients and their own vocational work from a wider perspective in order to uncover issues of meaning and purpose that may provide new alternatives to situations that feel hopeless (van Deurzen & Young, 2009). Existentially oriented supervision practices rely on the phenomenological method to help supervisees learn to explore the worldview assumptions and realities of their clients from an attitude of openness, curiosity, and profound respect to assist clients in taking a broader view of their current problems from the perspective of the human condition: "The objective of supervision is then to let the light of life and of consciousness shine in the darkest corners of human experience" (van Deurzen & Young, 2009, p. 3). For supervisors, "it means coming to the supervisory encounter with an attitude of wonder and doubt, ready to be amazed by new discoveries but also ready to be confronted with our usual bias and blind spots" (van Deurzen & Young, 2009, p. 199).

Exploring issues of meaning and purpose is foundational to an existential approach to supervision. Supervisors adopt an existentially oriented attitude to help supervisees listen for the hidden meanings and issues of existence that are inevitably present in the clinical situation. Socratic or hermeneutic questioning is used as a primary supervision technique:

> Existential supervision is a time to take stock and elucidate our usually all too vague understanding of the complexities of human existence. This means that supervisors will ask many questions of their supervisees so as to inspire them to explore, amplify and clarify their understanding of their client's reality over and over again. They will, as we have said, follow Socrates' tracks by hermeneutic questioning, assuming that in doing so it is possible to bring out the hidden knowledge that is already there in the situation. . . . Such questioning does not analyse or search for causes and explanations, but it makes clear, reorganises thought and brings things back into a natural order, so that the flow of the therapy and of the client's life make sense and can come back into their own once more. (van Deurzen & Young, 2009, p. 6)

As supervisees learn to help clients connect with a sense of meaning and order in their lives, they also have the opportunity to forge meaning and connection with their own sense of purpose. Existentially oriented supervision makes this an explicit focus of the supervision process through helping supervisees reconnect with their original calling and vocation:

> Therapists who work with people who feel out of touch with their lives often become somewhat disconnected themselves, dried up, parched, and starved. In supervision, they can quench and quell their thirst for new knowledge and understanding and recuperate their vitality, providing supervision generates the wisdom of careful thought that comes from collaborative remembering of

the things that matter in life. Existential supervision then needs to go to the source in order to reconnect therapists with the force of life and the power of human awareness. (van Deurzen & Young, 2009, pp. 6-7)

For existentially oriented supervisors, this includes attention to all the domains of "being in the world" (Heidegger, 1962) for the supervisee and their clients, including the physical, social, personal, and spiritual. Guided reflection on the spiritual dimensions of the work of the clinician are particularly helpful for facilitating a sense of meaning and purpose for supervisees. Moja-Strasser (2009) suggests the use of questions for this exploration: "I ask my supervisees questions such as: Who do you think you are when you call yourself a therapist? In what way is your life being enriched by engaging in the activity called 'therapy'? Is being able to be a therapist a gift? Or do we just do it because we have a qualification? What are the possibilities and limitations of therapy?" (Moja-Strasser, 2009, p. 37). Existentially oriented supervision approaches can help supervisees develop habits and practices that can lead to a sustained sense of meaning and purpose for their vocational endeavors as clinical experiences are viewed through the lens of larger existential, philosophical, and spiritual perspectives. Existential questions can provide professionals with a constant reminder of why we do what we do. While times of professional dryness and discouragement are inevitable, we remain hopeful when we consider the whole of our human existence and the potential for our profession to be beneficial to others. Our professional work is certainly beneficial to us as it prompts us to engage continually in a process of growth and self-exploration.

CHRISTIAN INTEGRATIVE APPROACHES TO FOSTER THE DEVELOPMENT OF HOPEFUL CLINICIANS

A Christian integrative approach to clinical supervision adds something more to the development of hopeful clinicians who can benefit society by incorporating explicitly Christian practices into the clinical training experience. Three supervision practices are recommended toward this aim: fostering reliance on the Holy Spirit, linking clinical work to Christian vocation, and thinking developmentally about integration competencies and goals.

Reliance on the Holy Spirit

One of the most hope-giving core beliefs for the Christian supervisor and therapist is that the Holy Spirit is the primary agent of growth and transformation. As stated in the Catholic catechism cited earlier, hope as a virtue is in part based on the belief that we do not rely on our own strength (which leads to acedia, according to Pieper) but on the transforming work of the Holy Spirit. As supervisors, we have the opportunity to help our supervisees understand that it is the Spirit's active work that is foundational for their own growth and sanctification, as well as the growth and change of their clients through the therapeutic process. McMartin (2015) encourages clinicians to integrate the Holy Spirit's work in perfecting all of creation, including human development and growth, with the process of growth in therapy: "Unlike their unbelieving counterparts, Christian therapists ground their hope for change on a well-defined agent (the Spirit) and a personal knowledge of that agent. The growth process is not founded on a vague wish, but on hope in a divinely given promise (Rom. 5:3-5)" (p. 225). It is both reorienting and hope-giving to consider that growth and transformation do not rely on our own human efforts but are dependent on the work of the Spirit. Our supervisory efforts, therefore, partner with the Spirit in producing growth. We remind our supervisees that the same is true of growth through the process of therapy.

Christian psychologist Siang-Yang Tan has written extensively on the work of the Holy Spirit in and through the Christian counselor (Tan, 2011b; Tan, 1999). He reminds us that the Spirit is actively involved in providing wisdom, power, and healing for the therapist and client during psychotherapy. Tan suggests three primary ways that the work of the Holy Spirit is evident in Christian life and ministry. First, the Spirit's power is the source of spiritual strength and empowerment for the Christian clinician. As clinicians are filled with the Holy Spirit, we exhibit the gifts of the Spirit toward more effective ministry. Second, the Spirit's truth guides the clinician and the client in good discernment. The Spirit can help shed light on the key issues and problems for the client that need to be addressed. Tan encourages Christian counselors to also consider the role of spiritual oppression and warfare in considering a client's current difficulties. Third, the Spirit's fruit, especially agape, are powerful tools for the Christian counselor as an expression of ministry. Tan reminds us that the Holy Spirit is also at work growing the clinician and the client in Christlikeness toward personal and spiritual maturity.

Christian integrative supervision practices that ground the supervisor and the supervisee in the Spirit's power and work include the following:

- Start supervision with a prayer of acknowledgment of dependence on the Spirit's wisdom and guidance.

- Pause during supervision for prayerful listening.

- Listen for acedia (supervisees taking too much responsibility); affirm responsibility but gently encourage greater dependence on the Spirit.

- Review Scripture together that reorients the Christian to reliance on God's empowerment.

By helping supervisees develop habits and practices of turning toward God for strength and empowerment, supervisors foster hope and expectation that God will complete in them the good work he has started (Phil 1:6). Ultimately, our hope is in God's sanctification process through the power of the Holy Spirit, transforming us into Christlikeness. This hope is the true anchor for our souls.

Support and Model Clinical Work as Christian Vocation/Calling

Hope-oriented Christian integrative supervision encourages supervisees to consider every aspect of their life and vocation as "building for God's kingdom" (Wright, 2008, p. 193). Incorporating a biblical and theologically grounded perspective into the supervision process enables us to help supervisees live in the "already but not yet," engaging deeply with human suffering through their clinical work while holding on to the hope of Christ's kingdom. Supervisors can help their trainees consider how they are reflecting God's image to a hurting world in their clinical and professional roles, whether they are doing implicit or explicit integration of faith and clinical work. Helping supervisees develop a practical theology of hope as part of their Christian vocation will assist them in mitigating the acedia and despair that can come from dealing with human suffering day in and day out.

Supervisees wrestle with many important questions related to their Christian identity and clinical vocation that rise to the surface during clinical training. Does alleviating suffering interfere with God's transforming work in the life of the client? When is it permissible to share my faith and values with a client, or my faith narrative? What do I do when my client's therapy goals are at odds with my Christian values? How is psychotherapy different from spiritual direction or discipleship? With a trusted supervisor, trainees can raise these critical questions. Although it is tempting to respond with quick answers and remind supervisees of ethical guidelines (and sometimes this is necessary), a wise supervisor will see this as an opportunity to facilitate a way of thinking about clinical work as Christian vocation that can help guide supervisees to resources and wisdom from Christian history and tradition. Directing students to the literature on soul care, for example, helps them see their professional trajectory as part of a long history of pastoral care in the church.

Clinical supervision also provides the opportunity for vocational mentoring as we encourage supervisees to consider God's unique call on their life. Amy Sherman's *Kingdom Calling* (2011) is an excellent resource to help supervisors with this task. Sherman encourages believers to be stewards of their vocational gifts and abilities for the sake of the kingdom. She writes that Christians should integrate faith and vocation through identification of their "vocational sweet spot," which is the intersection of (1) our abilities, passions, and gifts, (2) God's kingdom priorities as established in Scripture and the life of Jesus, and (3) the needs of the world around us. As we mentor clinicians in training, we can help them pay attention to these areas as they begin to identify their unique clinical skills and abilities, determine populations of interest, and develop their understanding of kingdom priorities. Most important, as supervisors we foster hope by expressing our faith in their potential to live out this calling.

Thinking Developmentally About Christian Integration Competencies and Goals

A Christian integrative approach to supervision fosters hope and positive expectancy by helping supervisees think developmentally about their growth toward integration competencies in counseling, psychology, and marriage and family therapy. Consistent with the Integrative Developmental Model, Gingrich and Worthington (2007) propose that supervisors should consider the developmental stage of the supervisee in formulating integration goals across different domains of integration, including worldview, theory, intervention, the supervisory and therapeutic relationship, and the personal/professional functioning of the therapist. For example, in the domain of intervention, a beginning-level supervisee may have some awareness but little ability to consider religion and spirituality in case conceptualization and intervention. However, supervisees move toward greater ability and comfort with the integration of spirituality into all aspects of clinical intervention from assessment to intervention. Aten and Hernandez (2004) also suggest using the domains of the IDM model to guide the development of supervisee competence in working with religious clients. Supervisors facilitate increasing knowledge and skills in religious and spiritual competencies in assessment, intervention, case conceptualization, use of theoretical models, treatment planning, diversity

competence, and ethical decision making (Aten & Hernandez, p. 154).

Similarly, Ripley, Jackson, Tatum, and Davis (2007) encourage supervisors to consider supervisees' moral and faith development utilizing Kohlberg's moral development theory and Fowler's stages of faith development to inform a developmental approach to integrating religious and spiritual issues in supervision. Supervisees who are in the early stages of Kohlberg's and Fowler's developmental theories, for example, may be limited in their self-awareness and concerned with the right and wrong ways to function as a clinician. Consequently, supervision approaches should provide a greater degree of structure, directivity, and education for addressing religious and spiritual issues in clinical work and should help the supervisee grow in self-awareness of the impact of their own faith journey on their work with clients. Supervisees in later stages of their moral and faith development will likely be ready to manage and even appreciate the religious and spiritual differences between themselves and their clients with humility, self-awareness, and a desire to learn from others (Ripley et al., 2007).

Developmental models can provide a hopeful vision of future growth in maturity as a Christian clinician. It is important that we model this virtue as supervisors and continue investing in our own growth and development of new knowledge, skills, and applications. While often our growth feels too slow and inconsistent, supervisors can encourage developmental thinking as a spiritual and professional "habit" that encourages forward movement and a "steadfast turning" toward the person and professional that God has called us to be, one step at a time.

SPIRITUAL DISCIPLINES FOR DEVELOPING THE VIRTUE OF HOPE: INDIVIDUAL AND COMMUNITY PRACTICES

Finally, we nurture hope in our supervisees by inviting them to consider spiritual formation practices that deeply connect them to God's purpose for their lives. Two formation practices are particularly important for the maintenance of hope: keeping the Sabbath and engaging in individual and corporate worship.

Sabbath: "Eternity Utters a Day"

Just as God has given us the gift of the theological virtue of hope, he gives us the gift of the Sabbath, in which we are invited to rest, enjoy, and reconnect with all that brings life and hope to us. Mental health professionals who spend their days dealing with the pain and suffering of others are particularly in need of rhythms of rest and reengagement with God, friends and family, and ourselves in order to sustain our sense of meaning and purpose. Our souls are nourished by God's provision of the Sabbath, and we are renewed for engagement in the work he has called us to do: "In the tempestuous ocean of time and toil there are islands of stillness where man may enter a harbor and reclaim his dignity. The island is the seventh day, the Sabbath. A day of detachment from things, instruments and practical affairs as well as of attachment to the spirit" (Heschel, 2003, p. 20).

Abraham Joshua Heschel's spiritual classic *The Sabbath* invites believers to enter into the Sabbath not merely as a day of rest or abstention from activities but as a taste of eternity that we will one day enjoy with God. Through engaging in those activities that are most life-giving, we reconnect with God and with our very souls, and this reconnection infuses our labor on the other six days with a sense of meaning and purpose. Heschel (2003) writes: "Six days a week we wrestle with the world, wringing profit from the earth; on the Sabbath we especially care for the seed of eternity planted in the soul. The world has our hands, but our soul belongs to Someone Else" (p. 1). Our yearning for the Sabbath during our weekdays of labor is a reminder of our desire for the "eternal Sabbath all the days of our lives" (p. 83). Thus, Heschel suggests that a rhythm of living that embraces the Sabbath helps us maintain a vision for all of life as a pilgrimage toward eternity with God.

Heschel (2003) asserts that by resting on the seventh day of creation, God has sanctified this time and space as a "palace in time" where "eternity utters a day":

> On the Sabbath it is given us to share in the holiness that is in the heart of time. Even when the soul is seared, even when no prayer can come out of our tightened throats, the clean, silent rest of the Sabbath leads us to a realm of endless peace, or to the beginning of an awareness of what eternity means. There are few ideas in the world of thought which contain so much spiritual power as the idea of the Sabbath. Aeons hence, when of many of our cherished theories only shreds will remain, that cosmic tapestry will continue to shine. (p. 93)

This hopeful vision of Sabbath encourages us not only to withdraw from our labors but also to engage with our Creator and with others who celebrate and worship him.

When we refuse to take time to reconnect with God and ourselves, we fall prey to the vice of acedia, as a refusal to accept our humanness and limitations. Mental health professionals who pour themselves out for others with no respite set themselves on the path to personal and professional burnout. Developing good habits related to the Sabbath cannot wait until after completion of graduate school. Too often we continue to live our professional lives the way we lived in graduate school. Too easily, the promise to ourselves that "I'll start practicing Sabbath after graduate school" (after licensure, after I get established in my career, etc.) is postponed again and again until exhaustion, burnout, or even leaving the profession occurs. As professional models and mentors, supervisors offer the invitation to begin living differently *now*.

Supervisors can encourage Sabbath-keeping through the following:

- inquiring about activities and practices that have been renewing and life-giving for supervisees in the past and present

- sharing with supervisees our own successes and failures in the practice of Sabbath and what we have found to be life-giving activities for personal and spiritual renewal

- modeling rhythms of rest and retreat from work through refraining from seeing clients, emailing, or doing assessment reports on the Sabbath

- refraining from requiring supervision homework first thing Monday morning to encourage Sabbath-keeping and church involvement on Sunday

- encouraging supervisees to start small in their practice of the Sabbath by initially setting aside a couple of hours a week and eventually building up to a full 24 hours of rest and renewal each week

- encouraging involvement in church, worship, and Christian community as part of Sabbath-keeping practices

Worship: Celebrating Our Life and Purpose in Christ

We discussed the importance of church and community for spiritual formation in the last chapter. One aspect of community that is especially important in fostering hope is worship. In worship we bring our whole being experientially into God's presence with a complete focus on him and all he has done for us. Our hearts are opened to receive God's gift of hope for ourselves, others, and the suffering world. We can experience a renewal of connection, gratitude, and engagement. Because we spend six days a week engaged in psychology and science, it is especially important for mental health professionals to engage in regular worship practices that employ heart, mind, soul, and the senses. One wise mentor regularly exhorted students to "spend as much time in worship as you do in self-examination!" (F. White, personal communication).

Around the world, community worship is a symbol of hope in the darkest places and a celebration of God's larger purposes for the world and the body of Christ. The underground church in Prague that now freely worships near the location where Christians were interrogated and persecuted for their faith under communism. The small church in Kathmandu where Nepali Christians, who make up less than 1 percent of the population and are often cast out of their families when they convert, join together to sing and dance with joy to the Lord. The weekly chapel service where students and faculty come together across departments and disciplines to sing, pray, and hear God's Word together. These are the holy moments that affirm our identity as Christ-followers first (and counselors, MFTs, and psychologists second) and remind us why we are studying, teaching, re-searching, and counseling. Worship reminds us why we are here and connects us with the Source of all faith, hope, and love for our work and our lives.

Worship is one component of the "virtuous circle" of activities necessary for the formation of Christian character emphasized by Wright (2010). Worship is both individual and corporate; it involves daily individual disciplines of prayer as well as community practices of reading Scripture together, singing hymns, sharing the Lord's Supper, celebrating baptisms, and following the liturgical calendar. Wright notes:

> Central to the practices of the Christian faith, as I have said all along, is shared worship. I assume that all serious Christians worship and pray in private, day by day; certainly little growth in virtue, or anything else for that matter, is likely to happen without this. But I assume, too, that serious Christians will worship and pray *together*. . . . The sheer act of coming together in worship, week by week, says in effect, "We, together, hope and intend to be part of God's royal priesthood, and we are here to draw wisdom and strength from Jesus himself." Thus, before a hymn has been sung or a word spoken, the habit of the heart is being formed: a community that together intends to work on faith, hope, and love. (p. 278)

Worship can involve a multitude of creative activities that bring us into God's presence, including reading the Psalms, singing, creating art, engaging with nature, and writing poetry. Calhoun (2015) writes, "The heart of worship is to seek to know and love God each in our own unique way" (p. 50). The following are some suggestions for individual worship activities that may be especially helpful for mental health professionals:

- Regular reading and memorization of the Psalms as sacred poetry that embraces the whole human experience. Reading one psalm a day, or reflecting on one psalm for the week, invites deeper engagement in worship.

- Embodied worship practices that engage the whole self in a physical way to enhance worship. Simple practices include attending to our posture during prayer (kneeling, opening our hands, walking prayer), creating a physical space in our homes set apart for quiet worship, engaging all the senses (through music, lighting a candle during prayer, etc.), and enhancing our focus on God.

- Use of sacred poetry, art, and literature to stimulate worship and prayerful reflection. Richard Foster (2011) calls these practices an act of "sacred imagination" that can aid the practice of contemplative prayer.

- *Visio divina*, or "divine seeing," a spiritual practice of seeking God in prayer through attentiveness to the beauty around us. Calhoun (2015) writes, "It is a way to pray with the eyes" (p. 47). Enjoying nature, prayerfully contemplating a work of art, and using painting or drawing as an expression of prayer are all practices where we allow our hearts to be moved to praise and worship through beauty.

- Singing and listening to songs, hymns, and spiritual songs that believers throughout history have composed for the sake of worship

Engaging in regular acts of worship, individually and corporately, is essential for the nurturing of Christian hope as we remind ourselves and each other of the true meaning and purpose of our life and work. Applications to supervision can include initiating discussion of meaningful worship practices and learning from each other, for example. Or a group supervisor could offer a brief worship devotional as part of a group supervision experience and discuss the importance of worship as an act of Christian hope and "steadfast turning" toward Christ.

CONCLUSION

What signs and symptoms indicate that supervisees are at risk for losing hope in God, themselves, and mental health work as beneficial to society? Supervisees may raise questions about beneficence and the profession: Is change truly possible? Is counseling really effective? Are families able to maintain the gains they have made in therapy? They may also question themselves and wonder, Am I really cut out for the work of a psychologist? Can I really make a difference? Supervisors should watch for signs of acedia, or "work-engendered depression" (Bartlett, 1990) as we have defined it above, which include poor work-life balance, inability to take a Sabbath, loss of joy in leisure activities, and too much self-reliance.

Supervisors have the opportunity to encourage their trainees to develop the character disposition of hope as a "steadfast turning" toward the purposes of God for their life and calling. Through use of developmental, positive psychology, and existential models and techniques of supervision, supervisors foster a hopeful vision for professional development and who the supervisee is becoming, step by step. Through Christian integrative approaches emphasizing reliance on the Holy Spirit, supervisors encourage the development of habits and practices that serve as a constant reminder that God is the source of all healing as he invites us to partner with him to build his kingdom. We offer vocational mentoring for our supervisees as we invite them to consider the work of counseling, psychology, and marriage and family therapy as Christian vocation toward strengthening families and communities and serving the church.

Finally, we engage in spiritual disciplines and practices to anchor our souls in hope. Keeping the Sabbath and engaging in individual and community worship turns our hearts and minds toward Christ, and our strength is renewed for the work he has called us to do. We can take Paul's blessing in Romans to heart as we engage wholeheartedly in the life and vocation that God has called us to, by the power of His Spirit: "May the God of hope fill you with all joy and peace as you trust in him, so that you may overflow with hope by the power of the Holy Spirit" (Rom 15:13).

CHAPTER SUMMARY / SUPERVISION GUIDE

Virtue	• **Hope**
Description	• Turning toward God as our purpose and the source of our meaning and toward his kingdom as the good that we desire
Scripture	• "Therefore, since we have been justified through faith, we have peace with God through our Lord Jesus Christ, through whom we have gained access by faith into this grace in which we now stand. And we boast in the hope of the glory of God. Not only so, but we also glory in our sufferings, because we know that suffering produces perseverance; perseverance, character; and character, hope. And hope does not put us to shame, because God's love has been poured out into our hearts through the Holy Spirit, who has been given to us" (Rom 5:1-5).
Ethical principle	• **Beneficence:** working for the benefit and good of others, promoting health and well-being in society
Supervision best practices	• Developmental models of supervision • Positive psychology supervision and promoting an efficacious vocational narrative • Existential supervision and vocational meaning
Christian integration focus	• Reliance on the Holy Spirit • Clinical work as Christian vocation • Developmental models of teaching integration competencies
Spiritual practices	• Sabbath • Worship
Desired outcome	• Hopeful clinicians who maintain a vision for mental health work as benefiting individuals, families, and communities, and who see their place in serving Christ's kingdom through promoting health and hope

CHAPTER 5

LOVE

Relational Competence and Ethic of Care

Follow God's example, therefore, as dearly loved children and walk in the way of love, just as Christ loved us and gave himself up for us as a fragrant offering and sacrifice to God.

EPHESIANS 5:1-2

Therefore, as God's chosen people, holy and dearly loved, clothe yourselves with compassion, kindness, humility, gentleness and patience. Bear with each other and forgive one another if any of you has a grievance against someone. Forgive as the Lord forgave you. And over all these virtues put on love, which binds them all together in perfect unity. Let the peace of Christ rule in your hearts, since as members of one body you were called to peace. And be thankful.

COLOSSIANS 3:12-15

WE NOW COME TO the third and greatest of the theological virtues, the virtue of love. As beings created in love for love, love is absolutely central to our growth in Christ and our professional calling. Jesus teaches that the greatest commandments are to love God with heart, mind, soul, and strength, and to love neighbor as self (Mk 12:28-31). Paul writes that while faith, hope, and love abide, the greatest of these for the Christian life is love. No matter how skilled we become in our psychological knowledge, clinical competency, and supervision mastery, without love our efforts are empty and nothing but a resounding gong or clanging cymbal (1 Cor 13).

Similarly, no other professional virtue is more important for clinical work than the ability to maintain healthy, respectful, and warmly engaged relationships with colleagues, supervisees, and clients. While trust and secure attachment provides a good beginning, emotional intelligence and relational competence are essential for long-term effectiveness in all areas of professional practice. Alternatively, poor relational competencies that manifest in lack of respect, boundary violations, over-involvement, or lack of engagement can result in significant harm to our clients, supervisees, and colleagues. Each one of us has stories of harm we have experienced in professional relationships, and at the same time we must confess that we ourselves have caused harm to others when we have failed to love and respect them in the way we know we should. Thus, effective supervision will need to pay attention to disciplines of the mind and heart that facilitate love as evidenced by relational competence. Cultivating the virtue of love in professional practice develops clinicians who consistently treat all persons as beings of great worth, created in the image of God, and deserving of dignity, respect, and care.

In this chapter, we examine the theological virtue of love and the corresponding professional value of demonstrating respect for others through relational competence. We explore psychological perspectives on the character strengths related to humanity, including altruism, compassion, emotional intelligence, and forgiveness. We will look at the role of clinical supervision in the development of relational competencies. Supervision strategies and spiritual formation practices can be incorporated into the supervision process to help us "walk in love" in our personal and professional lives.

LOVE: BIBLICAL AND THEOLOGICAL PERSPECTIVES

"God is love" (1 Jn 4:8) provides the starting point for our understanding of this most central theme in Scripture. The Bible teaches that loving God and others are the two greatest commandments and the foundation of true Christian vocation. Love is holistic and involves heart, mind, soul, and strength (Mk 12:30). It is our response to being loved by God (1 Jn 4:19). Love is more than simply words; it involves action too (1 Jn 3:18). And it is also more than good deeds, as our work is empty without love (1 Cor 13). Love is defined in detail by the apostle Paul in the familiar passage in 1 Corinthians 13 as patient, kind, never jealous or envious, never boastful or proud, but bearing, believing, and enduring all things. The Christian virtue of love is articulated in the New Testament using the Greek word *agapē*, and Christian tradition has often used the Latin word *caritas*, sometimes translated as "charity" (Kaczor, 2008).

Charity is the most important virtue, from which all the other virtues emanate, according to Aquinas. Love is unique among all the virtues, as it is the only one that is said to be "identical with God" (Pieper, 1997, p. 163). As an infused virtue, love is a gift from God, and we are only able to love others because we are first loved (1 Jn 4). The *Catechism of the Catholic Church* (2003) defines the virtue of charity in this way:

Charity is the theological virtue by which we love God above all things for his own sake, and our neighbor as ourselves for the love of God. Jesus makes charity the new commandment. By loving his own "to the end," he makes manifest the Father's love which he receives. By loving one another, the disciples imitate the love of Jesus which they themselves receive. Whence Jesus says: "As the Father has loved me, so have I loved you; abide in my love." And again: "This is my commandment, that you love one another as I have loved you."

"If I . . . have not charity," says the Apostle, "I am nothing." Whatever my privilege, service or even virtue, "If I . . . have not charity I gain nothing." Charity is superior to all the virtues. It is the first of the theological virtues: "So faith, hope, charity abide, these three. But the greatest of these is charity.

The *Catechism* also describes the unique role of charity among the virtues:

> The practice of all the virtues is animated and inspired by charity, which "binds everything together in perfect harmony"; it is the form of the virtues; it articulates and orders them among themselves; it is the source and the goal of their Christian practice. Charity upholds and purifies our human ability to love, and raises it to the supernatural perfection of divine love.
>
> The fruits of charity are joy, peace, and mercy; charity demands beneficence and fraternal correction; it is benevolence; it fosters reciprocity and remains disinterested and generous; it is friendship and communion: Love is itself the fulfillment of all our works. There is the goal; that is why we run: we run toward it, and once we reach it, in it we shall find rest. (para. 1822-23, 1826-27, 1829)

In the *Summa Theologica*, Aquinas writes that charity is the "mother" of the virtues because she conceives it within herself from another (God) and then emanates and sustains the other virtues through love. Thus, love inspires and holds the other virtues together. For Aquinas, love is an act of the will rather than an aspect of emotion or intellect. In fact, it was out of his fervent love for God and for humankind that Aquinas invested his life in writing the *Summa* as a guide for godly living (Kaczor, 2008). Similarly, the catechism rightly states that love is both the "source and goal" of all who practice Christian virtue. The highest form of love remains "disinterested" in that we love others for their own sake, because they are loved and created by God, without expectations or demands that come from our own self-interest (Mackey, 1997).

There are many important theological and philosophical works on love well beyond the scope of this chapter. Here we explore three important contemporary understandings of this central virtue that are most applicable to our thinking about clinical supervision: love as a continuation and imitation of God's creative act, love as an expression of God's love existing in the Trinity, and love as an expression of the incarnation.

Love as an Imitation of God's Creative Act

In his profound treatise on love, Pieper (1997) writes that all forms of Christian love, particularly agape/caritas, are expressions and imitations of God's original love for creation expressed in Genesis 1, an "echo of the divine, creative, prime affirmation" (p. 171). Through grace, God has infused his creative love in us that allows us to respond to others with the attitude, "It is *good* that you exist; how wonderful that you are!" (p. 174). Pieper writes:

> It is God who in the act of creation anticipated all conceivable human love and said: I will you to be; it is good, "very good" (Gen. 1:31), that you exist. He has already infused everything that human beings can love and affirm, goodness along with existence, and that means lovability and affirmability. Human love, therefore, is by its nature and must inevitably be always an imitation and a kind of repetition of this perfected and, in the exact sense of the word, *creative* love of God. (p. 171)

Pieper also links this source of love back to faith. Through faith, we believe in God's creation of the universe and human beings as a part of that creation. Faith, then, is essential to love:

> And there are many indications that, when the senses no longer observe beauty and the intellect can no longer detect any meaning or value, what ultimately sustains love and

remains believable as its real justification is the conviction that everything existing in the universe is creatura, creatively willed, affirmed, loved by the Creator and for that reason is really—in the most radical sense that the word "really" can possibly have—*really* good and therefore susceptible to, but also worthy of, being loved by us. (p. 199)

This love for creation encompasses God's "infused" love through grace for all of the creation as well as human beings' love for self, each other—in various forms (*eros* and *philio*)—and God. Pieper suggests that acts of caritas and mercy are also expressions of "how good it is that you exist," as exemplified in Mother Teresa of Calcutta's attitude toward the dying.

This moment of recognition of the eternal value and beauty of the other is beautifully articulated by author Marilynne Robinson in the Pulitzer Prize–winning novel *Gilead*. Clinicians will likely relate to her description of this moment that occurs in counseling. In *Gilead*, an aging minister, reflecting on his life and work, journals the following passage:

A great part of my work has been listening to people, in that particularly intense privacy of confession, or at least unburdening, and it has been very interesting to me. . . . When people come to speak to me, whatever they say, I am struck by a kind of incandescence in them, the "I" whose predicate can be "love" or "fear" or "want," and whose object can be "someone" or "nothing" and it won't really matter, because the loveliness is just in that presence, shaped around "I" like a flame on a wick, emanating itself in grief and guilt and joy and whatever else. But quick, and avid, and resourceful. To see this aspect of life is a privilege of the ministry which is seldom mentioned. (Robinson, 2004, pp. 44-45; see Jeffrey, 2009, for other reflections on *Gilead* and virtue.)

What a privilege it is to glimpse the imago Dei, the beauty of creation through the loving eyes of the Creator in the supervisees and clients we serve. This, then, is the essence of love.

Love as the Divine Essence of the Trinity

According to theologian and ethicist Stanley Grenz (1997), the foundation of a Christian ethic of love is God's trinitarian nature, in which Father, Son, and Holy Spirit are bound together in self-giving agape love. Grenz proposes that John's assertion in 1 John 4:8 that "God is love" suggests that love is the "divine essence" (p. 284), the "eternal dynamic of the triune God" (p. 285). Grenz writes:

Through all eternity God is the social Trinity, the community of love. The God who is love cannot but respond to the world in accordance with God's own eternal essence—love. Hence, *agapē* is not only the description of the eternal God in all eternity, it is likewise the fundamental characteristic of God in relationship with creation. With profound theological insight, therefore, John burst forth, "For God so loved the world that he gave" (Jn 3:16). (p. 285)

Just as God loves us in a self-giving way consistent with his very nature, so we are called to love "after the manner of God" (Grenz, 1997, p. 285) as those created in his image. While agape is primary and remains foundational to a Christian ethic of love, Grenz encourages Christians not to lose sight of the importance of other types of love in applications of Christian ethics.

In the context of medical caregiving, for example, Grenz (1997) suggests that the "agapaic" ethical principles of beneficence and nonmaleficence alone without other forms of love can lead to "austere paternalism" in professional caregiver to patient relationships. He says that agape alone does not capture the emotional sensitivity of care and concern needed for compassionate and emotionally engaged medical care. Rather, all types of love are needed in the professional context:

> Putting the matter in Christian theological terms, the kind of love that lies at the heart of the Christian agapaic ethic is an *agapē* informed by a "sensing with" others as those whom God has created with the goal of participating in an eternal community. As the Holy Spirit mixes the self-giving impulse (*agapē*) with a compassionate familial concern for (*storgē*), plus a sincere desire to enjoy friendship of (*philia*) and true communion with (*eros*) each other in God's eternal fellowship, the Spirit of the relation between the Father and the Son leads us into the fullness of the Christian love ethic. It is this kind of comprehensive love that characterizes truly *Christian* caregiving relationships, not only in the medical realm but in every context. (Grenz, 1997, p. 293)

Grenz provides us with an important link between a theological understanding of the virtue of love and professional caregiving with implications for developing a well-rounded ethic of love and compassion in mental health care.

God's Love in and Through the Incarnation

A third way that the church throughout history has understood God's love is the incarnation: God loving humankind and becoming one of us to save us. The incarnation, God becoming human and experiencing all human sufferings, then, becomes the deepest expression of love imaginable. "For God so loved the world . . ." Through this act of supreme love, God imbues humanity with dignity, sacredness, and worth.

Gushee and Stassen (2016) examine the parable of the sheep and goats in Matthew 25 as particularly important for understanding the incarnation and the sacredness of life. The "sheep" cared for are the least of these, and Jesus separates them out in the final judgment. They write:

> In a profoundly important twist on the theme of incarnation, Jesus here suggests that God enters humanity not just in one human, but in all people, especially the most needy. Jesus teaches us to see in the face of every person his own face. This judgment parable (if it is a parable!) particularly instructs us to see Jesus Christ in and through the face of every *suffering person*, everyone who counts as among "the least of these," enumerated here as those who are hungry, thirsty, strangers, naked, sick, and imprisoned. (Gushee & Stassen, 2016, p. 158)

The authors emphasize that the agape love taught in the New Testament is a *delivering love* where God rescues humankind from bondage and sin, liberating us to love in community. God's actions provide a template for our own loving action in the world: demonstrating compassion, seeking deliverance, and bringing into community those who are in bondage of sin and suffering (Gushee & Stassen, 2016, pp. 123-24). This perspective on incarnational, delivering love adds an important dimension to our consideration of the ethic of love as a propensity to seek justice, fairness, and equity for "the least of these."

To summarize, the virtue of love (caritas and agape) can be understood as an embodiment of God's very nature, the Trinity, and as an imitation of God's creative act toward others and toward creation—an expression of "how good that you exist!" God's self-giving love is expressed through the incarnation as he took on human form to save us. God infuses us with the gift of love for him, for creation, and for others. We can also enact this virtue by cultivation of a reverence for others as created in God's image, and therefore of inestimable worth and value, prioritizing "the least of these" in our professional work.

In clinical supervision, love involves commitment to an ethic of care for the holistic well-being of our supervisees, delighting in who God created them to be and desiring their good. Love requires coming alongside our supervisees in their professional journeys with respect for their autonomy and right to privacy. It also involves a commitment to helping them develop the interpersonal skills and competencies that are necessary for long-term care of others in professional relationships, helping them learn to care for others with respect and the highest regard. If faith is the essential starting point of establishing trust in supervision, and hope is the sense of meaning and purpose that sustains us professionally, then love is the ever-present attitude of agape and caritas through which all learning in supervision is mediated.

PSYCHOLOGICAL PERSPECTIVES: ALTRUISTIC LOVE AND SOCIAL/EMOTIONAL INTELLIGENCE

From a psychological perspective, the character virtue of love has been operationalized in several ways. Positive psychologists Peterson and Seligman (2004) have designated character strengths of "humanity"—including love, kindness/altruism, and social intelligence—as the traits that are involved in caring for others. *Love* is viewed as the emotional and cognitive bond in relationships that can be best understood through the lens of attachment theory. *Kindness* or *altruistic love*, according to Peterson and Seligman, involves traits of generosity, nurturance, care, and compassion. They write, "Kindness and altruistic love require the assertion of a common humanity in which others are worthy of attention and affirmation for no utilitarian reasons but for their own sake" (p. 326). The authors describe this type of love as consistent with agape love as taught by the Christian tradition. Correlates of altruistic love include empathy, moral reasoning, and social responsibility. *Social intelligence*, the third character strength of humanity, is used to describe the category of traits concerned with emotional, personal, and social reasoning and intelligence. A distinction is made in their categorization between *emotional intelligence*, which involves the ability to identify, understand, and respond to human emotions; *personal intelligence*, which involves self-awareness and regulation of one's own experience; and *social intelligence*, which describes the ability to understand and respond adeptly in social interactions.

Social and emotional intelligence have been widely studied in psychology with applications in parenting, education, and organizational psychology. Particularly intriguing is the growing field of social neuroscience or interpersonal neurobiology, which examines the impact of early caregiver relationships on brain development and the ability to relate to others (Narvaez, 2014). Findings suggest that early caregiver relationships affect brain development and ultimately our ability to relate to others, including the ability to demonstrate empathy, self- and other-awareness, and moral capabilities. Research in brain plasticity suggests that neural pathways are not fixed but rather can be affected by new relational experiences, and these findings been applied to counseling and psychotherapy (Ivey, Ivey, & Zalaquett, 2014). Good listening skills and empathy provide a therapeutic environment that helps clients (as well as supervisees) develop improved interpersonal relationship capabilities.

Research in moral and social psychology has also contributed to our understanding of the character trait of compassion. Considered to be both a state and trait, compassion is defined as "the feeling that arises in witnessing another's suffering and that motivates a subsequent desire to help" (Goetz, Keltner, & Simon-Thomas, 2010, p. 351). It is considered a facet of empathy, but differs from empathy in that it goes beyond the experience of feeling another person's distress and activates the desire to act on these feelings of concern. Contemporary perspectives consider compassion to be "an active, motivated choice" (Cameron & Rapier, 2017, p. 373) by which individuals consider goals, priorities, and context in deciding to engage in helping behaviors, suggesting compassionate action may be guided by prudence. Clinical interventions to cultivate compassion include mindfulness meditation practices that focus attention on the present moment, which can increase compassionate motivations. Cameron and Rapier (2017) suggest, "By encouraging focus on the present moment and the active cultivation of compassion, these programs are likely to clarify and dispel motivations to avoid compassion, and illuminate the benefits of extending compassion to others" (p. 396). This line of research and suggested interventions has valuable implications for the use of mindfulness to foster compassion in the clinical supervision process. For example, suggesting a supervisee pause to engage in a brief mindfulness exercise when

discussing a difficult client has the potential to foster compassion.

One additional area of research related to the virtue of love is the psychological research on forgiveness. Forgiveness is defined as "a prosocial change toward a perceived transgressor, and includes the reduction of negative (and in some cases the increase of positive) thoughts, emotions, and motivations toward the offender that might eventuate in changed behaviors" (Davis, Worthington, Hook, & Hill, 2013, p. 233). Forgiveness is conceptualized as both a state of forgiveness for a specific incidence and a trait of forgivingness over time (Worthington et al., 2012). Empirical research has consistently demonstrated physical, psychological, and relational health benefits from forgiveness (see Toussaint, Worthington, & Williams, 2015, for an excellent overview of this research). A positive relationship has also been demonstrated in the research between religion and forgiveness as a state (Fehr, Gelfand, & Nag, 2010). Recent research also suggests a moderate relationship between trait forgiveness and religiosity, as well as contextual religious/spiritual factors and forgiveness (Davis et al., 2013). Religion may contribute to forgivingness, and therefore overall health, in a number of ways by encouraging forgiveness as a virtuous, consistent practice. In addition, religious communities provide the doctrinal support, guidelines, rituals, and motivation that help individuals develop consistent and wise forgiveness practices over time (Worthington et al., 2012). As a prosocial behavior, the practice of forgiveness can be beneficial for personal and professional relationships.

From a psychological perspective, therefore, the character strengths of humanity are influenced by early relationships with caregivers but can be further developed by learning and practicing emotional regulation and empathy and are demonstrated by prosocial actions such as compassion and forgiveness. We build on these important findings as we consider how to develop the virtue of love through the clinical supervision process.

PROFESSIONAL ETHICS: DEMONSTRATING RESPECT AND RELATIONAL COMPETENCE

An incarnational understanding of the ethic of love allows clinicians to be with their clients in moments of deepest suffering while respecting their dignity, autonomy, and right to privacy. We "walk in love" in our professional conduct by aspiring to the ethical *ceiling*, that is, the highest level of ethical behaviors and attitudes, and not just the ethical *floor* in our respect for our client's dignity and worth (Pomerantz, 2012, p. 311). We enact the virtue of love when we approach all the ethical guidelines from an *ethic of care* through bringing a relationally oriented morality to ethical decision making that keeps our client's benefit always in mind as the highest good (Ng, 2013). In this section, we review the ethical principle of respect and the professional value of relational competence as areas of important focus for clinical supervision.

Respect

Professionally, we demonstrate the ethic of love when we respect the dignity and worth of all persons, including their right to privacy, autonomy, and self-determination. The ACA, APA, and AAMFT ethical codes all emphasize the importance of professional attitudes and behaviors that are consistent with this ethic of positive regard. In fact, client welfare is the most important responsibility for counselors, psychologists, and MFTs and provides a foundation for all other ethical mandates. As stated in the ACA Code of Ethics, "The primary responsibility of counselors is to respect the dignity and promote the welfare of clients" (American Counseling Association, 2014, p. 4). The Canadian Psychological Association Guidelines for Ethical Supervision articulate well the ethical responsibility of respect for persons in the supervision process:

> The principle of Respect for the Dignity of Persons requires supervisors and supervisees to demonstrate respect for each other as well as for all other persons with whom they relate in their psychological activities. Respect involves valuing the innate worth of persons and not using them solely as a means to an end. Respect is an essential characteristic in the relationship between supervisors and supervisees. The supervisee shares the responsibility for respect, even though the supervisor has the greater responsibility for modelling and maintaining a respectful relationship and for addressing problems that may arise. The power differential adds to the complexity of the supervisory relationship. (Canadian Psychological Association, 2009, p. 5)

An ethic of respect for client welfare will also lead to appropriate protections of their privacy and right to confidentiality. Beyond compliance with HIPAA guidelines, clinicians who respect the dignity and worth of their clients will take great pains to ensure that confidential records, session recordings, and psychological assessment results are well protected. Clinicians can approach the process of informed consent as an opportunity to facilitate "informed collaboration" and empower clients to be true partners in the clinical setting (Pomerantz, 2012, p. 311).

Supervisees take their cues from supervisors and mentors about how to interact with others in ways that demonstrate the highest levels of respect. Even the way in which we discuss clients outside the therapy office reflects our level of respect for their dignity and worth. Developing respectful habits and practices toward client care begins early in our professional lives and is fostered by the attentive supervisor. Demonstrating respect for our supervisees and clients occurs through acts of hospitality and consideration, such as offering a beverage, inviting them to sit in a comfortable seat, and inquiring respectfully about their general well-being before moving into clinical material. These small gestures communicate love in the best sense to supervisees and clients alike: "It is *good* that you exist; how wonderful that you are!"

Relational Competence

Competency in relationships is not only desirable for clinical practice; it is a necessary benchmark goal for counselors, psychologists, and MFTs. Relational competence is considered foundational to all other areas of clinical competence (Mangione & Nadkarni, 2010). Demonstrated capabilities include developing and maintaining a therapeutic alliance, showing empathy and respect, dealing with alliance ruptures, working effectively with others in consultation and collaboration, demonstrating a capacity for self-reflection on relational impact on others, and managing transference and countertransference issues.

Each mental health discipline prioritizes unique but complementary relational competencies. MFT supervisors prioritize the development of the supervisee's understanding of the web of relationships in which family therapy occurs, as well as the ability to employ relational and systemic models of change in psychotherapy (Todd & Storm, 2014). Counseling professionals emphasize the importance of the development of self-reflective practice, which includes "knowledge about self and interpersonal behavior" (Bernard & Goodyear, 2014, p. 6). Psychologists use a competency-based approach in education and supervision to help trainees develop the empirically supported relational competencies that have demonstrated impact on the therapeutic process (Mangione & Nadkarni, 2010). In fact, the APA has developed a comprehensive description of relationship-competency benchmarks for psychologists, with a corresponding rating form that can be used by supervisors and supervisees to assess progress (see table 4).

Relational competence is essential in the mental health disciplines as research has demonstrated the importance of the therapeutic alliance on successful therapy outcomes. Empirically Supported Relationship variables (ESRs) suggest that the "common factor" relationship qualities will have as much, if not more, impact on the therapeutic process than theory-specific techniques (Norcross, 2011). We do our supervisees a great disservice if we do not make them aware of these relationship factors and foster their ability to implement common factors across theoretical orientations and modalities.

Table 4. Relational competency benchmarks in professional psychology (APA, 2011, p. 5)

5. Relationships	Relate effectively and meaningfully with individuals, groups, and/or communities.		
	Readiness for Practicum	**Readiness for Internship**	**Readiness for Entry to Practice**
5A. Interpersonal Relationships	Displays interpersonal skills	Forms and maintains productive and respectful relationships with clients, peers/colleagues, supervisors and professionals from other disciplines	Develops and maintains effective relationships with a wide range of clients, colleagues, organizations, and communities
5B. Affective Skills	Displays affective skills	Negotiates differences and handles conflict satisfactorily; provides effective feedback to others and receives feedback nondefensively	Manages difficult communication; possesses advanced interpersonal skills
5C. Expressive Skills	Communicates ideas, feelings, and information clearly using verbal, nonverbal, and written skills	Communicates clearly using verbal, nonverbal, and written skills in a professional context; demonstrates clear understanding and use of professional language	Verbal, nonverbal, and written communications are informative, articulate, succinct, sophisticated, and well-integrated; demonstrates thorough grasp of professional language and concepts

SUPERVISION MODELS AND METHODS FOR FACILITATING RELATIONAL COMPETENCE

The interpersonal dynamics of individual, triadic, and group supervision provide the ideal context to facilitate relational competencies as interpersonal strengths and areas for growth inevitably manifest in both clinical work and the supervisory relationship. In a secure and trusting supervisory relationship marked by mutual respect, concern, and unconditional positive regard, supervisees can examine the relational patterns that foster or hinder their professional work and develop the habits of mind and heart necessary to sustain a long-term ethic of care for others. As these competencies are "caught" rather than "taught," the supervision context is likely to be the best vehicle for assessing and developing relational competencies necessary for effective mental health practice. In this section, we examine models and methods of supervision that guide best practices for fostering relational competence.

Humanistic/Experiential Models of Supervision

Many of the supervision models that prioritize the development of relational competencies can trace their roots back to Carl Rogers's work on the facilitative conditions necessary for effective psychotherapy, which include empathy, warmth, respect, genuineness, and unconditional positive regard (Rogers, 1957). Contemporary humanistic/experiential approaches to clinical supervision also prioritize these indispensable competencies as foundational to effective clinical practice. Several specific approaches are described here.

The helping skills training approach (Hill, 2014b) teaches beginning therapists the basic therapeutic skills as part of a three-stage model of therapy that includes exploration, insight, and action. Ideal for a small group format, helping skills are introduced through didactic teaching and then practiced in small groups. Trainees benefit from practicing, taping, and then transcribing their sessions, followed by a self-evaluation of their growing competencies. Hill (2014b) suggests that helping skills are crucial before trainees begin to see clients "because trainees are learning to shift from communication that is appropriate in friendship to communication that is appropriate for therapy. Hence, they must learn to move from evenly shared conversations to listening more, giving less self-disclosure and less opinion, and interrupting less" (Hill, 2014b, p. 337). The helping skills model can also be taught with advanced graduate students supervising practice sessions (with faculty supervisors providing the "supervision of supervision") and thus developing supervision skills at the same time.

A group supervision activity to foster empathy involves the supervisor role-playing a client while each group member takes a turn in the therapist role practicing reflective listening. Burke and Hohman (2014) suggest that the activity begin with a brief discussion of the purpose of reflective listening, why it is important in facilitating empathy, some common "traps," and the role of reflective listening in fostering empathy. During the role-playing, the supervisor responds to the supervisee in the client role but also calls a pause or timeout in the role-playing when a supervisee uses a nonreflective response (e.g., advice giving, probing questions). Supervisors facilitate participant reflection on their own reactions and struggles with reflective listening as potential barriers to the development of empathy.

Another group supervision activity for teaching empathy involves use of actual clinical material (Parker & Blackburn, 2014). A supervisee presents a case including a video clip of a session with an individual or family. Then group members each describe the feelings and experiences of the client(s). To include an affective component with the empathy, Parker and Blackburn (2014) suggest that the supervisor can ask if the supervisee has personally experienced a similar situation and what that felt like. Supervisors facilitate discussion of the experience of empathizing with the client(s) and what reactions and challenges occurred for each supervisee in this process.

Farber (2014) suggests that supervisors keep in mind the core competencies of the humanistic/existential approach to therapy and utilize these skills in supervision to provide supervisees with a firsthand experience of the relational competencies. First, supervisors utilize an experiential orientation to help supervisees develop competencies in phenomenological inquiry and here-and-now relational processing. Second, supervision aims to cultivate a "person of the psychotherapist" focus through development of abilities to be self-reflective in clinical and professional relationships. A third essential outcome involves the development of competencies in relational capacities that have been demonstrated to produce change, including empathy, genuineness, unconditional positive regard, and respect. Finally, supervision seeks to develop existential values and orientation including a holistic view of persons emphasizing human agency, uniqueness, self-determination, with respect for differences. Primary supervision interventions include adopting a collaborative stance (which then generalizes to the supervisee's approach with the client), modeling phenomenological assessment and inquiry, and mutual exploration of themes in the client's life and the meaning of symptoms.

Transgenerational (TG) Family Systems Approaches

TG approaches to clinical supervision in MFT are particularly instrumental in developing therapist relational competencies. In TG family therapy, couple and family relational patterns are viewed as expressions of generational behavioral patterns. This historical understanding and context is critical to the change process and helps families make sense of behavioral patterns and issues (Brooks & Roberto-Forman, 2014).

Likewise, TG supervision examines supervisee relational patterns in the context of their own family of origin (FOO) and explores the impact of relational strengths and challenges on relationships with clients. TG supervision emphasizes self-of-the-therapist work through encouraging supervisees to reflect on relational experiences, family history, and their cultural context. The goal of TG is to develop relational competencies in supervisees by fa-cilitation of a high level of differentiation, a Bowenian concept that refers to the ability to sustain emotional connections while maintaining a sense of personal autonomy, authority, and efficacy. The assumption of TG supervision is that well-differentiated therapists are more able to promote change as they can join with a family and yet maintain a sense of separateness that is crucial to efficacious therapeutic actions in family therapy.

TG supervision utilizes the following interventions to encourage examination of relational patterns and foster self-of-the-therapist growth in relational competency:

- Use of experiential interventions and facilitative questions to explore supervisee reactions to clinical material and videotape review, and to elicit stories of supervisee family-of-origin experiences.

- Introduction of the genogram in supervision as a tool for the identification of relational patterns, cultural context, and strengths in the supervisee's family of origin with the goal of fostering mastery of the use of the genogram in theory.

- Use of group supervision as an opportunity for interpersonal growth, learning from others' perspectives, and practicing the art of giving (and receiving) input and feedback as TG skills of assessment and intervention are practiced.

- Co-therapy with supervisor initially taking the lead and then encouraging supervisee autonomy and authority as they are developmentally ready. This format provides opportunities for here-and-now experience of relational patterns and interactions. Time devoted to debriefing sessions afterward is a critical component of this approach to supervision.

- Use of Aponte's person-of-the-therapist supervision instrument (Aponte & Carlsen, 2009) as a helpful tool for facilitating use of self in supervision.

Psychoanalytic Supervision Models

Contemporary psychoanalytic models of supervision are relationally focused, viewing the relationship as the primary crucible where change and growth occur (Frawley-O'Dea & Sarnat, 2001). In psychoanalytic supervision, the relationship is co-constructed and intersubjective with both supervisor and supervisee offering their unique voice and perspective on the relational experience. Transparency and openness about the inherent power differential are explicit, modeling for supervisees how this power dynamic can be managed with clients. Supervisors pay close attention to relational dynamics with clients that may be repeated in the supervisory relationship as enactments of past or present relational experiences experienced by the supervisor, supervisee, or client. Frawley-O'Dea (2003) describes the approach in this way:

> A relational approach, however, assumes that supervision is an analytic endeavor in and of itself (Rock, 1997). Fiscalini (1997), for example, puts it well when he says, "The supervisory relationship is a relationship about a relationship about other relationships" (p. 30). As happens between therapist and patient, supervisor and supervisee engage in enactments of conscious and unconscious, verbal and nonverbal transference and countertransference constellations cocreated by them during the supervisory process. In addition, supervisor and supervisee may enact relational configurations that, although bespeaking elements of their own relationship, represent as well currently

unformulated features of the treatment relationship. The relational supervisor holds that it is crucial to live out mindfully with the supervisee and eventually to make explicit with him relational patterns set in play within their relationship. Herein lie the excitement, the richness, the potential, and the terror of supervision. (p. 363)

Psychodynamic approaches to supervision have contributed important understandings of enactments in terms of parallel process and countertransference, which are now generally used terms to describe the therapist's personal reaction to clients (Shafranske & Falender, 2008). Let us explore each of these processes in more detail, as each provides a key opportunity for facilitation of relational competence in supervision.

Countertransference. Exploring supervisees' personal feelings and reactions to clients is a fundamental task of clinical supervision (Shafranske & Falender, 2008). Examples include feelings of attraction, repulsion, judgment, bias, and even boredom that are evoked in the context of counseling, consultation, and assessment. Unaddressed, countertransference reactions can be an obstacle to effective treatment and even cause harm to the client if feelings and reactions are acted on. It is the responsibility of the supervisor to establish a safe and non-shaming supervisory relationship where these countertransference reactions can be explored and understood. Addressing personal conflicts in supervision for the sake of more effective treatment is appropriate, but supervisors have to be mindful that supervision does not become personal therapy. In this way, clinical supervision can be "therapeutic" for the supervisee without becoming "therapy" (Atkinson, 1997). Maintaining a supervision frame where the welfare of the client is always primary helps uphold this boundary. In the event that supervisees experience ongoing personal reactions and conflicts that interfere with their professional functioning, a referral for personal therapy is warranted (Falender & Shafranske, 2004). Supervisors pay attention to interactions that feel out of character, surprising, or particularly intense for the supervisee and consider whether it is occurring also in the supervisory relationship.

Parallel process. Parallel process occurs in supervision when a relational dynamic is unconsciously repeated in the supervisory relationship by either the supervisor or supervisee (Frawley-O'Dea & Sarnat, 2001). For example, a supervisee who is working with a client who feels depressed and helpless may manifest depressed and helpless behavior in supervision. Also called "isomorphs" in the family therapy literature, this process provides the opportunity for recursive relational patterns to be addressed in the context of the supervision relationship (Bernard & Goodyear, 2014). Parallel process is bidirectional; thus supervisors can model or intervene with a supervisee in the manner in which they would like the supervisee to respond to the client(s). For example, a supervisor could respond to the helpless and stuck supervisee with empathy, but also foster self-efficacy and competence, a relational dynamic that would then be repeated by the supervisee with his or her client. Supervisors can also directly intervene by calling attention to the possibility that parallel process is occurring and explore this possibility with the supervisee. Generally, addressing parallel process is most helpful in supervision when there is a strong supervision alliance and with a more experienced supervisee, as this can be overwhelming for beginning supervisees who are focused on just mastering the basics of the clinical process (Bernard & Goodyear, 2014).

Existential Therapy Supervision

Existential psychotherapy supervision approaches are perhaps the most similar to the theological definitions of love discussed above, as one of the explicit goals is to foster in supervisees an attitude of profound respect for the humanity of their clients as fellow "beings in the world" (van Deurzen & Young, 2009). Supervisors seek to relate to their supervisees not as objects to be evaluated and observed (an *I-It* relationship, according to Martin Buber) but rather "'with our whole being' in an *I-Thou* manner" (Barnett, 2009, p. 57). This attitude on the part of the supervisor is one of deep respect for the uniqueness and potential of who the supervisee is created to be. Inspired by the writings of Kierkegaard on love, Moja-Strasser (2009) asserts that this essential attitude of the existential supervisor is one of love and concern for the supervisee's soul, the spiritual dimension of their being. She writes:

> Loving the person of the supervisee, is to show them, not directly but indirectly, what possibilities are there for them that have not yet been realized and also encourage them towards gaining enough trust in themselves so that they rely more and more on self-understanding. . . . I offer my supervisees my willingness to listen and attend to their concerns, my ability to be present and sensitive; I make myself available to the way they experience their being-in-the-world, and in turn the way they are relating to their clients and to myself, the supervisor. I would call this an attitude towards another human being; a way of relating; an attitude towards my supervisee that is inspired and guided by love. (Moja-Strasser, 2009, p. 42)

Existential supervision approaches encourage attentiveness to the deepest, most human parts of our supervisees as we encourage them to explore and access their unique potential. In the next section, we explore what this loving and respectful approach to supervision might look like from a Christian integrative orientation.

Concluding Comments on Relationally Oriented Supervision Models

As the above models and methods illustrate, the supervision relationship itself provides the optimal context for supervisees to grow in their awareness of their interpersonal strengths and areas for needed growth. Growth in relational competence best occurs in an interpersonal learning environment where inevitable relationship challenges and dynamics can lead to relationship ruptures that must be mended. It is the responsibility of the supervisor to initiate exploration and repair of any ruptures. This can provide supervisees with an important opportunity to learn metacommunication skills as the supervisor invites exploration of here-and-now supervision relational dynamics (Falender & Shafranske, 2004). Triadic and group supervision formats provide unique opportunities for the development of supervisee self-awareness and relational skills in a small group format with other trainees. In the context of group supervision, supervisees learn to give and receive feedback, practice

new skills, and grow in their awareness of their relational impact on others.

In order to accurately assess relational competencies of supervisees and the quality of their therapeutic alliances, it is important for supervision to occur as close to the actual clinical work of the supervisee as possible. Co-therapy, live supervision, and review of taped sessions are ideal supervision methods for assessing and intervening in the development of relational skills. Having access to supervisees' actual clinical work is consistent with APA ethical guidelines, which state that "psychologists evaluate students and supervisees on the basis of their actual performance on relevant and established program requirements" (American Psychological Association, 2010, 7.06). Likewise, AAMFT guidelines for supervision of trainees for licensure or clinical membership in the AAMFT state that supervision should focus on "raw data" through a combination of co-therapy, live observations and supervision, and viewing recorded sessions (American Association for Marriage and Family Therapy, 2014).

Providing supervision through online or video conference formats can pose a challenge to assessing relational competence and facilitating intervention. Supervisors should ensure that technology is sophisticated enough so that face-to-face, synchronous supervision is possible.

CHRISTIAN INTEGRATIVE APPROACHES

A Christian integrative approach brings something more to the supervision process by developing relational competencies as a part of a Christian ethic of love. Biblical and theological perspectives on the virtue of love from incarnational and trinitarian theological

perspectives form a foundation for the development of loving and respectful habits and practices that express to others, "How good it is that you exist!" As supervisors, we help our trainees learn to "walk in love" as a characteristic way of being in our personal and professional lives. Several resources from the integration literature are particularly relevant to this endeavor.

Empathy as Incarnational Love

A Christian integrative approach to clinical supervision encourages the primacy of empathy in clinical practice as an expression of incarnational love. As God loved humankind through sharing in our suffering in the person of Christ, so we encourage our supervisees to share deeply in the suffering of their clients as foundational to the provision of competent Christian counseling. Benner's classic article on the metaphor of the incarnation for the work of psychotherapy is relevant here. Benner (2007) uses object relations therapy to shed light on the role of the therapist who absorbs the patient's projections, struggle, and pain in a way that promotes healing. Benner writes:

> But perhaps it is more parsimonious to view the curative factor in this basic process as love. Love involves giving of oneself to another, making oneself available to bear someone else's burdens and share in their struggles. This is not "sloppy sentimentalism" but rather tough, disciplined, and personally costly love. Its mode of communication is involvement. Its effect is healing. . . . In one way or another all these (and other) modalities then encourage the patient to put inner confusion and chaos onto the therapist who then attempts to consider it less chaotic and frightening, more intelligible and benign. This assumption and transformation of the patient's inner world constitutes the incarnational element of psychotherapy. (p. 248)

Benner also emphasizes the importance of Christian community and the church for Christian therapists, who can only practice incarnational therapy when they are receiving support and care from God and others. Benner quotes 2 Corinthians 1:4 here: God "comforts us in all our troubles, so that we can comfort those in any trouble with the comfort we ourselves receive from God" (p. 249).

Similarly, Kwon (2012) recommends a practical theology of the incarnation as a foundation for the development of the virtue of empathy in pastoral counselors. Kwon writes:

> The incarnated image of a human Jesus enhances the clinical behavior of empathizing with a wounded client in pastoral counseling. The act of understanding a certain person is similar to the incarnation process in which Jesus Christ "suffered into" earth as a human being. . . . Understanding another person can be described as "understanding" on the very bottom floor of the person's pain and suffering. The true model of "under-standing" was presented by God, who became human to stand "under"—i.e., at the very bottom of human reality, at a place of suffering and death. (p. 4)

Kwon notes common mistakes in "false empathy" made by beginning counselors, including disclosing their sufferings to the client (which takes the focus away from the client), generalizing the client's suffering, and empathizing with a third party in the client's narrative (rather than the client). Counselors are encouraged to stay with the emotional experience of the client in seeking deeper understandings of the issues that are at the heart of the suffering. This, Kwon suggests, personifies the true heart of Christ in taking on our own sufferings.

Trinitarian Theology and Relational Competencies

Balswick and Balswick (2006, 2007) draw from trinitarian theology to propose relational principles that are characteristic of the Trinity and serve as a model for the way we should love each other in family, marriage, and all human relationships. Based on the premise that Christ calls us to love others as we are loved (Jn 13:34), the Balswicks' model identifies four pillars of trinitarian love that provide a guide for human relationships. *Covenant* love is the principle of secure, unconditional love that is not dependent on the actions of the other. *Gracing* love establishes acceptance and forgiveness as an essential component of Christlike relationships. *Empowering* love highlights the aspect of love where we use power in relationships to serve each other toward the goal of becoming all that we were created to be. *Intimate* love encourages Christians to know and be known by others. On the basis of the trinitarian relationship, the Balswicks propose "differentiated unity" as a model for Christian couple and family relationships where there is both connection and a separate sense of autonomy.

While the Balswicks apply this model to couple and family relationships, these principles provide a wonderful guide to the relational qualities of trinitarian love that we should seek to incarnate in all our personal and professional relationships. Certainly, the notion of a supervisory relationship marked by security and trust (covenant), acceptance and forgiveness for errors and shortcomings (grace), use of power to serve the other (empowering), and relational authenticity and genuineness (intimacy) is consistent with what we know to be ideal qualities of the effective supervisory alliance. These trinitarian relational principles can also serve as a guide for our supervisees on how to live out an ethic of Christian love that will truly foster the welfare of others.

Concluding Thoughts

A foundational theological anthropology is essential to developing character strengths of love and respect for others. As we see our supervisees and clients as marvelous creations, prized and loved by God, we can genuinely approach those we are called to serve with an attitude of "how good that you exist!" And we can begin, by the grace of God, to imitate his incarnational and sacrificial love through empathy, respect, and relational competence. We do this in both large and small ways. For example, Bufford (2007) encourages the development of an "internal dialogue" about our clients that is humanizing and honoring, reflecting their creation in the image of God. This attitude is in stark contrast to the temptation to dehumanize clients by focusing on their psychopathology or diagnostic labels alone.

As we love our supervisees and delight in their creation and calling, we express the love of God to them. We prize their questions, their challenges, and their developmental process. We offer a faithful, hopeful, and loving presence that encourages them on in their quest to walk in love.

SPIRITUAL DISCIPLINES FOR THE FORMATION OF LOVE: COMMUNITY AND INDIVIDUAL PRACTICES

God's gift of his very essence of love to us through Jesus Christ provides a foundation for all our efforts to love others in our personal and professional lives. Our ability to consistently practice any ethic of love and care for others must grow from an unshakeable knowledge that we are loved and cherished by God. Contemplative prayer, meditation on passages of Scripture affirming God's love for us (e.g., Rom 8), and images of secure attachment as discussed in chapter three are all essential to securing ourselves in his love.

The relational intensity of clinical work inevitably reveals areas for growth and development for us to improve our abilities to love. Learning to love others beyond our emotional reactions, countertransference, and annoyances requires divine intervention. Devoting ourselves to regular spiritual practices is necessary to develop and strengthen an ethic of love, so that it becomes second nature to us. In this section, we look at spiritual disciplines that are particularly applicable to love of God and neighbor.

Incarnating Christ's Love in Community

Experiencing the love of God and manifesting it to others best happens in community. Learning in community, living in community, and worshiping in community will inevitably provide opportunities for challenge and growth in agape and caritas. For this reason and many others, it is important to encourage our supervisees to engage deeply in community and seize every opportunity to grow in their ability to love through practicing compassion, forgiveness, boundary setting, and truth speaking. We can encourage supervisees to reflect on their experiences and look for patterns that may also be emerging in their clinical work and the supervisory relationship. We can ask supervisees: What themes do you see across your relationships in terms of your relational competencies and areas for growth? Where do you need to grow in loving God and others? In this way, supervision becomes one part of God's overall formation and transformation of our supervisees as they grow in their ability to experience God's love and incarnate this love to others. Recognition and confession of relational sins and shortcomings is the first step toward relational competency.

Calhoun (2015) offers spiritual disciplines for incarnating the love of Christ. She writes that as we are "rooted" in Christ's love for us, we are able to grow in our ability to love our neighbor. "Love always gives birth to more love," Calhoun suggests (p. 197). Spiritual practices for incarnating Christ's love to others include the following:

- *Blessing*—expressing words of appreciation, delight, and encouragement to others and speaking well of them; making it a practice to build others up as an expression of God's love for them

- *Forgiving*—continually practicing forgiveness of self and others for sin and wrongdoing, including not holding on to grudges or nursing resentment and hatred in personal and professional relationships

- *Speaking truth*—demonstrating respect for others by speaking the truth with love

Eck (2002) identifies interpersonally oriented spiritual disciplines that can be incorporated into psychotherapy to foster client growth in relationally oriented issues. These disciplines would be highly relevant to encouraging growth in relationship for supervisees. Eck groups interpersonally oriented spiritual disciplines into three main categories:

- spiritual disciplines that cultivate *repair of relationships*, such as forgiveness and confession

- disciplines that foster *connection to others* in Christian community, including worship, fellowship, and Eucharist

- spiritual disciplines that promote *spiritual healing in the context of relationship*, including intercession, healing prayer, and witnessing

Encouraging supervisees to practice spiritual disciplines to develop their capacity to express God's love to others is important for cultivating the spiritual relationship competencies as taught by Scripture and modeled in the lives of Christ and the disciples. As areas for relational growth emerge in the context of supervision, supervisors can provide an introduction to interpersonally oriented spiritual disciplines and invite supervisees to prayerfully consider a particular spiritual practice.

Intercessory Prayer

A Christian community either lives by the intercessory prayers of its members for one another, or the community will be destroyed. I can no longer condemn or hate other Christians for whom I pray, no matter how much trouble they cause me. In intercessory prayer the face that may have been strange and intolerable to me is transformed into the face of one for whom Christ died, the face of a pardoned sinner. That is a blessed discovery for the Christian who is beginning to offer intercessory prayer for others. As far as we are concerned, there is no dislike, no personal tension, no disunity or strife that cannot be overcome by intercessory prayer. Intercessory prayer is the purifying bath into which the individual and the community must enter every day. (Bonhoeffer, 2004, p. 90)

Dietrich Bonhoeffer reminds us of the transformative power of intercessory prayer on behalf of others. In clinical supervision we have the opportunity to introduce supervisees to the important spiritual intervention of intercessory prayer for those we serve. Through intercessory prayer, we bring our clients and supervisees before the Father in love to ask for his care for them. We ask Jesus to go before the Father to intercede for those we serve—for their healing, growth, forgiveness of sin, self-awareness, courage, and hope. Foster (1992) writes: "If we truly love people, we will desire for them far more than it is within our power to give them, and this will lead us to prayer. Intercession is a way of loving others" (p. 191). Foster writes that it is a "sacred obligation" and a priestly responsibility for all believers to pray for others with regularity and specificity. Foster's suggestions for practicing the spiritual discipline of intercessory prayer applied to the context of clinical supervision are as follows:

- Pray in the name of Jesus—prioritizing his desires and concerns for people and accessing his power as he goes before the Father to intercede for us.

- Pray for our enemies and those who we perceive as persecuting us.

- Pray in the Spirit—wait for the Holy Spirit to bring to mind people and concerns. Ask the Spirit to express the needs of others that are too deep for words.

- Keep a list of people and prayer needs.

- Picture those we are praying for and hold them up to the Father.

- Pray individually and corporately.

We can encourage supervisees to practice the discipline of intercessory prayer for clients by praying during supervision as the Spirit leads. In addition, we can initiate discussions about use of prayer with clients—both implicitly and explicitly.

Developing habits of intercessory prayer for our clients is a discipline of love. It is a way to continually express our dependence on the one true Healer who loves our clients and supervisees more than we can ever aspire to.

CONCLUSION

The virtue of love in supervision provides both a guide for the ideal qualities of the supervisory relationship and a clear direction for the development of relational competencies that are necessary for effective clinical practice. As we experience the love of God in our own lives, we are able to approach each supervisee and client with wonder and curiosity, as a precious creation of God. Our love for God compels an ethic of care where we engage in professional activities of charity and mercy as an expression of God's delivering love. Love provides the essential motive for our growth in Christian maturity and Christlikeness as we respond to God's love with gratitude and love for others.

The aspirational ideals of love also serve as a reminder of just how challenging it is to love God, our neighbor, and ourselves. We must confess in humility how often we fall short of charity because of our own self-interest and the repetition of relational patterns from our own histories. It is important to acknowledge just how easy it is to go through the motions of an outward show of love and respect for others, and at the same time disparage and disrespect others with our thoughts, biases, and attitudes. If we do not deal with these barriers to love, our relationships will ring false like the clanging gong Paul writes about in 1 Corinthians 13. To truly delight in others as God delights in them requires more than professional skills and social intelligence; it requires the kind of character change that only God can bring about. For most of us, this means lifelong enrollment in the "school of charity" and all her corresponding virtues through daily faithfulness to the spiritual disciplines that foster love.

Saint Teresa of Ávila, one of the great saints who has taught us much about love of God and others, once wrote a line about love that is probably the best advice we can give to therapists in training: "The important thing is not to think much but to love much; and so do that which best stirs you to love. Love is not great delight but desire to please God in everything" (2008, p. 101).

May this be our guiding principle as we care for those we supervise, and in turn teach them to love others who are in their care.

CHAPTER SUMMARY / SUPERVISION GUIDE

Virtue	• **Love:** charity
Description	• "Charity is the theological virtue by which we love God above all things for his own sake, and our neighbor as ourselves for the love of God" (*Catechism of the Catholic Church*, 2003, para. 1822).
Scripture	• "Therefore, as God's chosen people, holy and dearly loved, clothe yourselves with compassion, kindness, humility, gentleness and patience. Bear with each other and forgive one another if any of you has a grievance against someone. Forgive as the Lord forgave you. And over all these virtues put on love, which binds them all together in perfect unity. Let the peace of Christ rule in your hearts, since as members of one body you were called to peace. And be thankful" (Col 3:12-15).
Ethical principle	• Respect for the dignity, rights, and inherent worth of all people to privacy, autonomy, confidentiality, and self-determination
Supervision focus	• Humanistic and experiential models of supervision • Transgenerational models of supervision • Psychoanalytic supervision: countertransference and parallel process • Existential therapy supervision
Christian integration focus	• Empathy as incarnational love • Trinitarian theology and relational competencies
Spiritual practices	• Incarnating Christian love in community: interpersonal spiritual disciplines • Intercessory prayer
Desired outcome	• Loving clinicians who have a deep sense of respect for the dignity and worth of all as created in the image of God, and who demonstrate empathy, positive regard, and respect for the rights of others through honoring the privacy and confidentiality of those they serve

CHAPTER 6

PRACTICAL WISDOM

Competence and Ethical Decision Making

But the wisdom that comes from heaven is first of all pure; then peace-loving, considerate, submissive, full of mercy and good fruit, impartial and sincere. Peacemakers who sow in peace reap a harvest of righteousness.

JAMES 3:17-18

IN THE WAKE OF THE largest cheating scandal in Harvard's history, cognitive and educational psychologist Howard Gardner (2012) described the incident as an example of the "thinning of the ethical muscle" of smart and ambitious young Americans. Gardner observed that many high achieving students have been habituated to the pursuit of success above all else, often at the expense of virtues such as honesty, fairness, and love of learning. What, he asks, has happened to the classic virtues of wisdom, beauty, truth, and goodness as the goal of education?

A similar challenge is evident in the training of mental health professionals, where students often enter graduate school with a passion for learning and a heart for service but quickly become burdened by the demands of their coursework and the soul-wearying experience of dealing with human suffering that is an essential part of clinical work. As clinical supervisors, we often witness how the rigors of graduate school contribute to a gradual erosion of a trainee's love of wisdom and learning as an

end in itself. A virtue-informed approach to clinical supervision aims to address this problem by cultivating professional habits that lead to lifelong learning, including intellectual curiosity, a commitment to competence, and good practical judgment. In this chapter, we examine the character virtue of wisdom from theological and psychological perspectives and provide specific supervision methods and spiritual practices that foster wisdom as an explicit goal of the supervision process. A Christian integrative approach to supervision seeks to develop wise clinicians who are lifelong learners, curious, and able to tolerate complexities, who value God's Word and science-informed practice, are competent and ethical, and are able to apply knowledge and make good clinical judgments with practical wisdom and discernment.

Wisdom is related to the character virtue of prudence, which is concerned with the development of habits and practices related to practical wisdom. Wisdom is about knowing the right thing to do at the right time. In counseling, psychology, and marriage and family therapy, this involves the practical application of scientific findings, theoretical knowledge, and moral principles to clinical practice. Applying knowledge learned in the classroom to the clinical setting is a primary task of the clinical supervision process and requires the cultivation of practical wisdom as a character strength and professional value. In this section, we deepen our understanding of biblical, theological, and scientific understandings of wisdom as a foundation for supervision practices.

WISDOM: BIBLICAL AND THEOLOGICAL PERSPECTIVES

For the believer, Scripture points the way to the true source and foundation of wisdom. The Old Testament Wisdom literature found in the book of Proverbs provides practical wisdom for everyday living:

> for gaining wisdom and instruction;
>   for understanding words of insight;
> for receiving instruction in prudent behavior,
>   doing what is right and just and fair.
>   (Prov 1:2-3)

In the books of Ecclesiastes and Job, we learn about the wisdom that comes through adversity from the experiences of King Solomon and Job as they seek to trust God in the midst of human suffering. We are instructed that ultimately God's ways are mysterious and beyond the comprehension of human beings (Farley, 1995).

New Testament understandings of wisdom direct the believer to the person of Jesus Christ, the incarnation of divine mystery and the source of all wisdom. John 1 describes Jesus as the divine Logos, creator and sustainer of the universe:

> In the beginning the Word already existed.
>   The Word was with God,
>   and the Word was God.
> He existed in the beginning with God.
> God created everything through him,
>   and nothing was created except through
>   him.
> The Word gave life to everything that was
>   created,

> and his life brought light to everyone.
> The light shines in the darkness,
>   and the darkness can never extinguish it.
>   (Jn 1:1-5 NLT)

In John 14:26, Jesus tells his followers that the Holy Spirit will be sent to them by the Father as a source of wisdom: "But the Advocate, the Holy Spirit, whom the Father will send in my name, will teach you all things and will remind you of everything I have said to you." The first chapter of the book of James is also a reminder to Christ's followers that wisdom is a gift from God. James 1:2-4 encourages patience and perseverance in suffering toward the goal of Christian maturity. This is the context for verse 5: "If any of you lacks wisdom, you should ask God, who gives generously to all without finding fault, and it will be given to you." Believers are encouraged to maintain God's transcendent perspective on human suffering, a gift of wisdom that can only come from him (Nystrom, 1997).

Aristotle identified wisdom as a classic virtue and made a distinction between *phronesis* (practical wisdom), *episteme* (scientific wisdom), and *techne* (technical wisdom or craftsmanship) (Chase, 1847). Aquinas believed prudence to be the rule or *regula* that guides the practice of the other moral virtues (Westberg, 2015, p. 152). The definition of wisdom found in the *Catechism of the Catholic Church* (2003) summarizes Aquinas and the early church teaching on practical wisdom:

Prudence is the virtue that disposes practical reason to discern our true good in every circumstance and to choose the right means of achieving it; "the prudent man looks where he is going." "Keep sane and sober for your prayers." Prudence is "right reason in action," writes St. Thomas Aquinas, following Aristotle. It is not to be confused with timidity or fear, nor with duplicity or dissimulation. It is called auriga virtutum (the charioteer of the virtues); it guides the other virtues by setting rule and measure. It is prudence that immediately guides the judgment of conscience. The prudent man determines and directs his conduct in accordance with this judgment. With the help of this virtue we apply moral principles to particular cases without error and overcome doubts about the good to achieve and the evil to avoid. (para. 1806)

According to Aquinas, the exercise of prudence requires the practice of important subvirtues, which include memory, intelligence (understanding), docility (teachableness), shrewdness, and reason. Other subvirtues important for the application of practical wisdom include foresight, circumspection, and caution (Aquinas, *Sum* IIa-IIae, q. 49). Essential for prudence is the gift of *counsel* from the Holy Spirit to guide believers in practical wisdom. As described by Kaczor and Sherman (2009): "God's counsel, in the case of the infused virtue of prudence, or human counsel, in the case of acquired prudence, helps our intelligence, i.e., aids our understanding in doing what is right" (p. 38, footnote). As we learn to practice intellectual habits of prudence guided by the counsel of the Holy Spirit, we develop the practical wisdom necessary to make right choices for a virtuous and happy life.

Contemporary theological understandings of practical wisdom include the writings of theologian Ellen Charry. Charry draws on the writings of Augustine to advocate for a return to the practical theology of the early church fathers and mothers:

> Modern academic theology has largely limited itself to *scientia*. While it is essential for pointing seekers in the right direction, in Augustine's view, *scientia* alone is unable to heal us. The goal of *scientia* is to move the seeker to *sapientia*, wisdom. *Sapere* in Latin originally meant "to taste or smell things" and was carried over into the cognitive realm to mean "to discern, think, or be wise." . . . Augustine pressed Christians not just to celebrate what God has done for them but also to taste and enjoy God. (1997, p. 133)

Charry proposes sapiential theology as an applied approach to theology that focuses on the spiritually and personally formative aims of Christian doctrine to offer wisdom in living a skilled and excellent life. In *God and the Art of Happiness* (2010), Charry describes a practical theology of happiness that involves living a life of virtue and obedience to God in love through becoming wise in his commandments and teachings, which results in a state of blessedness. From the perspective of sapiential theology, spiritual growth can be envisioned in this way:

> Christian growth in sapience, then, is a dialectical movement that at one turn nurtures insight or existential encounter with God by grounding them in scripture, doctrine, and tradition (*scientia*) and at the next enlivens that *scientia* with prayerful insight nurtured through reflective prayer and service. (Charry, 1997, p. 243)

A theological understanding of practical wisdom includes trust in God and his Word, with the hope that developing habits of good moral judgment will lead to a virtuous and blessed life. From a theological perspective, then, wisdom is inseparable from faith, hope, and love.

A biblical and theological understanding of wisdom emphasizes the importance of developing mental health professionals who are humbly reliant on God for his gift of wisdom and who consider human suffering and adversity from the perspective of God's greater purposes and plans. In clinical supervision, we encourage wisdom through reliance on God's written Word, through the guidance of the Holy Spirit, and most of all through following the Lord Jesus Christ, the divine mystery and Logos incarnate. This is our greatest and only hope of true wisdom.

WISDOM: PSYCHOLOGICAL PERSPECTIVES

Psychological theories consider wisdom to be a combination of personal intelligence, life experience, practical reasoning, and consideration of the common good. Positive psychologists describe wisdom and knowledge as cognitive strengths that are used for the purpose of living a good life and include the character traits of creativity, curiosity, open-mindedness, love of learning, and perspective (Peterson & Seligman, 2004). Some scholars advocate for returning to an Aristotelian perspective that views practical wisdom as more than an individual character strength; rather, it is the executor of the virtues that are required for *eudaimonia*, or the happy life (Schwartz & Sharpe, 2006). From this perspective, practical wisdom is based on good judgment rather than rule following, and it is developed through experience: "One becomes wise by confronting difficult and ambiguous situations, using one's judgment to decide what to do, doing it, and getting feedback. One becomes a wise practitioner by practicing being wise" (Schwartz & Sharpe, 2006, p. 388).

In contemporary wisdom research, there has been a movement away from wisdom as a cognitive construct toward the concept of "personal wisdom," which involves an interaction between the character traits of self-awareness, mindfulness, and emotional intelligence (Staudinger & Glück, 2011). Wisdom is viewed as an experiential state of being where one draws from both thoughts and feelings in the moment. Staudinger and Glück (2011) write, "Wisdom is conceived of as the perfect integration of mind and character for the greater good" (p. 221). According to science writer Stephen Hall (2010), recent findings in contemporary brain science suggest eight "neural pillars" of wisdom, which include emotional regulation, practical judgment, moral reasoning, empathy, altruism, patience, and dealing with uncertainty. In one of the few empirical studies of the virtue of practical wisdom, Krause and Hayward (2015) examined the relationship between practical wisdom, which they define as a "higher order virtue" (p. 738), and nine virtues. Better practical wisdom was found to have a positive association with increased hope and self-esteem. In addition, practical wisdom had a stronger relationship than other virtues with compassion and altruistic behaviors towards strangers.

How do individuals develop wisdom? Current developmental theory finds that personality, motivational, and contextual factors all contribute to the acquisition of wisdom. Staudinger and Glück (2011) suggest, "Generally, the development of wisdom is a dynamic process in which cognitive, affective, and motivational resources develop interactively through the reflection of experience" (p. 230). Glück and Bluck (2013) propose the MORE model of gaining wisdom through life experiences. In their model, wise individuals demonstrate a *mastery* orientation in their ability to cope with experience, are *open* and curious about new experiences and views, demonstrate *reflective capacities* and the ability to consider their own and others' perspectives, and demonstrate *empathy* and *emotional regulation* through care and consideration for the feelings of others and themselves. This model is certainly applicable to learning through experience in clinical training of mental health professionals. Wisdom in the practice of psychotherapy is inseparable from compassion and is developed through increased self-awareness and mindfulness (Germer & Siegel, 2012).

The theory and research on moral and ethical decision making is particularly relevant for our understanding of developing practical wisdom in supervision. Contemporary research in cognitive science has challenged our notions that logic and reason are the primary guides for ethical decision-making processes. Instead, intuition, emotion, personal bias, and other mostly unconscious processes appear to play a larger role in moral decisions than we would like to think (Greene, Morelli, Lowenberg, Nystrom, & Cohen, 2008). Greene and colleagues have proposed a *dual process theory* that suggests there are two pathways to ethical decision making (Greene, Sommerville, Nystrom, Darley, & Cohen, 2001). The first system is a fast, efficient, intuitive, and emotional system that processes moral decisions according to overlearned moral rules and trial-and-error learning experiences. The second decision-making process is slower, consciously controlled, and

reasoned, and considers the best moral outcome for the situation. Greene (2014) uses the metaphor of the automatic and manual settings on a camera to explain the differences in moral decision making: for familiar situations, the efficient "point and shoot" approach leads to satisfactory outcomes, while novel moral dilemmas require a manual approach to decisions that involves a more conscious and reasoned process. The author suggests that slowing down the moral decision-making process is particularly important in ethical situations to counter the impact of cognitive biases, emotional reactions, contextual factors, and personal proximity to the issue—factors that have been demonstrated to affect the ethical decision-making process. Because there is significant overlap and interaction between cognitive processing systems, cognitive scientists advocate for the importance of moral flexibility when dealing with tensions between normative ethical principles and considerations of best outcomes for the most people (Bartels, Bauman, Cushman, Pizarro, & McGraw, 2015).

Theory and research from the cognitive science of religion are relevant to our understanding of practical wisdom. Automatic, unconscious, and overlearned processes in decision making underscore the importance of the development of virtuous habits and practices that also become automatic and guide our cognitive processing. Van Slyke (2015) suggests that the church plays a key role in fostering practices that can provide a moral foundation for ethical decision making. In addition, the church can ideally provide moral exemplars who model behaviors that can be imitated and simulated:

> Formative practice, habits, and time play a highly determinate role in moral development. Imitation and simulation set up

some of the foundational aspects of moral identity and eventually mature to form moral schemas that constrain the enactment of scripts based on contextual and environmental cues. The Christian church has an important role to play in the types of schemas and scripts persons enact based on the types of examples provided both by leaders and everyday members. (Van Slyke, 2015, p. 212)

As an example, Van Slyke refers to research on the L'Arche community members, who sought to intentionally practice a reverent attitude toward individuals often marginalized because of their disabilities. Researchers tracked the descriptors that caregivers used to characterize themselves and compared these with moral character traits (Landauer, McNamara, Dennis, & Kintsch, 2007). The authors surmise that a sense of moral identity among caregivers may be an important component in sustaining altruistic moral behaviors.

Practical wisdom from a psychological perspective, then, is a multifaceted and complex human quality with cognitive, physiological, and behavioral components. Psychological perspectives suggest the interconnectivity of wisdom to other character traits and skills including compassion, patience, and altruism. Research on cognition and moral decision making underscores the importance of slowing down the ethical decision-making process and developing virtue to influence the overlearned and intuitive decision-making processes. Knobel (2015) makes an important distinction between an Aristotelean view of practical wisdom as a mark of individual virtue and excellence and a Christian view of practical wisdom where the prudent individual recognizes the need for divine guidance in situations requiring moral judgment. Wisdom is attributed to God, rather than viewed as an individual character strength or achievement. Knobel proposes that a Christian perspective on virtue contributes something more to our understanding of practical wisdom through recognizing our dependence on our Creator as the source of true wisdom.

PROFESSIONAL ETHICS: WISDOM AND THE PURSUIT OF COMPETENCY

What are the characteristics of a wise clinician? The virtue of practical wisdom in the mental health professions is best exemplified by habits and practices that lead to a lifelong commitment to two key professional virtues: maintaining professional competence and developing effective ethical decision-making skills. Professional competence and ethical decision making involve knowledge, good judgment, and contextual discernment about the appropriate application of clinical skills at the proper time. They require a commitment to lifelong learning and staying current with contemporary standards and practices. Prudence in professional practice is also characterized by awareness of one's limitations and need for consultation and continuing education. In this section, we review the role of clinical supervision in the development of competence and ethical decision making.

Competence

Bernard and Goodyear (2014) suggest that contemporary understandings of competence in the health care professions are similar to Aristotle's notion of *phronesis*, or practical wisdom, as it involves the development of skills pertaining to good judgment. The authors offer a comprehensive definition of competence from Epstein and Hundert (2002) that is valuable to reiterate here: "The habitual and judicious use of communication, knowledge, technical skills, clinical reasoning, emotions, values, and reflection in daily practice for the benefit of the individual and community being served; [it relies on] habits of mind, including attentiveness, critical curiosity, awareness, and presence" (Epstein & Hundert, 2002, p. 227, as cited in Bernard & Goodyear, 2014, p. 8). Competent mental health professionals demonstrate "meta-competence," which is the ability to conduct an honest self-evaluation about areas of strength and weakness including the need for additional training and education. While most mental health licenses require professionals to accrue continuing education hours for renewal of their license, meta-competence is important in discerning the type and topic of training needed to maintain clinical competence. Clinical supervisors can foster meta-competence by encouraging supervisee self-assessment as part of the evaluation process.

The clinical supervision literature has identified *cognitive complexity* as an important predictor of successful clinical development. Cognitive complexity involves various cognitive skills related to knowledge, reasoning, differentiation, and observation. Owen and Lindley (2010) propose a Therapists' Cognitive Complexity Model (TCCM) as a developmental approach to fostering cognitive skills in clinical practice. Using this model, supervisors target and assess the development of cognitive skills in three domains: session thoughts (i.e., basic cognitions about clients such as data used in case formulations), meta-cognitions (i.e., self-awareness and assessment of impact of therapist interventions on the client), and

epistemic cognitions (i.e., theories about the nature of knowledge itself that are foundational for supervisees). Supervisors pose questions during supervision that facilitate the development of the trainee's cognitive skills in all three areas with the goal of increasing overall cognitive complexity.

Competence in mental health practice is also linked to the application of scientific knowledge to clinical work. Evidence-based practice can be defined as "the integration of the best available research with clinical expertise in the context of patient characteristics, culture, and preferences" (American Psychological Association, 2005). Evidence-based clinical supervision facilitates the development of science-informed clinical judgment with careful consideration of client context and preferences and also utilizes current research on effective clinical supervision to guide the experiential learning process in supervision (Milne, 2009). It includes the use of empirically supported treatments but also utilizes psychotherapy outcome research to develop the basic clinical skills and attitudes that have been demonstrated to improve therapy outcomes (Hill, 2014a). Through clinical supervision, trainees develop professional skills and habits that lead to the ability to apply relevant research in the appropriate context. This includes consideration of treatment approaches with demonstrated effectiveness when clinically indicated.

Ethical Decision Making

An integral component of competence in counseling, psychology, and marriage and family therapy is ethical decision making. Knowledge of the ethical codes alone, while important and necessary, does not provide the comprehensiveness, specificity, and nuance necessary for ethical decision making in all circumstances. As stated by Kitchener and Kitchener (2017), "Following the APA code is not sufficient for general ethical behavior" (p. 7). Contemporary research from cognitive science on moral decision making underscores the importance of training mental health professionals to use models of ethical decision making that activate the analytical, deliberate, "manual" cognitive processes. In addition, the development of consistent habits of ethical decision-making processes can decrease the likelihood that unconscious biases, emotional reactions, and irrelevant contextual factors will unduly influence the process. Good ethical decision making requires an in-depth understanding of ethical principles and codes of conduct, experience with a variety of ethical situations, and use of a clear ethical decision-making approach that decreases the risk of ethical decisions based on intuition or personal values alone.

What school or approach to ethics fosters the most competent and effective decision making? Cottone (2012) identifies the three approaches or "intellectual movements" that continue to guide our efforts to develop ethical decision-making competencies (p. 100). *Principle ethics* emphasizes a deep understanding and familiarity with both general moral principles and specific codes of ethics that provide guidance for navigating ethical dilemmas. *Virtue ethics* makes a case for the importance of the moral character of the decision maker that has been developed over time through moral habits and practices. *Relational ethics* encourages clinicians to consider sociocultural factors in ethical decision making and emphasize clinician awareness of their own contextual influences. Cottone also highlights the impact of the multicultural competence

movement on ethical decision making and advocates for the consideration of cultural context as an integral part of all ethical considerations. Approaches to ethical decision making are not mutually exclusive; in fact, some of the strongest models include consideration of multiple approaches to ethics.

One such comprehensive model is provided by Kitchener and Kitchener (2012), who propose a two-level model of ethical decision making. First, the *immediate level* is the automatic moral decision-making response based on the situation and "ordinary moral sensibilities and virtues": "Our ordinary moral sense is based on a combination of what we have learned about being moral over a lifetime and the development of our moral character (much in the way Aristotle suggested). In ideal circumstances, it predisposes us to act in morally appropriate ways and leads to sound ethical choices, but in ambiguous or confusing cases, it may not" (Kitchener & Kitchener, 2012, p. 25). When the immediate level is insufficient, the *critical-evaluative level* of decision making comes into play. This level consists of four "plateaus": moral rules (such as the APA ethics codes), ethical principles (beneficence, nonmaleficence, etc.), ethical theories (principle ethics, virtue ethics, etc.) and finally metaethics, in which the decision maker reflects on the appropriate moral approach from the options above. Kitchener and Kitchener propose that as professionals grow and mature, we can develop "moral wisdom" that gradually improves our immediate responses to ethical situations. Moral wisdom develops through facing ethical issues, reflecting on our experience, and continuing to develop the moral virtues through professional education and training. However, complex ethical dilemmas or situations involving conflicts between two or more of the ethical principles (e.g., autonomy and beneficence) will continue to require use of the critical-evaluative level of ethical decision making. Consistent with the cognitive research on ethical decision making, this level slows down the decision-making process to allow more careful consideration of guiding principles and ethics.

Positive psychology approaches to supervision focus on the development of supervisee character strengths as an efficacious approach to fostering competence and ethical decision making. A "positive" approach to ethical behavior encourages the development of professional habits of thought, feeling, and action to produce clinicians who strive to exemplify the values of the profession and not just avoid malpractice (Knapp, VandeCreek, & Fingerhut, 2017). Fowers (2005) critiques contemporary ethical codes and models of ethical decision making as inadequate because of vague language, omissions in the codes themselves, and conflicting guidelines, and suggests that an approach based on *episteme* or rule following is inadequate. An approach to ethical behavior based on *phronesis*, according to Fowers, connects more deeply with the way mental health professionals live their lives as it promotes the practice of making the right decisions in the right context at the right time. He writes, "Fully ethical practice will depend more on the character and judgment of the psychologist than on guidelines found in the Ethics Codes" (p. 185). As discussed in chapter one, Fowers's perspective reflects a *virtue ethics* approach to ethical decision making that focuses on character development as an educational priority, in addition to the *principle ethics* orientation that prioritizes the ability to apply broad principles to ethical situations (Jordan & Meara, 1990). As discussed previously, principle ethics focuses on the question "What should I do?" while virtue ethics asks the question "Who shall I be?" (Jordan & Meara, 1990).

In summary, practical wisdom in professional practice is reflected in the mental health professional's commitment to competent and ethical practice. Clinical supervision research suggests that developing the supervisee's capacity for meta-competence, cognitive complexity, and evidence-based practices is an important supervision goal. Developing practical wisdom involves attention to both virtue and principle ethics, as clinicians develop wise judgment and professional habits that facilitate sound ethical decision making over time.

CLINICAL SUPERVISION MODELS AND METHODS TO PROMOTE COMPETENCE

In this section, we examine supervision models and techniques that are particularly suited to the development of practical wisdom, competence, and ethical decision making in supervisees. Competent supervisors resist doing therapy through their supervisees by simple instruction. Rather, we recognize that by fostering the development of practical wisdom, we have the opportunity to inform lifelong habits of thinking and practice for our supervisees that will affect present and future clients. We will look at several supervision models and methods for cultivating competence: competency-based supervision, cognitive behavioral supervision, existentially oriented supervision, and MFT supervision.

Competency-Based Supervision

Falender and Shafranske's competency-based model of clinical supervision (2004; 2008) provides a structured framework for assessing and developing clinical competence. Drawn from competency-oriented models of education in other health care professions, this approach organizes clinical supervision around the identification and development of specific clinical skills that are recognized collaboratively by the supervisor and trainee. The emphasis is "on the ability to apply knowledge and skills in the real world" (Falender and Shafranske, 2004, p. 20). Competency-based supervision draws from developmental, psychotherapy, and integrative models of supervision and incorporates many of the best practices in clinical supervision gleaned from supervision research. It can be implemented using the following steps:

1. Establish a good supervisory alliance and consider supervisee characteristics, including developmental factors.

2. Facilitate supervisee self-assessment of competencies to identify specific areas for skill development. This can occur through discussion or through use of paper and pencil assessments or rating forms.

3. Collaboratively develop a supervision contract, identifying clinical competencies that will be the focus of supervision, activities for learning competencies, and how supervisee progress will be assessed.

4. Commence supervision, with supervisors using "collaborative inquiry" to explore the supervisee's clinical experiences and client outcomes.

5. Assess effectiveness of supervisee competence through direct observation and review of video and audiotapes.

6. Perform ongoing assessment and feedback.

A competency-based approach is especially useful when supervision is focusing on the development of specific and identifiable clinical skills such as competence in use of assessment instruments, clinical interviews, basic counseling skills, or a new approach/modality of psychotherapy.

Cognitive-Behavioral Supervision to Promote Competence

Another model of supervision that provides excellent structure and methods for promoting competence derives from cognitive-behavioral therapy (CBT). CBT supervision models focus on developing supervisees' learning capabilities and technical mastery and are especially effective for promoting competence with empirically supported treatments that rely on careful adherence to treatment manuals for effective use (Bernard & Goodyear, 2014).

CBT approaches to supervision generally focus on two areas: teaching a CBT theoretical understanding of human behavior and problems, and the development of CBT skills and techniques. Each supervision session follows a similar structure that parallels the structure of a CBT psychotherapy session. A typical CBT supervision session includes some version of the following: setting an agenda, review of homework, didactic teaching, role-playing, review of tapes or direct observation, and assigning new homework. An important goal is to explore supervisee cognitive schemas related to the practice of therapy and the supervision experience (Liese & Beck, 1997; Pretorius, 2006). CBT approaches also invite the supervisee to first experience the tool or technique through self-practice before using the intervention with clients (Bennett-Levy, Thwaites, Chaddock, & Davis, 2009). For example, a supervisor may walk a trainee through a mindfulness exercise in supervision, encourage practice of the technique as a supervision homework assignment, and then review the experience during the next supervision session.

Existential Supervision: Finding the "Golden Mean"

Existential models of supervision apply the "wisdom of the ages" to clinical practice by framing clients' current problems in the context of the overall human condition (van Deurzen & Young, 2009). Existential supervisors draw from historical and contemporary philosophy to help supervisees and clients engage in deeper exploration of their own humanity and the issues of existence that are inevitably confronted by all (Yalom, 1980). Supervisees learn to listen for the existential themes that are inevitably present in clients' presenting concerns and to encourage acceptance, responsibility, and meaning making.

Macaro (2009) applies Aristotle's theory of virtue to clinical supervision and suggests the primary role of the supervisor is to facilitate training in practical wisdom or good clinical judgment. She writes:

> This can be done through a joint investigation of the reasons for thinking about the client in particular ways, or favouring certain interventions over others, and the likely consequences of such conceptualisations. It will involve reviewing all relevant considerations—theoretical and therapeutic, ethical, personal and organizational. In this sense the aim of supervision could be to facilitate the therapist's ability to reach the right judgement, all things considered, as a first step towards developing virtue. By regularly talking through our reasons, training the right attitudes and practicing the right actions, the ability to perceive and follow the appropriate course of action should eventually become second nature. (Macaro, 2009, p. 25)

Macaro (2009) proposes Aristotle's doctrine of the "golden mean" as the primary supervision technique for facilitating practical wisdom. Aristotle proposed that virtuous action often lies in pursuing the middle ground between two extreme positions. Through use of Socratic questioning, the supervisor facilitates an exploration of the supervisee's thoughts, reasoning, and considered actions for various clinical questions, helping them avoid both extreme positions and dogmatic "rules" for therapeutic practice. Macaro provides an example of common supervisee questions about the appropriate level of emotional involvement with clients. The supervisor poses questions to help the trainee think wisely through exploring the risks of too much detachment and lack of emotional engagement on the one hand, which can result in poor alliances with clients, and the risks of too much involvement with clients on the other hand, which can result in poor boundaries or controlling behaviors on the part of the therapist. Macaro reminds supervisors that there are, of course, some ethical "absolutes" with no middle ground, such as prohibitions against any form of sexual relationship with clients or supervisees.

An Ethical Decision-Making Process from MFT

There is tremendous value in teaching supervisees a specific ethical decision-making model to slow down the process of ethical decisions and facilitate application of knowledge and judgment. A helpful framework for teaching ethical decision making in clinical supervision comes from the MFT supervision literature. Haug and Storm (2014) propose a three-step process for supervisors. First, the supervisor helps the supervisee *identify and define* the various ethical issues involved, key stakeholders, and their own values and beliefs that may affect the decision-making process. Second, the supervisee is encouraged to *consider* applicable ethical principles, systemic therapy guidelines and best practices, potential unintended consequences (on other members of the family system, for example), and their personal integrity as it relates to the ethical decision. Finally, supervisees are instructed to *act and reflect* through implementing the clinical decision, considering the result, and learning from the experience and outcome.

In addition to utilizing an ethical decision-making model, other specific suggestions for promoting ethical decision making include the following:

- During supervision, discuss the use of the general ethical principles and aspirational goals as they apply to clinical material. For example, facilitate a discussion in supervision about how the principle of doing no harm is relevant in a given situation while exploring potential unintended consequences. Ethical prin-

ciples from faith-based organizations can also be integrated into the supervision process as ethical practices are linked to core professional and religious values.

- Bring in ethical dilemmas from your own cases and facilitate the use of a specific ethical decision-making process to determine a course of action. Follow up in a future supervision session with a discussion of the outcome and model reflective practice as you consider what you have learned from the experience.

- Facilitate exploration of personal biases and assumptions for both you and your supervisee to make potential unconscious cognitive biases more conscious.

- Ask a colleague with expertise in a certain area to come in during a supervision session to model the practice of seeking consultation around ethical decisions.

Good ethical decision making includes both principle ethics and virtue ethics with a dual focus on "what I should do" and "who I should be." Effective supervision facilitates the development of character *and* competence.

A CHRISTIAN INTEGRATIVE APPROACH TO SUPERVISION: FACILITATING COMPETENCY

A Christian integrative approach to supervision actively promotes competency in the applied integration of Christian belief and practices with counseling, psychology, and MFT as part of the clinical supervision process. Integration research underscores the importance of this endeavor. Ripley, Jackson, Tatum, and Davis (2007) found that Christian supervisors are more likely to use abstract versus applied approaches to addressing religious and spiritual issues in

clinical work. Likewise, Aten, Boyer, and Tucker's (2007) sample of supervisors reported more frequent use of implicit spiritual practices (praying for a supervisee, for example) rather than explicit spiritual practices (praying *with* a supervisee) in clinical supervision. These findings highlight the need for supervision guidelines and practices to foster supervisee development of applied, explicit integration competencies.

Developing Religious and Spiritual Competencies

Fortunately, a burgeoning literature on religious and spiritual competencies for mental health professionals can guide supervision practices and priorities. Vieten et al. (2013) used surveys and focus groups to identify sixteen competencies for mental health practitioners in addressing spiritual and religious issues. In a follow-up study, the researchers surveyed mental health professionals and found a high level of agreement with the sixteen competencies, but over half of the surveyed professionals acknowledged minimal training in the identified areas (Vieten et al., 2013). Highly rated competencies include empathy and respectful attitudes, knowledge, and skills for effective clinical work with clients from diverse religious backgrounds. In addition, competent clinicians help clients access religious and spiritual resources as part of the therapeutic process. Professionals are aware of the impact of their own religious background and beliefs on their clinical work.

Hull, Suarez, and Hartman (2016) recommend specific supervision tools for addressing each of the spirituality competencies proposed by ASERVIC, which include increasing self-awareness, improving understanding of religion and spirituality, incorporating spirituality into assessment and interventions, and practicing effective and accurate communication around spirituality issues. Similarly, the SACRED model proposed by Ross, Suprina, and Brack (2013) describes a progressive approach to addressing spirituality in supervision. First, supervisors establish *safety* by providing informed consent for inclusion of spirituality issues in supervision. Second, supervisors facilitate *assessment* practices that consider

clients' religion and spirituality. Third, *case conceptualization* incorporates the role of religion and spirituality in client concerns. Fourth, supervisors facilitate *reflection* on the impact of supervisees' own religious belief systems on their clinical work. Fifth, the *emerging congruence* between clinical work and spiritual needs of clients are considered in formulating interventions. Finally, supervision attends to *development* in spiritual intervention skills and in one's own spiritual and religious identity by both supervisee and supervisor.

Competence in Use of Spiritual Interventions

Supervisors can incorporate spiritual interventions into the supervision process as an opportunity for experiential learning. For example, a supervisee wondering how to pray with a client in session would likely benefit from experiencing supervisor-initiated prayer during a supervision session followed by the opportunity to reflect on the experience. Supervisors also assess their trainees' effectiveness in the use of spiritual interventions through live observation, review of taped sessions, or cotherapy, and offer specific formative feedback. Similar to the development of competence and confidence with any therapeutic intervention, facilitating competence with spiritual interventions involves teaching, experiencing, practicing, and assessing outcomes.

For an introduction to spiritual interventions, supervisors and supervisees are encouraged to review McMinn and Campbell's (2007) *Integrative Psychotherapy*, which provides a practical guide to the integration of Christian theology with psychology theory and technique in the process of assessment, case conceptualization, and treatment planning. Aten and Leach's (2009) *Spirituality and the Therapeutic Process* also provides an in-depth look at how spirituality, broadly defined, can be incorporated throughout the treatment process. Several excellent books are available that detail specific spiritual interventions and provide guidelines for competent application in clinical practice (Aten, McMinn, & Worthington, 2011; Worthington, Johnson, Hook, & Aten, 2013; Walker & Hathaway, 2013).

Christian Integrative Supervision and Ethical Decision Making

A Christian integrative approach to supervision affirms and upholds the ethical principles of our professional guilds and encourages supervisees to be above reproach in their understanding of and adherence to ethical standards. In addition, supervision facilitates ethical decision making and practical wisdom in the unique situations that may arise in clinical practice in faith-based settings with Christian clients (see Sanders, 2013, for an excellent introduction to ethics in Christian counseling). We can bring the Christian resources of prayerful discernment and biblical wisdom to our ethical decision-making practices. Most important, we encourage our supervisees to be faithful in their commitment to develop mature Christian character, as this will have the greatest impact on their ethical decisions and practices over the course of their professional careers.

A number of authors have thoughtfully explored the ethical guidelines and considerations for the use of explicitly religious or spiritual interventions in counseling and psychotherapy (Richards & Bergin, 2005; Plante, 2009; Hathaway, 2011; Hathaway & Ripley, 2009; Vieten et al., 2013). APA's Division 36 charged a task force with proposing preliminary guidelines, and the task force conducted interviews with experts and exemplars in the use of religious and spiritual interventions (Hathaway, 2011). The following is a summary of key ethical guiding principles:

- Respect for the welfare of clients requires clinicians to develop competencies in assessment and intervention practices that consider the client's religious and spiritual traditions and practices.

- The client's right to autonomy and self-determination requires clinicians to obtain informed consent from clients before incorporating any religious or spiritual practices or interventions into the treatment process. Clinicians should provide clear and accurate descriptions of any interventions, including the purpose and any risks associated, so clients can make an informed choice.

- Religious or spiritual interventions should benefit the client, should be in line with clinical and treatment goals, and should not be used in exclusion of other standard and well-supported treatments.

- Clinicians should be competent in the use of religious or spiritual interventions for the purpose they are intended and seek consultation from more experienced peers as well as religious leaders in the client's tradition.

- Clinicians should ensure that their use of religious and spiritual issues is consistent with their professional role as a mental health provider and does not conflict with the role of clergy or religious leaders (i.e., assuming inappropriate spiritual authority with a client).

Summary

A Christian integrative approach to clinical supervision promotes competence in applied integration of Christian faith and clinical practice. Through facilitating competency, we encourage the next generation of Christian clinicians to consistently and regularly consider the explicit use of spiritual interventions in counseling and psychotherapy. We now examine spiritual discipline practices that can be incorporated into the supervision process toward the cultivation of wisdom.

SPIRITUAL DISCIPLINES FOR THE FORMATION OF WISDOM: INDIVIDUAL AND COMMUNITY PRACTICES

The transforming of our minds toward Christian maturity and Christlikeness is part of God's ongoing work of sanctification in our lives. We are invited to participate in this work through regular practice of individual and corporate spiritual disciplines. As supervisors, we have the responsibility of demonstrating in word and deed to our supervisees the importance of dependence on God as the source of all wisdom along with the proper use of scientific knowledge and ethical practice. Supervisors encourage their trainees to develop spiritual habits and practices that lead to knowledge of and love for God's Word, an ever-deepening theological understanding, a discerning mind and heart, and the ability to be spiritually sensitive to the leading of the Holy Spirit. In this final section of the chapter, we consider two disciplines that are essential for the cultivation of wise character: Scripture study and meditation, and spiritual discernment.

Scripture Study and Meditation

Knowledge and understanding of God's Word are essential for the development of the virtue of wisdom. Dallas Willard (1998) defines the role and function of the spiritual discipline of Scripture study in this way:

> Study as a spiritual discipline is, in general, the focusing of the mind upon God's works and words. In study our mind takes on the order in the object studied, and that order invariably forms the mind itself and thereby the soul and the life arising out of it. Thus the law of God kept before the mind brings the order of God into our mind and soul. The soul is "restored" as the law becomes the routine pattern of inward life and outward action. We are integrated into the movements of the eternal kingdom. (p. 108)

It is especially important that we remain engaged in the personal and corporate study of Scripture during the graduate school experience, as Willard's words remind us that regular study of God's Word forms our inward and outward habits of thinking and action toward God's kingdom. Required theological study, which is a part of many faith-based graduate programs, does not take the place of personal Bible study and meditation, although supervisors can encourage students to integrate the theological knowledge they are learning in the classroom to clinical material.

Calhoun (2015) provides four spiritual practices for hearing God's Word, including Bible study, devotional reading, meditation on Scripture, and memorization. Such practices develop knowledge of Scripture as well as the personal application of biblical teaching in one's life. One meditative approach to Scripture that can be used individually or in a group is *lectio divina*, a Benedictine practice that involves the "sacred reading" of a passage of Scripture (see Foster, 1992, pp. 149-50, for a good introduction to this practice). Generally, *lectio divina* involves four steps: reading of a passage of Scripture, meditation on the passage, prayer, and contemplation. *Lectio divina* encourages the participant to use the imagination to place oneself in the biblical narrative and allow one's attention to be drawn to a particular word, phrase, or image. Memorization of Scripture is an important (but somewhat lost) discipline that is strongly encouraged by spiritual formation writers as a way of retaining and meditating on God's Word (Willard, 1988).

Corporate reading and study of Scripture is an essential practice for the development of wisdom. Reading, singing, studying, and meditating on God's Word in the context of a community of faith provides a critically important anchor point for students (and supervisors) who are immersed in human suffering through clinical practice. A deep knowledge and understanding of Scripture "in our bones" forms clinicians who can embody the wisdom of the Old and New Testaments as they work with suffering individuals and families. Knowing and trusting the God who inspired the wisdom in Proverbs, Ecclesiastes, and Job, for example, allows supervisees to approach hurting clients with wisdom and understanding. Supervisors encourage the practice of spiritual disciplines through teaching, modeling, inquiry, and bringing practices into the supervision experiences.

Wise Discernment

The spiritual discipline of discernment is also an important practice to aid in the development of wisdom and judgment. Ruth Haley Barton provides a helpful introduction to the spiritual practice of discernment in *Strengthening the Soul of Your Leadership*. She writes:

> Discernment is first of all a habit, a way of seeing that eventually permeates our whole life. It is the journey from spiritual blindness (not seeing God anywhere or only seeing him where we expect to see him) to spiritual sight (finding God everywhere, especially where we least expect it). Ignatius of Loyola, founder of the Jesuits and best known for developing a set of exercises intended to hone people's capacity for this discipline, defined the aim of discernment as "finding God *in all things* in order that we might love and serve God in all." (Barton, 2008, p. 111)

Barton's thoughtful and balanced process for prayerful discernment includes submission to God's will and guidance, collecting and considering data, inner reflection and confirmation, and action. This practice can be especially meaningful when it is done in a community of two or more people. It is easy to incorporate into the supervision process and is a good way to practice discernment with supervisees so they may develop the practice of seeking God in all things as they make important decisions that will impact people's lives. When discussing a tricky clinical situation in supervision, for example, a supervisor may initiate a moment of quiet prayer, reflection, and meditation before moving toward a treatment plan. Certainly, we also strive to be discerning supervisors, seeking God's wisdom and guidance about how to best be a part of his formative work in the lives and souls of our supervisees.

CONCLUSION

In this chapter, we explore the cultivation of practical wisdom in clinical supervision as essential to the development of wise clinicians who bring God's wisdom, science-informed competence, and a discerning spirit to their work with hurting and vulnerable individuals, families, and communities. Clinical supervision fosters the development of professional habits that lead to a lifelong pursuit of wisdom, which is essential in the mental health disciplines where new knowledge and better clinical interventions are constantly emerging. Encouraging and incorporating spiritual disciplines into the supervision process connects us with the source of all wisdom and reminds us that virtue is not an end in itself. Rather, we seek to become wise so we may love and serve God and our neighbor to the best of our abilities. May God richly bless our clinical mentoring and generously give us the wisdom we need to be wise and discerning supervisors.

CHAPTER SUMMARY / SUPERVISION GUIDE

Virtue	• **Practical Wisdom:** prudence, reasoning, understanding, circumspection, foresight, teachability, memory, shrewdness
Definition	• Right reason in action
Scripture	• "But the wisdom that comes from heaven is first of all pure; then peace-loving, considerate, submissive, full of mercy and good fruit, impartial and sincere. Peacemakers who sow in peace reap a harvest of righteousness" (Jas 3:17-18).
Ethical principles	• Competency • Ethical decision making
Supervision focus	• Competency-based supervision • Cognitive behavioral supervision • Existential supervision: finding the golden mean • Ethical decision-making processes
Christian integration focus	• Competencies in using religious and spiritual interventions • Ethics for use of religious and spiritual interventions
Spiritual practices	• Scripture study and meditation • Discernment
Desired outcome	• Wise clinicians who are lifelong learners, curious, able to tolerate complexities; who value God's Word and science-informed practice; who are competent and ethical, able to apply knowledge and make good clinical judgments with practical wisdom and discernment

CHAPTER 7

JUSTICE

Diversity Competence, Hospitality, and Openness to the Other

Learn to do right; seek justice.
Defend the oppressed.
Take up the cause of the fatherless;
plead the case of the widow.

Isaiah 1:17

THE PURSUIT OF GRADUATE training in counseling, psychology, and marriage and family therapy is for many people a response to God's call to care for the vulnerable, marginalized, and suffering. We hope to gain the knowledge and skills that will help us make a difference in the world today with our vocational choice. However, actualizing this call with real-world clinical situations requires the disorienting experience of recognizing and dealing with our own biases and blind spots. Clinical supervisors play a formative role as supervisees develop diversity awareness, competence, and advocacy skills. We must be able to cultivate the character strength of justice to prepare our supervisees for long-term engagement and service to "the least of these" in our diverse and globalized world.

This chapter describes the theological and professional virtue of justice and proposes supervision methods and spiritual formation practices to develop professional habits of fairness, eliminating bias, diversity competence, and advocacy. The personal transformation necessary for lifelong "openness to the other" starts from a foundation of understanding our role as stewards of God's good creation and embodying his love for the poor and marginalized. Clinical supervision facilitates the development of the knowledge, skills, values, and attitudes necessary for diversity competence and advocacy. The spiritual disciplines of Christian attentiveness, hospitality, and service cultivate a justice-oriented character that leads to servant-practitioner-scholar integration for the long haul. As supervisees grow in their openness to the other, they are better able to manage the value conflicts that are inevitably present in the therapeutic encounter.

JUSTICE: BIBLICAL AND THEOLOGICAL PERSPECTIVES

The virtue of justice is defined by Aquinas as the ongoing commitment to "render to each person that which is his or her right, what is due to each person, what each person ought to receive" (Kaczor & Sherman, 2009, p. 59). In comparison to the other cardinal virtues that are viewed as individual characteristics and practices, justice is an other-oriented virtue that involves development of habits related to fair and just treatment of others as individuals and in society. Gratitude is a subvirtue of justice, as we recognize and honor what we have received from God and others. The Catholic catechism provides this definition of the virtue of justice:

> Justice is the moral virtue that consists in the constant and firm will to give their due to God and neighbor. Justice toward God is called the "virtue of religion." Justice toward men disposes one to respect the rights of each and to establish in human relationships the harmony that promotes equity with regard to persons and to the common good. The just man, often mentioned in the Sacred Scriptures, is distinguished by habitual right thinking and the uprightness of his conduct toward his neighbor. "You shall not be partial to the poor or defer to the great, but in righteousness shall you judge your neighbor." (*Catechism of the Catholic Church*, 2003, para. 1807)

Classical definitions describe three aspects of justice that are the focus of virtuous actions: *general justice* pertains to a person's duties and responsibilities to society, *distributive justice* concerns the society's responsibilities to its people, and *commutative justice* pertains to people's reciprocal responsibilities to each other as part of the community (Waddams, 1964; Pieper, 1966).

Justice is due to other human beings because all persons are created by God in his image and loved by God for all eternity. It is because persons have eternal value that they are to be treated as an end in themselves and not as means to an end to be exploited and misused (Waddams, 1964). As stated by Pieper (1966): "Man has inalienable rights because he is created a person by the act of God.... Something is inalienably due to man because he is a *creatura*. Moreover, as a *creatura*, man has the absolute duty to give another his due" (p. 51). Justice is considered an expression of Christian love; however, it is different than Christian love in that the object of justice is that which is experienced as "other" (Jones, 1994).

Justice also involves giving to God what is due. Aquinas viewed religious expression in a just society as an act of honoring God for what he has done for us through expressions of worship and gratitude: "Religion, then, is not a matter simply for 'religious' or 'spiritual' people. Rather, all people, in virtue of being created by God and sustained by God, owe God worship out of justice.... To fail to render God his due is to be a moral failure" (Kaczor & Sherman, 2009, p. 63). Righteous individuals give God his due through offering God their time (Sabbath-keeping) and money (tithing) and seeking him at all times in prayer (Westberg, 2015). Justice also compels us to recognize and be thankful for the contribution of others in our lives—for example, responding with gratitude and filial piety toward family members and others who have provided for us.

In *Generous Justice*, Tim Keller (2010) provides a theological foundation for justice and asserts that justice is a necessary outcome of the Christian faith. First, the doctrine of creation teaches us to honor and love others as created in the image of God, understanding that the well-being of all humanity is precious to God. Additionally, our recognition of God's ownership over all creation and our role as stewards should motivate us toward generous care for others evidenced by seeking justice. Second, Keller suggests that as we fully recognize our own spiritual poverty and need for God's grace, we are motivated to generously seek justice on behalf of others. In other words, embracing the full meaning of our justification by faith in Jesus Christ will lead to acting justly. Keller unpacks the teaching in James 2 that "faith by itself, if it is not accompanied by action, is dead" (James 2:17):

> If you look at someone without adequate resources and do nothing about it, James teaches, your faith is "dead," it is not really saving faith. So what are the "works" he is talking about? He is saying that a life poured out in deeds of service to the poor is the inevitable sign of any real, true, justifying, gospel-faith. Grace makes you just. If you are not just, you've not truly been justified by faith. (Keller, 2010, p. 99)

What characterizes just persons in their relationships with others? Westberg (2015) examines Old Testament passages related to the virtue of justice. Psalm 15 describes the righteous as those who speak truth, keep promises, and refrain from slander, revenge, or taking bribes. In addition, the righteous hate wickedness and give honor to those who are God-fearing. Justice as a character virtue is evident when we express gratitude and thankfulness to God and others for the blessings and care we receive from them. Westberg suggests that we "owe" others friendliness, words of truth, and integrity to maintain social harmony and order in relationships. Gushee and Stassen (2016) look to the example of Jesus and con-

clude that the just person practices "kingdom ethics" through challenging the wealthy and powerful to protect the poor, confronting violence and domination as unjust, and opposing religious exclusiveness. A Christian ethic of justice involves "always assess[ing] ethical dilemmas, issues, and situations with a view to whether injustice is present and how it might be confronted, and what a just outcome (justice from below) would look like in terms especially of greed/economic injustice, domination, violence, and exclusion from community" (Gushee & Stassen, 2016, p. 147).

Fundamentally, practicing the Christian ethic of justice is an expression of God's love for the world. Grenz (1997) articulates this beautifully:

> The desire to mirror God's love mandates Christian involvement in social issues, including the quest for justice in its many forms. We are attentive to justice issues simply because we share God's loving concern for all creation, and therefore we desire to be the vehicles through which God expresses that love to all. Our desire to be vehicles of God's love leads to attempts to transform social structures that work against God's loving purposes. To this end we become God's advocates in confronting evil, and we champion the cause of the weak, the marginalized and the downtrodden, just as Jesus has shown us by his own example. (p. 262)

Historical and contemporary understandings of the character strength of justice provide a biblical and theological foundation for a Christian integrative approach to supervision. As supervisors, we aspire to promote the development of justice-oriented clinicians who engage in the work of counseling, psychology, and MFT as an expression of God's love for all creation, especially the vulnerable and marginalized.

JUSTICE: PSYCHOLOGICAL PERSPECTIVES

Peterson and Seligman (2004) describe the character strength of justice as an interpersonal quality concerned with the relationships between the person and their community. Three character traits are included in this classification: citizenship, fairness, and leadership. Individuals with the character strength of *citizenship* demonstrate social responsibility as they look beyond their own needs to the larger interests of their group or community and are committed to the common good. The virtue of *fairness* is developed through moral reasoning and results in the treatment of all persons equally and without bias. The character strength of *leadership* involves the ability to organize and influence others toward achievement of a common goal. Justice-oriented virtues, from a psychological perspective, are civic-minded and focus on the relationships *among* people in a community or social group, whereas strengths of humanity, according to Peterson and Seligman, focus on relationships *between* people (p. 357).

Empirical research in the social sciences related to the virtue of justice has focused on the development, personality factors, motivations, and correlates of prosocial traits. Duffy and Chartrand (2017) offer the following definition: "Prosocial affect and prosocial cognition are psychological processes that connect us with other people . . . and . . . increase the likelihood of prosocial behavior: a voluntary action intended to help others" (p. 439). Prosocial traits include gratitude, benevolence, helping orientation, and a willingness to forgive. Prosocial attitudes and behaviors are associated with the personality trait of *agreeableness*, which involves a general interpersonally oriented and positive social orientation (Graziano & Tobin,

2009). Motivation for prosocial behaviors includes a combination of moral cognitions, such as internalized values and principles, as well as moral emotions, which include compassion and empathy (Carlo & Davis, 2016). Research has demonstrated a two-way causal relationship between religiosity and prosocial behaviors: religious affiliation provides activation and motivation of prosocial attitudes and behaviors, and individuals who have prosocial personality orientation are drawn to religious systems that emphasize altruism and other-oriented values (Saroglou, 2013).

How do individuals develop the character strength of justice? Social scientists, philosophers, and political scientists have explored the development of moral reasoning in human beings and examined how individuals acquire capacities for moral judgments and behaviors. Historically, cognitive developmental theorists proposed that individuals progress through predictable states of development in the acquisition of moral reason (Piaget, 1948; Kohlberg, 1984). Kohlberg's (1984) model outlined six stages of development that progress from egocentric decisions around moral issues to the highest stage, where universal moral principles are applied. Feminist critiques of Kohlberg such as that of Carol Gilligan (1982) argue for the legitimacy and value of moral reasoning strategies that prioritize care for others as part of ethical decision making. *Care reasoning* proposes that moral decision-making skills that are interpersonally and relationally oriented are just as legitimate as a philosophical or objective orientation toward moral reasoning. Current theories emphasize the importance of moral emotions such as benevolence in the development and motivation of prosocial attitudes and behaviors (Carlo &

Davis, 2016). Benevolence, viewed as an experience of empathy and compassion for others, is both an intrinsic character trait and a developmental process that is affected by modeling, socialization, and imitation/mimicry (Eisenberg, Fabes, & Spinrad, 2006; Duffy & Chartrand, 2017). Interestingly, research suggests there may be a stronger relationship between sympathy and prosocial behaviors than between moral reasoning and prosocial behaviors across age groups and situations (Carlo & Davis, 2016). The authors state that "moral emotions are sometimes more relevant than cognitions, depending on the characteristics of the individual and the situation. . . . Benevolence, via sympathy, plays a powerful role—equal to that of justice and other moral motives—in understanding morality" (Carlo & Davis, 2016, p. 267).

Contemporary theory and research in interpersonal neurobiology emphasize the role of attachment and early caregiving experiences on the development of moral character. Narvaez (2014) suggests that the capacities for empathy and moral reasoning are developed through a combination of interpersonal, cognitive, and affective experiences early in life. Transformative interpersonal experiences later in life, such as those with mentors, religious institutions, and educators, also have the potential to reshape moral character toward the development of moral wisdom and virtue (Narvaez, 2014). Certainly, clinical supervision has the potential to be one such experience as supervisors facilitate the development of attentiveness, empathy, and concern for the fair and just treatment of others.

The contextual family therapy model developed by Boszormenyi-Nagy provides a systemic understanding of fairness and justice dynamics in couples, families, and larger systems. Family and social system develop trust and mutuality through seeking to balance a fair and equitable experience of fundamental human rights among members of the system (Boszormenyi-Nagy, Grunebaum, & Ulrich, 1991). Thus, Boszormenyi-Nagy proposes that *relational ethics* are the primary dynamic motivation in relational systems. This dynamic view of trust and health as primary relational motivators differs greatly from transactional or "quid pro quo" understandings of relationship ethics and approaches something more akin to the ethic of care that characterizes feminist theories of care reasoning described above.

The study of gratitude has received considerable attention in the empirical literature and contributes to our understanding of the virtue of justice as giving others what is due to them. Gratitude has been defined as "a feeling that occurs in interpersonal relationships when one person acknowledges receiving a valuable benefit from another" (Emmons & Mishra, 2012, p. 10). Gratitude has been investigated as both an emotion and as an enduring character trait or virtue. As a prosocial emotion, it is hypothesized to provide a moral barometer, a moral motive, and a moral reinforcement for prosocial behaviors (McCullough & Tsang, 2004, p. 125). As a virtue, the disposition of gratitude has been positively linked to health benefits including physical and psychological well-being, prosocial behaviors, and positive interpersonal interactions (Emmons & Mishra, 2012). The authors hypothesize that gratitude improves well-being by improving spiritual awareness, decreasing stress, increasing positive interpersonal experiences, and providing protection from negative emotions. Interventions designed to foster gratitude tend to focus one's attention on remembering and recognizing benefits that have been received, and they share the general strategy of "mindfulness practice that leads to a greater experience of being connected to life and awareness of all of the benefits available" (Emmons & Mishra, 2012, p. 19). Dispositional gratitude has also been found to be positively associated with spirituality and religiosity (Emmons & Kneezel, 2005) as well as prosocial religious behavior (Saroglou, 2013). Religious scriptures, rituals, and practices provide opportunities for remembering God's acts of love and care for the believer and encourage expressions of gratitude through caring for others as one has been cared for by God.

Psychological perspectives provide important considerations for the development of the character virtue of justice in clinical supervision. Through the clinical supervision process, we foster fair and just treatment of others through facilitating the integration of moral reasoning and application of ethical principles with the moral emotions of benevolence, empathy, and compassion. We cultivate civic-minded professional behaviors through moral exemplars and modeling in the context of the supervisory relationship. And we consider the role of gratitude in fostering prosocial behaviors through focusing on the benefits we have received from God and others.

JUSTICE AS A PROFESSIONAL VALUE: DIVERSITY COMPETENCE AND ADVOCACY SKILLS

A virtue-oriented approach to clinical supervision prioritizes the development of an ethic of "generous justice" as an expression of God's love and concern for the world, especially the marginalized. We mirror God's love through addressing the barriers that stand against his love and purpose, including the barriers within ourselves that hinder our ability to render fair and equitable professional care. Two ethical principles and practices are central to the virtue of justice: diversity competence and advocacy skills. In this section, we review the ethical guidelines and then describe the role of clinical supervision in fostering diversity and advocacy competencies.

Ethical Guidelines

The promotion of justice and equity is a core professional value for counselors, psychologists, and MFTs. The ACA code of ethics includes both "honoring diversity" and "promoting social justice" as the core values that motivate ethical counselors to uphold the foundational principle of "justice, or treating individuals equitably and fostering fairness and equality" (American Counseling Association [ACA], 2014, p. 3). ACA includes a specific ethical admonition for counselors to engage in advocacy for social justice in ethical principle A.7.a: "When appropriate, counselors advocate at individual, group, institutional, and societal levels to address potential barriers and obstacles that inhibit access and/or the growth and development of clients" (ACA, 2014, p. 5). ACA's *Multicultural and Social Justice Counseling Competencies* (Ratts, Singh, Nassar-McMillan, Butler, & McCullough, 2016) describes proficiencies in four domains: counselor self-awareness of personal beliefs and attitudes, counselor knowledge and understanding of the client's worldview, counselor awareness and actions regarding the impact of power and privilege on the therapeutic relationship, and counselor ability to advocate with and for clients. ACA also provides specialty guidelines for competency in the treatment of diverse groups including LGBT clients, transgender clients, multicultural career counseling, and treatment of religious and spiritual issues in counseling (see www.counseling.org/knowledge-center/competencies).

The APA Ethical Principles also specify justice as a core value (American Psychological Association [APA], 2010). Psychologists commit to equal access and quality of services for all persons as an issue of justice. In addition, psychologists commit to self-monitoring of any biases or areas of incompetence: "Psychologists exercise reasonable judgment and take precautions to ensure that their potential biases, the boundaries of their competence and the limitations of their expertise do not lead to or condone unjust practices" (APA, 2010, p. 3). APA provides a detailed description of ethical guidelines and competencies for multicultural practice, research, and education (APA, 2003; APA, 2008). Consistent with its commitment to multicultural competency in practice, APA has also developed practice guidelines for providing clinical services to transgender and gender-nonconforming individuals, LGBT clients, girls and women, older adults, and individuals with disabilities (see http://www.apa.org/practice/guidelines/).

Likewise, marriage and family therapists embrace "diversity, equity, and excellence" (American Association for Marriage and Family Therapy [AAMFT], 2015) as core aspirational values. AAMFT's Standard 1 pertains to MFTs' responsibility to clients that prohibits any practice of discrimination, stating, "Marriage and family therapists provide professional assistance to persons without discrimination on the basis of race, age, ethnicity, socioeconomic status, disability, gender, health status, religion, national origin, sexual orientation, gender identity or relationship status"

(AAMFT, 2015). MFTs are encouraged to consider larger societal and systemic factors that maintain power, privilege, and unjust treatment of others through development of a critical consciousness that considers the impact of injustice on clinical issues (Almeida, Hernandez-Wolfe, & Tubbs, 2011).

Diversity Competence

What exactly do the ethical standards mean by the terms *diversity* and *multicultural competence*? APA provides the following working definition:

> The terms "multiculturalism" and "diversity" have been used interchangeably to include aspects of identity stemming from gender, sexual orientation, disability, socioeconomic status, or age. Multiculturalism, in an absolute sense, recognizes the broad scope of dimensions of race, ethnicity, language, sexual orientation, gender, age, disability, class status, education, religious/spiritual orientation, and other cultural dimensions. All of these are critical aspects of an individual's ethnic/racial and personal identity, and psychologists are encouraged to be cognizant of issues related to all of these dimensions of culture. The concept of diversity has been widely used in employment settings.... It has since evolved to be more encompassing in its intent and application by referring to individuals' social identities, including age, sexual orientation, physical disability, socioeconomic status, race/ethnicity, workplace role/position, religious and spiritual orientation, and work/family concerns. (APA, 2003, p. 380)

Social justice values in psychology, counseling, and MFT are operationalized in the benchmarks for graduate training programs. Demonstration of multicultural competence and advocacy skills as educational outcomes are required in the education and training of all mental health professionals. Competency benchmarks include the development of knowledge, skills, values, and attitudes that foster equitable, fair, just, and competent treatment for all. Graduate programs establish specific student learning outcomes related to multicultural competence and provide coursework and supervised practicum/ internship experiences with diverse client populations to promote diversity competence and provide opportunities to evaluate student progress. Service learning has also been identified as an "out of the classroom" opportunity for the development of multicultural competence and advocacy skills (Maxwell & Henriksen, 2011).

Training in multicultural competence requires clinicians to consider not only the impact of individual dimensions of diversity on the client's identity and experience but also *intersectionality*—how the interaction between various aspects of identity can lead to greater marginalization and discrimination (Hernández & McDowell, 2010).

Advocacy Skills

Counselors, psychologists, and MFTs have embraced the pursuit of social justice through social advocacy as integral to the role of the mental health professional. Based on belief in a just society and a desire for equal access for all to mental health treatment, the counseling profession in particular has identified advocacy and social justice counseling as a "fifth force" in the counseling movement (Ratts, 2009). Advocacy counseling is "an empowerment stratagem that counselors and psychologists use to fully empathize with their clients to exact social change" (Green, McCollum, & Hays, 2008, p. 15) with the goal of identifying and removing the barriers to human growth

and development that exist for each client. The ACA has identified specific advocacy competencies to promote the effective and ethical engagement of counselors with clients and with the public (Ratts & Hutchins, 2009; Ratts, Toporek, & Lewis, 2010). Advocacy competencies include the use of empowerment and advocacy strategies to promote change in clients, communities, and societal domains.

The APA competency benchmarks for professional psychologists include proficiencies in advocacy as part of the required skills for management and administration in mental health settings. Advocacy is defined as "actions targeting the impact of social, political, economic or cultural factors to promote change at the individual (client), institutional, and/or systems level" (APA, 2011, p. 17). Competencies include the knowledge and skills necessary to empower clients to effect change in their environment. In addition, psychologists develop awareness of systemic and societal barriers and are able to intervene at a systemic level to impact institutions and communities.

Educational and training benchmarks provide a natural starting point for identifying diversity competence and advocacy goals for clinical supervision. Supervisors encourage the development of just habits and professional practices that ensure fair and equitable treatment of others.

Virtue-Ethics Approach to Multicultural Competence

As an alternative to the educational and skill-development approach to diversity competence, Fowers and Davidov (2006) focus on the development of character strengths that are foundational to a lifelong commitment to diversity competence. The aim of a virtue-oriented approach is to develop clinicians who "recognize and embody the ethical importance of multiculturalism and internalize its aims of social justice, cultural respect, and mutual affirmation . . . toward making cultural competence second nature" (Fowers & Davidov, 2006, p. 591). This approach to diversity competence places the emphasis on the development of the character traits of personal self-awareness, self-evaluation, and transformation that lead to a lifelong commitment to valuing other worldviews and perspectives while maintaining a sense of one's own. Fowers and Davidov write:

> We suggest that a character development approach captures the richness and personally transformative aspects of cultural competence more fully than a straightforward skills perspective. At its best, cultural competence involves becoming a particular kind of person or developing one's character toward excellence in responding to cultural matters. In other words, cultural competence is not simply the possession of self-knowledge, information about culture, and behavioral capacities that may or may not alter the psychologist as a person. Rather, one must internalize and embody this knowledge in a profound way, making it part of one's character, not just an addition to one's behavioral repertoire. This transformation of character makes it possible for psychologists to extend respect and affirmation to people with various heritages spontaneously and reliably and to do so in an informed and appropriate manner. Multiculturalists are calling on us not just to improve our therapeutic technique but to elevate our humanity. (p. 588)

This hopeful vision provides aspirational goals for a justice-oriented clinical supervision. As supervisors, we can add "something more" to the supervision process by inviting supervisees to pursue a transformation of character that leads to diversity competence and advocacy as a way of life.

SUPERVISION MODELS AND METHODS: DEVELOPING DIVERSITY COMPETENCY AND ADVOCACY SKILLS

Clinical supervision aimed at the formation of the character strength of justice helps supervisees move beyond "political correctness" to a deep and abiding commitment to fairness and equity in all areas of professional functioning. A review of professional values, ethics, and competencies supports the assertion that "multicultural competence is considered an ethical and practice imperative"; however, "attaining such competence as individuals and within the supervision relationship has proven to be daunting" (Falender, Shafranske, & Falicov, 2014, p. 7). Falender and Shafranske (2004) provide the following definition for diversity competence in supervision:

> We believe that diversity competency includes incorporation of self-awareness by both supervisor and supervisee and is an interactive process of the client or family, supervisee-therapist, and supervisor, using all of their diversity factors. It entails awareness, knowledge, and appreciation of the interaction among the client's, supervisee-therapist's, and supervisor's assumptions, values, biases, expectations, and worldviews; integration and practice of appropriate, relevant, and sensitive assessment and intervention strategies and skills; and consideration of the larger milieu of history, society, and sociopolitical variables. (p. 125)

This section provides an overview of the best practice guidelines for developing diversity competence and advocacy skills through the process of clinical supervision. Rather than focus on models of supervision, the following summarizes principles and suggested techniques that represent supervision practices that promote multicultural competence in counseling, psychology, and MFT.

Establish the Supervision Relationship as a Safe Space for Diversity Discussions

Fostering diversity competence begins with the establishment of a trusting supervision alliance where honest disclosure and discussion of values, attitudes, and biases can occur. In a Delphi study, Dressel, Consoli, Kim, and Atkinson (2007) found that expert clinicians rated supervision alliance as the most important factor in successful multicultural supervision behaviors. Initial supervision sessions can invite the supervisor and supervisee to share their own cultural and worldview values and assumptions, while at the same time recognizing the supervisee's privacy and right to nondisclosure of personal information (Falender et al., 2014). Consider the following specific supervision techniques for creating a safe space:

- The initial supervision contract should include reference to the importance of discussing issues of diversity in supervision and provide informed consent that this is a necessary and required component of professional development.

- Supervisors can use their professional disclosure statement to share their own diversity and justice commitments. For example, supervisors may describe how their work in a community-based setting informs their use of systemic interventions to implement change.

- The supervision contract can also identify specific goals for the development of specific diversity competencies and tie these goals to the supervisee's long-term vocational aspirations. For example, a supervisee interested in specializing in intimate partner violence would benefit from a focus on the intersection of gender, culture, religion, and socioeconomic status as contextual factors and exploration of their own biases and worldview assumptions in these areas.

- Keep in mind that research suggests oversensitivity to culture can result in ineffective supervision (Constantine & Sue, 2007). Initial conversations about culture and worldview are important to diffuse awkwardness and invite diversity considerations as a normal component of supervision sessions. APA supervision guidelines suggest, "Viewing diversity as normative, rather than as an exception, aids supervisors in being sensitive to important similarities and differences" (APA, 2014, p. 17).

Foster Cultural Self-Assessment, Personal Awareness, and Reflective Practice

Foundational to the development of diversity competence in supervisees is self-awareness of their own worldview assumptions, biases, and areas of needed growth. Diversity "meta-competence" is defined as "knowing what one knows and what one does not know" (Falender et al., 2014, p. 274). Clinical supervision research suggests that the supervisee's level of racial identity development demonstrates a significant relationship with their multicultural competence, based on self-report (Ladany, Inman, Constantine, & Hofheinz, 1997). Thus, supervisors should encourage personal exploration of self as a person of culture (for the supervisee and supervisor). An important outcome of growth in self-awareness is cultural humility and an attitude of curiosity, openness, and exploration in regard to client worldview differences and experiences. "Cultural humility requires supervisors and supervisees to learn about other religions, social classes, ethnic groups, and so on without generalizing characteristics, but maintaining openness to learn from each other and clients" (Hernandez-Wolfe & McDowell, 2014, p. 49).

The following supervision tools and techniques are recommended to promote cultural self-awareness:

- Supervisees can be encouraged to complete a self-assessment of cultural competence and then formulate specific goals for supervision based on assessed strengths and areas for growth. Free self-assessment tools are available (see SAMHSA, 2014).

- A commonly utilized tool in MFT supervision to encourage self-of-the-therapist work is the cultural genogram (Hardy & Laszloffy, 1995). Supervisees can be given the assignment of completing their own cultural genogram outside supervision, or a supervision session can be devoted to completion of the genogram by the supervisor, supervisee, or supervision group.

- Supervisors can model cultural humility by discussing a recent professional encounter where they recognized their limited knowledge of an aspect of diversity.

- Supervisors can assign books, articles, movies, or videos that increase cultural knowledge and self-awareness. Supervision groups can read or view the resources together and then discuss reactions. For example, watch C. N. Adichie's (2009) TED talk "The Danger of a Single Story."

Incorporate Attention to Issues of Diversity into All Aspects of Clinical Practice

Supervisors look for ways to attend to diversity issues in all areas of clinical practice; these include but are not limited to establishment of therapeutic alliance, assessment and psychological testing practices, case conceptualization and treatment plans, and evaluation of outcomes. This requires supervisors to be competent and knowledgeable about diversity competence. Falender, Shafranske, and Falicov (2014) suggest, "Supervisor competence includes knowledge, skills, attitudes, and values regarding the empirical base of multicultural diversity, and clinical supervision research and practice, including from an international frame" (p. 17). The following resources can be incorporated into the supervision process to develop good professional habits and practices in diversity competence.

- A widely used tool for considering dimensions of diversity in assessment and treatment is Hays's (2001) ADRESSING model. Clinicians consider the various overlapping dimensions of their own and their clients' diversity factors including age, disability, religion, ethnicity, social status, sexual orientation, indigenous heritage, nationality, and gender. Supervisors can introduce this tool and ask supervisees to consider each dimension in their clinical assessment and treatment interventions.

- The Outline for Cultural Formation (OCF) in the DSM-5 can be introduced and used as a tool for considering cultural factors in assessment and diagnosis (Lewis-Fernández, Aggarwal, Hinton, Hinton, & Kirmayer, 2015).

- Supervisors can encourage use of the APA and ACA specialty guidelines and competencies for diverse populations and access/utilize these guidelines during the supervision process.

- Supervisors should ensure that supervisees gain experience with diverse client populations and presenting problems. One of the benefits of triadic and group supervision is that supervisees have the opportunity to learn from their peers' experiences with diverse populations.

- Live observations or review of taped sessions should include attention to supervisees' competencies to form alliances with, assess, and treat diverse populations. Regular feedback on emerging strengths and weaknesses is important to promote growth.

Develop a Critical Consciousness

Supervisors facilitate awareness of issues of power and privilege and the effects these have on the clients and families they serve. This includes recognizing and challenging oppression and microaggressions when they occur. The following practices can be incorporated into the supervision process:

- Supervisors can introduce the use of the Critical Genogram (Garcia, Kosutic, McDowell, & Anderson, 2009). This tool maps out a family's experiences with power and privilege across generations by considering the intersection of diversity characteristics with larger social and systemic contexts. Hernandez-Wolfe and McDowell (2014) suggest that supervisors ask trainees to complete the genogram individually or in a supervision group. The tool can be used for therapist growth in developing a critical consciousness and can also be used with families to increase their awareness of the impact of oppression, power, and privilege.

- Supervisees can be encouraged to develop a regular practice of reflecting on diversity and justice issues through keeping a "critical incidents journal" (Lee & Vennum, 2010). Here, supervisees process critical interactions, thoughts, feelings, and reactions to clients that may be illustrative for their growth in developing a critical consciousness. Supervisees can be encouraged to process these experiences in supervision.

Provide Formative and Summative Evaluation of Diversity Competence

One of the primary ways we come to "know what we don't know" is through feedback about our blind spots and biases. Supervisors should be transparent in the initial supervision contract about the inclusion of diversity-competence assessment as an important aspect of overall competency (Falender et al., 2014). It is the responsibility of the supervisor to initiate discussions regarding diversity concerns and issues of power and privilege and to provide ongoing, formative feedback to supervisees. Supervisors provide formative, developmentally appropriate feedback regarding areas of needed growth, as well as affirmation of emerging strengths. Summative evaluations should include the specific evaluation of diversity competence consistent with educational benchmarks in counseling, psychology, and MFT.

Encourage the Development of Advocacy Skills

Clinical supervision is the ideal educational context for students to explore their roles and responsibilities as advocates for justice as they consider the unique contributions and challenges they can bring to the institutions and larger systems of which they are a part. Chang, Hays, and Milliken (2009) propose a three-tiered supervision model to promote the development of advocacy skills in supervisees. Using a social constructivist theoretical foundation, supervisors are encouraged to first facilitate the development of supervisees' self-awareness of their own cultural identity, values, and biases. As part of this awareness, supervisees are encouraged to develop a personal and vocational commitment to be agents of social change. Second, supervisors help trainees consider their clients' worldviews and experiences and how they can empower their clients to address environmental and societal factors that may inhibit growth and development. The third tier of supervision activities involves the development of community collaboration and advocacy skills so the supervisee learns to be involved in enacting needed changes on behalf of clients at the larger systemic level. The authors recommend the following specific supervision activities to develop social justice and advocacy competencies:

- Encourage supervisees to increase self-awareness through activities and questions designed to explore cultural identity,

experiences of privilege and oppression, attitudes toward counseling, and potential areas of bias. For example, in a group supervision format, supervisees are asked to bring in an item or prop that represents their cultural heritage (e.g., food, decorative item, poem, or song) and then respond to a series of questions about their cultural identification and the influence of their worldview on their counseling work.

- Implement the consideration of contextual factors in case conceptualization and elicit the supervisee's perspective on their clients' experiences of oppression, power, privilege, and potential barriers to growth and development.

- Facilitate the identification of techniques and strategies for empowering clients, including accessing resources, noting exceptions to symptoms in clients' behaviors, or fostering an externalization of the problem.

- Empower supervisees to develop a "voice" in regard to justice issues that may pose barriers to their clients' development and functioning. Encourage the development of strategies to address these barriers in the agency or community.

- Partner with supervisees in providing presentations, workshops, and so forth, to address identified issues.

- Pose questions for supervisees about the role of advocacy and social justice in the counseling profession to facilitate development of a personal philosophy.

- Consider service learning as an opportunity to facilitate the development of justice-oriented skills and experiences in students and supervisees such as opportunities for community projects and service activities.

Demonstrate Faithful Practice and Intentional Commitment

Fowers and Davidov (2006) remind us that there is no shortcut to the development of the character strength of justice and openness to others; it requires good examples and modeling, faithful and consistent practice, personal transformation, and just action. They write:

> This learning requires teaching, feedback, modeling, and guidance from those who already exhibit the character strength. One acquires character strengths intentionally, through gradual efforts, by practicing them, by identifying and counteracting contrary desires, by altering one's cognitions in line with one's knowledge about the virtue, and by becoming the kind of person who habitually engages in these cognitions and actions. (Fowers & Davidov, 2006, p. 586)

Likewise, Falender et al. (2014) note that commitment, intentionality, and practice are required to cultivate self-reflective practices regarding the embedded cultural context in which all supervision and clinical work occur. They write, "Indeed, the fish must make an effortful commitment (with a lot of reminders) to know the water in which it swims every day" (p. 279).

Through use of best practice supervision approaches and interventions, supervisors facilitate the personal and professional awareness and transformation that lay the foundation for a lifelong commitment to justice in one's professional life. Through supervision, clinicians in training develop cultural humility, critical consciousness, culturally reflective practice, and attentiveness to opportunities for advocacy on individual client and systemic levels. Good supervision aimed to develop justice-oriented values and multicultural competence should not only educate but also inspire students to engage in personal transformation, acquisition of knowledge, and skill development toward this end (Fowers & Davidov, 2006).

A CHRISTIAN INTEGRATIVE APPROACH TO DIVERSITY COMPETENCE AND ADVOCACY IN SUPERVISION

Clinical supervision models and methods that train supervisees in diversity competence and advocacy skills provide an important foundation for justice-oriented clinical practice. A Christian integrative approach provides something more by inviting supervisees to respond to the biblical and theological imperative for Christians to pursue justice and love mercy. The doctrine of creation compels us to view all people as precious to God, especially the widow, the orphan, the poor, and the oppressed. As stewards of God's good creation,

we are charged with expressing his "generous justice" to the hurting world. Clinical supervision provides the opportunity for putting biblical justice commitments into action through prioritizing diversity competence and advocacy as an integrative outcome.

A Christian integrative approach to clinical supervision facilitates the development of biblical, justice-oriented practices of thought and action in light of kingdom ethics and values, which view all persons as created in the image of God and worthy of dignity, respect, and care.

Diversity competence and advocacy skills are developed in response to the kingdom mandate to care for the poor and marginalized and to address issues of inequity. In the Christian integration literature, this has been termed "faith-praxis integration" (Bouma-Prediger, 1990) or "integration as service" (Canning, Pozzi, McNeil, & McMinn, 2000). Five practices are recommended for a Christian integrative approach to supervision: affirm a commitment to diversity competence, facilitate the development of "double vision," provide skills for managing value conflicts, incorporate Christian virtues, and encourage advocacy as an integrative outcome.

Affirm a Commitment to Diversity Competence

Injustice, discrimination, and exclusion are all incompatible with a Christian ethic of justice. It is imperative that a Christian integrative approach to supervision affirm a commitment to diversity competence and nondiscrimination through connecting the dots for students that diversity competence is both a theological imperative and a professional responsibility.

It is common for students to feel anxious, incompetent, and even confused about moving into unfamiliar territory in openness to the other in clinical practice. They may fear that embracing others with differing values will somehow compromise their own. Supervisees may hesitate to engage with social justice concerns out of a fear that virtues of tolerance and equity may supersede the virtue of love for God and others and obedience to the authority of his Word (Hook & Davis, 2012). The supervision relationship is the ideal professional development venue for addressing these unconscious biases, anxieties, and discomforts as students come face to face with differing worldviews through their clinical experiences.

Although the ability of faith-based graduate programs to train students in diversity competence and nondiscrimination has come under challenge (Smith & Okech, 2016), faith commitments and nondiscrimination commitments can go hand in hand. Sells and Hagedorn (2016) assert this position unequivocally and make a compelling case that religious liberty and nondiscrimination can both be upheld in the training of mental health professionals at faith-based institutions. They write: "We believe that discrimination, when exercised as institutionally sanctioned hatred toward any group, is immoral and contrary to both the standards that govern the counseling profession and the sacred texts that inform religious practice. Such practices run contrary to the principles of our professional ethics, our emerging laws, and the Christian religious commitments" (p. 266).

Survey research suggests that students in explicitly Christian doctoral programs report significantly more diversity training in religious and spiritual issues than students in secular programs; however, they report significantly less training in ethnic, racial, and socioeconomic diversity (McMinn et al., 2015). In this study, no significant differences in diversity training between faith-based and secular programs were found in the areas of gender, sexual orientation/identity, or age. The authors suggest that explicitly Christian programs are more effectively preparing students to work with clients with diverse religious and spiritual worldviews but need to pay special attention to developing student competence with racial, ethnic, and socioeconomic diversity.

Facilitate "Double Vision"

Christian integrative approaches to diversity competence can draw from the theological perspectives on social justice of Miroslav Volf to articulate a biblical imperative of inclusiveness and reconciliation as a foundation for the embracing of the other while maintaining one's own sense of differentiated identity (Eriksson & Abernethy, 2014; Sells & Hagedorn, 2016). In developing cultural competence and understanding of others' experiences, for example, Eriksson and Abernethy (2014) use the writings of Volf to encourage students to develop "double vision," where they see experiences through the eyes of the other in a deeply empathic way without sacrificing their own views and values. This approach is particularly important for students who may feel that in seeking to understand the position of the other, they are agreeing with or condoning views and behaviors that conflict with their own values (Eriksson & Abernethy, 2014). Research suggests that a degree of differentiation of self and others is important for student development in intercultural understanding, as it involves the ability to understand another's perspective without feeling that it threatens one's own (Sandage & Harden, 2011). Self-and-other differentiation is a developmental journey for supervisees that can be fostered through the process of Christian integrative supervision as students experience the otherness of their clients in clinical practice.

Manage Value Conflicts

Dealing with conflicting values is an inevitable task facing all clinicians. Students often worry about the ethical dilemma of working with clients on goals that are inconsistent with the values of the therapist. For example, supervisees may feel a conflict of values when providing divorce therapy to a couple, or premarital therapy to a cohabitating couple. Sells and Hagedorn (2016) recommend ethical

bracketing (EB) as a way for students to remain committed to diversity competence and non-exclusionary practice while maintaining integrity of their own faith values. Ethical bracketing is defined as "the intentional separating of a counselor's personal values from his or her professional values or the intentional setting aside of the counselor's personal values in order to provide ethical and appropriate counseling to all clients, especially those whose worldviews, values, belief systems, and decisions differ significantly from those of the counselor" (Kocet & Herlihy, 2014, p. 182). The ACA suggests EB as an important practice for counselors as they maintain fidelity to the new, more stringent ethical code with its admonition to refrain from referring clients to another practitioner based on value conflicts: "Counselors need to manage any discomfort with a particular client through consultation, supervision and continued education and to view referral as an intervention of last resort. It's about protecting the clients we serve and putting their needs first" (Martz & Kaplan, 2014, p. 1). ACA ethical standards are clear that a referral to another counselor should be based on the issue of competence alone versus counselor discomfort.

Competent supervision with value conflicts is especially important in the current cultural climate where "conscious cause" discussions permeate the professional and popular literature (see Wise et al., 2015, for a good introduction and discussion). Eriksson and Abernethy (2014) point out that this is where the virtue of prudence and practical wisdom is necessary to help the supervisor discern whether the supervisee's desire to refer is clinically indicated or is a reaction to a diversity issue that is outside their "zone of tolerance" and poses a justice issue regarding fair and equitable treatment.

Incorporate Christian Virtues

A Christian integrative approach to clinical supervision fosters the development of cultural humility as both a biblical and professional virtue. A cultural-humility approach encourages attitudes and practices that involve a secure sense of one's own worldview and cultural identity while at the same time developing the capacity to "take in" the experience of others. Supervisors model and practice curiosity, openness, and exploratory skills that lead to deepening their understanding of other worldviews. As Christians, we follow Christ's example of humility and self-sacrifice and the biblical admonition to practice humility (Dwiwardani & Waters, 2015).

Supervisors encourage and practice the virtues of kindness, gentleness, and self-control as difficult diversity conversations occur. This may be particularly important in group supervision or a classroom environment where students listen and respond to each other's perspectives. We need community to help us recognize blind spots, but these conversations can be tense and uncomfortable and lead to further feelings of marginalization for students. Eriksson and Abernethy (2014) encourage faculty to help students develop "multicultural muscles" (p. 181) by practicing grace, forgiveness, and reconciliation during difficult discussions around race, gender, and other multicultural issues. They write: "The Christian ethics of hospitality, compassion, and justice suggest a commitment to diversity that moves beyond mere practicality or functionalism. An integrative approach to teaching multicultural competency offers theological constructs where students might locate a faith-related motivation, as well as the grace for this educational journey" (p. 175).

Group supervision is a particularly important modality for fostering the development of cultural humility and inviting supervisees to practice Christian virtue in diversity conversations with each other. Encouraging students to reflect on their worldview assumptions, cultural experiences, religious convictions, and experience of discrimination and microaggressions provides opportunities to foster difficult dialogues between supervisees that can help them move beyond an intellectualized understanding of cultural difference to deeper and lasting change (Dwiwardani & Waters, 2015).

Encourage Advocacy as an Integration Outcome

As trainees come face to face with issues of inequity, social injustice, and unequal access to services, supervision provides the opportunity for them to engage in critical reflection on these realities and their potential role as agents of change. Supervisors can empower supervisees to engage in advocacy efforts as kingdom work as they wrestle with justice issues in their clinical practice.

Watson and Eveleigh (2014) suggest that teaching students to "advocate effectively" is an important outcome of the integration of psychological theories with Christian faith. A three-pronged approach to integration involves Christian appraisal of theories as the first task, applied integration as a second priority, and social advocacy as a third outcome:

> A third integration task fosters the development of service-oriented values and convictions and nurtures a passion for compassionate justice that results in *advocacy* for underserved and marginalized populations. . . . Students develop a vision for how psychological theory and Christian faith can be faithfully integrated into their larger calling to serve the church and build Christ's

kingdom through addressing the real needs in the world today. (Watson & Eveleigh, 2014, p. 200)

Suggestions for facilitating the development of integration as advocacy include the following strategies adapted from Watson and Eveleigh:

- Utilize Problem Based Learning (PBL) as an evidence-based teaching tool in individual or group supervision (Allen, Donham, & Bernhardt, 2011). Students are introduced to a social problem, and then the supervisor facilitates discussion, promotes critical thinking, and facilitates a problem-solving process. For example, a supervisor may follow up a case presentation involving intimate partner violence with the question "What can the church do to prevent violence in the family?"

- In a group setting, a supervisor can utilize a "think-pair-share" exercise. The supervisor poses a question, asks students to write down their thoughts and reactions, and then pairs students to talk through their ideas with each other.

- Supervisors assign the development of a "personal mission statement" incorporating social justice concerns and advocacy goals developed from clinical experiences and self-reflection.

Concluding Thoughts

One of the most impactful supervisory interventions we can provide in developing the character strength of justice is to share our own "justice journey" that has led to our professional priorities and commitments. We can also draw our supervisees' attention to exemplar colleagues who are making a difference in the world through their actions and advocacy efforts. It is important that we share not just our successes but also our honest, ongoing struggle with blind spots and areas of needed growth in multicultural competence. Most likely, these blind spots will emerge in the supervision relationship, and we will have the opportunity to model humility as we seek our supervisees' forgiveness for the ways we have missed or discounted their "otherness."

SPIRITUAL DISCIPLINES FOR THE DEVELOPMENT OF JUSTICE-ORIENTED CHARACTER

Christian spiritual disciplines offer time-tested individual and community practices for cultivating the ethic of just, fair, and inclusive treatment of others. Through engaging in spiritual disciplines, we ask God to transform our character toward the development of habits and practices that promote equality, eliminate bias, and advocate for the good of others. In this section, we consider the spiritual disciplines of attentiveness, hospitality, and service and how they can be incorporated into the supervision process.

Attentiveness

A faithful and long-term commitment to justice involves the regular practice of paying attention to the world around us. Bethany Hoang of International Justice Mission asserts that a deeply rooted, lifelong engagement with justice requires a faithful practice of opening our eyes to both the reality of injustice around us and the reality of the hope we have in God's redeeming work in the world. As we seek to see the world through God's eyes, we recognize the needs around us and can discern the role he would have us play. Hoang (2012) writes:

> As you commit to the spiritual discipline of drawing near to the suffering of others, it will mean committing yourself to looking intently at the reality of violent injustice in our world today, and to do so while asking God, continually, to show you how moving toward injustice can also bring you closer to the heart of God. Ask God to remove the despair-driven question "But what could I possibly do to make a difference?" and turn this question into an unceasing prayer—a prayer asking God to show you injustice with God's very own eyes, asking God to let you live from the mind of Christ that is within you, and asking God to bring his glory in greater measure as you step forward in daily obedience to God above all else. (p. 28)

Paying attention to issues of injustice as a spiritual discipline involves living out an "openness to the other" by listening to stories, learning about events, and participating in projects. In other words, attentiveness involves choosing to face the realities of injustice in our immediate communities and in the world around us. Annan, in *Slow Kingdom Coming* (2016), asserts that "we practice awakening to justice by choosing who we talk with, what stories we read, what trips we take, what art we take in" (p. 31). He writes: "Part of this practice of attention involves asking ourselves, What breaks my heart? In the world, my country, or my neighborhood, what makes me angry because it should be better? Questions like this can awaken our attention for how we're called to serve the kingdom" (p. 32).

We also must direct our attention to the God of justice who is Lord over all, and in doing so we recognize our dependence on his power to restore what is broken: "Justice is always connected to worship, because both worship and justice are about a right ordering of the world" (Hoang, 2012, p. 36). In worship we remember God's mighty acts of deliverance of his people with hearts of gratitude. We are inspired as we recall the courageous and faithful work of those before us whom God has used to bring his justice to the world.

We can incorporate the spiritual discipline of attentiveness to justice in clinical supervision as we listen carefully to what breaks our supervisees' hearts, encouraging them to pay attention to the issues of justice they encounter and to seek God's guidance about how they can make a difference.

Hospitality

The spiritual discipline of hospitality invites believers to develop a regular practice of welcoming others in; of creating a space, both metaphorically and physically, for those whom God brings into our lives: "Hospitality creates a safe open space where a friend or stranger can enter and experience the welcoming spirit of Christ in another" (Calhoun, 2015, p. 161). Practicing hospitality as a way of life involves "small increments of daily faithfulness" (Pohl, 1999, p. 37) as we learn to open ourselves up to welcoming others on a regular basis.

Pohl (1999) provides thoughtful reflections on the practice of Christian hospitality. As a foundation for hospitality, she points the reader to two important teachings of Jesus. First, Christian hospitality and care for others is integrally linked to our love for Jesus and our expression of gratitude for what he has done for us. In Matthew 25, Jesus teaches that in welcoming the stranger, the poor, the hungry, we are welcoming him. Seeing Christ in "the least of these" is foundational to the practice of Christian hospitality. As we recognize Jesus in those we welcome into our homes and communities, we reciprocally receive blessings and gifts from the encounter. Second, Christian hospitality is not practiced for the purpose of improving social standing or selfish gain, but as part of a Christian ethic of care for and protection of others. In Luke 14, Jesus encourages his followers to "invite the poor, the crippled, the lame, the blind, and you will be blessed. Although they cannot repay you, you will be repaid at the resurrection of the righteous" (Lk 14:13-14).

Pohl (2007) provides a number of practical suggestions for individuals, families, and churches who are seeking to practice hospitality as a way of life. Hospitality begins with gratitude and a recognition of what God has done for us. It is best practiced by individuals and communities as a way of life that involves faithful generosity to make room for others. It involves creating hospitable spaces in our churches and homes where meals, time, and attention are generously shared—acts that are certainly countercultural in our accomplishment-oriented world. We practice the spiritual discipline of hospitality when we respond prayerfully and sensitively to the needs around us through hospitable gestures including invitations, meals, acts of service, and giving and receiving gifts. We invite others into our groups and circles, prayerfully considering who might be the vulnerable stranger in our midst in need of connection and care.

In our professional lives, we cultivate hospitality as a spiritual practice when we interrupt tasks to devote our full time and attention to others. Ortberg (1997) calls this "the ministry of being interrupted." As supervisors, we can be hospitable and make room for the needs, anxieties, and interruptions of our supervisees, particularly when they come to us with a crisis situation. In turn, this models and teaches

them to practice hospitality and responsiveness to their clients. We practice hospitality when we help supervisees and clients feel welcome and comfortable in our office space through our choice of décor and through offering tea, water, and tissues. We can generously share our time and resources with others, giving them our full attention through silencing our phones and computers and minimizing other distractions.

Seeking God's transformation of our character through the discipline of hospitality increases our capacity for openness to the other, which is foundational to the development of diversity competence and biblical justice in clinical practice.

Service

The spiritual discipline of service involves "striv[ing] to meet all persons who cross our path with openness to service for them" (Willard, 1988, p. 184). It takes the character strength of "openness to the other" to a whole new level as we ask God to develop in us a consistent attitude of mind and heart that involves laying down our life for others in love. It is a particularly important discipline for those in positions of power (and our advanced degrees certainly place mental health professionals in this position), as it fosters humility, unselfishness, and responsible exercise of power. As Willard (1988) writes:

> To be "great" and live as a servant is one of the most difficult of *spiritual* attainments. But it is also the pattern of life for which this bruised and aching world waits and without which it will never manage a decent existence. Those who would live this pattern must attain it through the discipline of service in the power of God, for that alone will train them to exercise great power without corrupting

their souls. It is for this reason that Jesus told his disciples to wash one another's feet and set them an example (John 13:14). (p. 183)

Practicing the spiritual discipline of service involves asking God to use our time, talents, and energies for "the good of others and causes of God in our world" (Willard, 1988, p. 182).

Foster (1988) provides a number of excellent examples of the spiritual discipline of service. Responding to the immediate needs of others in a Spirit-led, hidden way leads to "the service of small things" (p. 135). We can engage in the service of protecting the reputation of those around us by refusing to engage in gossip, slander, and venting. Taking the time to listen deeply and attentively to the cares and concerns of others, certainly central to the work of the clinician, is a continual act of service that can lead to bearing one another's burdens.

Foster (1988) provides an important distinction between true service and "self-righteous service," which involves pursuing acts of service through our own efforts, when we feel like it, for external glory and reward, and with a focus on results: "Self-righteous service fractures community. . . . It centers in the glorification of the individual. . . . It puts others into its debt and becomes one of the most subtle and destructive forms of manipulation known" (p. 129). True service, however, is Spirit-led, hidden, and faithful; it privileges the marginalized, and it becomes a way of life for the believer: "It springs spontaneously to meet human need" (Foster, 1988, p. 129).

Practicing the spiritual discipline of service leads to cultivation of the character virtue of humility, and therefore it is not an easy path.

As Foster (1988) writes:

Nothing *disciplines* the inordinate desires of the flesh like service, nothing *transforms* the desires of the flesh like serving in hiddenness. The flesh whines against service but screams against hidden service. It strains and pulls for honor and recognition. It will devise subtle, religiously acceptable means to call attention to the service rendered. If we stoutly refuse to give in to this lust of the flesh, we crucify it. Every time we crucify the flesh, we crucify our pride and arrogance. (p. 130)

As supervisors, we seek opportunities to love and serve our supervisee through speaking well of them to others, making extra time for them when they are dealing with a crisis, and putting them forward for opportunities where they can succeed. Providing small acts of caring and support when they are overwhelmed, such as offering to score a psychological test for them or tracking down a resource for a client, can be a cup of cold water to supervisees struggling to stay afloat.

In this way supervisors seek to model servant leadership as a way of life for the mental health professional. We follow the example of Jesus, who resisted the temptation of power and popularity to lay down his life in love. Nouwen (1989) reflects on Jesus' model of servant leadership and challenges Christian leaders to follow Christ's example in practicing a model of spiritual leadership "in which power is constantly abandoned in favor of love" (p. 82). Through practicing the spiritual discipline of service, we ask God to develop in us a heart for justice and advocacy as a lifelong commitment.

CONCLUSION

A Christian integrative approach to clinical supervision brings something more to the development of justice-oriented clinicians, who prioritize service and advocacy for "the least of these" and practice diversity competence for the sake of the kingdom, so that there is fair access to mental health services for all. This is no small task and requires guidelines and practices from the supervision literature on diversity competence and advocacy, combined with spiritual wisdom from the integration literature. The Christian spiritual disciplines of attentiveness to injustice, hospitality and making room for "the other," and hidden acts of service are necessary for the formation of Christian character toward justice.

No modern-day saint has modeled a life of justice more than the late Mother Teresa of Calcutta. Mother Teresa teaches us to see Jesus in the "distressing disguise" of the poor in our midst. In our practice of an ethic of justice expressed through attention, hospitality, and service in our clinical work, let us pray as she did: "Dearest Lord, may I see You today and every day in the person of Your sick, and, whilst nursing them, minister unto You. Though You hide yourself behind the unattractive disguise of the irritable, the exacting, the unreasonable, may I still recognize you, and say: 'Jesus, my patient, how sweet it is to serve You'" (Mother Teresa, p. 284).

CHAPTER SUMMARY / SUPERVISION GUIDE

Virtue	• **Justice:** commutative justice, distributive justice
Definition	• Fair and just treatment of others both as individuals and in society
Scripture	• "Learn to do right; seek justice. Defend the oppressed. Take up the cause of the fatherless; plead the case of the widow" (Is 1:17).
Ethical principles	• Fairness, equity, equality, eliminating biases, respect for diversity and individual differences • Advocacy at individual, group, institutional, and societal levels (ACA, 2014)
Supervision focus	• Supervision relationship as safe space for diversity discussions • Cultural self-assessment, personal awareness, reflective practice • Attention to diversity in all areas of clinical practice • Development of critical consciousness • Formative and summative evaluation of diversity competence • Development of advocacy skills
Christian integration focus	• Affirm commitment to diversity competence consistent with a Christian ethic of justice • Facilitate "double vision" • Manage value conflicts through ethical bracketing • Encourage advocacy as integrative outcome

| Spiritual practices | • Attentiveness
• Hospitality
• Service |
| Desired outcome | • Justice-oriented clinicians who prioritize service and advocacy for "the least of these" and practice diversity competence for the sake of Christ's kingdom, so that there is fair access to mental health services for all |

CHAPTER 8

TEMPERANCE

Reflective Practice

For the Spirit God gave us does not make us timid, but gives us power, love and self-discipline.

2 TIMOTHY 1:7

DEVELOPING CHARACTERISTIC habits of temperance is a requisite professional practice for mental health professionals. Perhaps few other professions require the levels of self-awareness and self-regulation that are necessary for the practicing clinician. Our thoughts, feelings, and experiences are the primary professional instruments we bring to the task of clinical assessment and intervention. Through training and supervision, clinicians learn to regulate emotional reactions to clients, to use "self of the therapist" as a key instrument in the therapeutic process, and to monitor our own emotional and physical health for potential impact on our clients. We engage in regular evaluation and review of our own clinical work, and learn to give and receive feedback so that we become aware of our limitations and refrain from doing harm. We seek out our own personal therapy and spiritual direction to maintain psychological, spiritual, and relational health.

Consider the following common supervision scenario. Your supervisee starts out strong at his clinical placement and demonstrates good clinical skills. He is intuitive, is in-terpersonally sensitive, and develops excellent therapeutic alliances with his clients. However, as the semester progresses, you begin to notice that he has an increasingly difficult time paying attention in supervision, frequently looks at his phone, and does not follow through on homework or supervision assignments. You view recorded sessions with clients and notice a similar pattern where he seems distracted and impulsive and tends to over-self-disclose. Furthermore, his training site informs you that while he gets along very well with others on the team and shows excellent promise as a family therapist, he is weeks behind in his session notes and often late to meetings or sessions. All the signs are there that this supervisee needs your help in developing professional habits and practices related to temperance, self-awareness, and self-discipline.

In this chapter, temperance is proposed as a foundational character virtue that protects clinicians from inflicting harm on others through cultivating the disciplines of self-awareness, humility, and self-control. In counseling, psychology, and MFT, this professional value is operationalized in the professional standards for reflective practice and self-regulation. Clinical supervision encourages the development of reflective clinicians who utilize feedback and evaluation to grow in their self-awareness and ability to consider the person of the therapist in their clinical work. Supervision models and methods can foster reflective capabilities, mindfulness, and the ability to assess one's effectiveness and impact on others. A Christian integrative approach invites supervisees to practice the spiritual disciplines of examination of conscience and fasting to prayerfully attend to God's formation of our souls and his desire to empower us to order our desires so we can be more effective servants for God's kingdom.

TEMPERANCE: BIBLICAL AND THEOLOGICAL PERSPECTIVES

Temperance is the character strength pertaining to our relationship with the self and how we seek moderation and balance in our thoughts, appetites, needs, longings, and impulses. D. C. Jones (1994) provides this succinct but comprehensive definition: "Temperance is: the discipline of oneself to live a more ordered life for the glory of God and the service of others" (p. 99).

Nearly all biblical categorizations of the virtues include the character strengths of temperance such as self-control, humility, and chastity. Temperance is produced through the Holy Spirit's transforming work in the life of the believer and is identified as a fruit of the spirit in Galatians 5. Temperance is also formed by acts of the will as we respond to God's love with obedience and self-control. Paul uses the metaphor of the athlete in training in 1 Corinthians 9 to admonish believers to practice self-discipline: "Everyone who competes in the games goes into strict training. They do it to get a crown that will not last, but we do it to get a crown that will last forever" (1 Cor 9:25). Descriptions of the effective leader include the virtue of temperance; for example, the character qualities for appointing church elders are described in Titus 1:7-8: "Since an overseer manages God's household, he must be blameless—not overbearing, not quick-tempered, not given to drunkenness, not violent, not pursuing dishonest gain. Rather, he must be hospitable, one who loves what is good, who is self-controlled, upright, holy and disciplined." Proverbs 25:28 provides a vivid picture of the absence of this virtue: "Like a city whose walls are broken through is a person who lacks self-control." Scripture provides a clear description of self-control and obedience as a response to the love of God and as virtues that are embraced both to care for one's own soul and to better serve the church and ultimately the kingdom. Classical definitions describe the virtue of temperance in this way:

> Temperance is the moral virtue that moderates the attraction of pleasures and provides balance in the use of created goods. It ensures the will's mastery over instincts and keeps desires within the limits of what is honorable. The temperate person directs the sensitive appetites toward what is good and maintains a healthy discretion: "Do not follow your inclination and strength, walking according to the desires of your heart." Temperance is often praised in the Old Testament: "Do not follow your base desires, but restrain your appetites." In the New Testament it is called "moderation" or "sobriety." We ought "to live sober, upright, and godly lives in this world." (*Catechism of the Catholic Church*, 2003, para. 1809)

In the *Summa Theologica*, Aquinas includes fasting, chastity, self-control, and humility as subvirtues of temperance. As we as Christians develop "graced habits" related to moderation in the enjoyment of the senses and desires in a way that is consistent with God's divine law, Aquinas suggests that we can experience a sense of balance, harmony, and freedom from distress (Kaczor & Sherman, 2009, p. 298).

Pieper (1966) expands our understanding of temperance by describing this virtue as "selfless self-preservation" (p. 150) in that it requires the Christian to focus on the self in order to preserve and protect an inner ordering of desires and senses against selfishness and hedonism. Pieper suggests that ordering the inner world through fasting, chastity, and self-control is a purification process that leads to the ultimate fruit of purity of heart: "preserving man uninjured and undefiled for God" (p. 205). Temperance is in this way a "prerequisite" for the other virtues in that it provides the moderation and self-discipline necessary for the development of justice, courage, prudence, and the theological virtues to move the Christian toward perfection of character (Pieper, 1966, p. 175).

Wright (2010) also affirms the importance of self-control for cultivation of the Christian virtues. As discussed previously, Wright suggests that living the Christian life after you believe is about a lifelong commitment to character transformation as we grow in Christlikeness for service to his kingdom. Using the metaphor of the garden, Wright says that the fruits of the spirit do not grow healthy and independently without pruning, cultivation, irrigation. He writes, "If the 'fruit' were automatic, why would self-control be needed?" (p. 196). Rather, cultivation of Christian character involves self-control, choice, and self-

discipline acting in partnership with God's transforming work through the Spirit:

> Christian virtue, including the nine-fold fruit of the spirit, is *both* the gift of God *and* the result of the person of faith making conscious decisions to cultivate this way of life and these habits of heart and mind. In technical language, these things are both "infused" and "acquired," though the way we "acquire" them is itself, in that same language, "infused." . . . It is sufficient to note that the varieties of spiritual fruit Paul names, like the Christian virtues, remain both the work of the Spirit and the result of conscious choice and work on the part of the person concerned. (Wright, 2010, p. 197)

Humility, a subvirtue of temperance, has also been proposed as foundational for development of all the virtues as it is characterized by an acknowledgment of our human limitations and absolute dependence on God's power for transformation and change (Bollinger & Hill, 2012). For the Christian, humility is essentially a social virtue that involves seeking unity and the good of others and requires seeing Christ's sacrifice as the ultimate example (Austin, 2015). As Paul admonishes,

> In your relationships with one another, have the same mindset as Christ Jesus:
>
> Who, being in very nature God,
>   did not consider equality with God
>   something to be used to his own
>   advantage;
> rather, he made himself nothing
>   by taking the very nature of a servant,
>   being made in human likeness.
> And being found in appearance as a man,
>   he humbled himself
>   by becoming obedient to death—
>   even death on a cross! (Phil. 2:5-8)

The Christian virtue of temperance, then, involves the practices of self-discipline, self-control, and humility that enable believers to live in moderation and balance so that we are best able to love God and serve others. Let us examine psychological perspectives on temperance, specifically the subvirtues of self-control and humility.

TEMPERANCE: PSYCHOLOGICAL PERSPECTIVES

Positive psychologists define the character strength of temperance as a collection of traits that keep individuals from excessive behaviors and emotions and involve self-restraint for one's own benefit and for the good of others. Such traits include forgiveness, mercy, humility, modesty, prudence, and self-regulation. Self-regulation "refers to how a person exerts control over his or her own responses so as to pursue goals and live up to standards" (Peterson & Seligman, 2004, p. 500). While the terms *self-regulation* and *self-control* are often used interchangeably in the virtue literature, self-control is considered a type of self-regulation involving emotional or behavioral impulse control. Social scientists suggest that self-control is not just *a* virtue but *the* primary virtue or "internal restraining mechanism" that allows individuals to control their impulses and desires for the good of society:

> From the community's perspective . . . virtue consists of performing socially desirable actions. For the self, however, the intentions rather than the actions and outcomes are crucial, and so moral self-judgment may proceed quite differently than moral judgment of others. Thus, in terms of the inner personality processes, virtue consists of having the intention to carry out desirable actions as well as having the wherewithal to do so. The wherewithal . . . depends heavily on self-control. (Baumeister & Exline, 1999, p. 1170)

Psychologically, self-regulation is the process pertaining to the management of one's thoughts, emotions, and behaviors in a way that is consistent with personal and societal values and goals. The process of self-regulation includes the ability to exercise self-awareness and to determine the appropriate response in a given situation as one observes the social norms, expectations, and external threats, including the threat of social exclusion (Heatherton, 2011). Theorists have proposed that self-regulation of behavior and affect occurs as individuals self-correct their behavior and emotions on an ongoing basis in pursuit of personal goals; thus self-regulation operates through a "feedback loop" (Carver & Scheier, 2011). Cognitively, the prefrontal cortex is responsible for executive functions including self-control, and research suggests that the same neurological processes are involved in the self-regulation of emotions, thoughts, and behaviors (Heatherton, 2011). Studies have found that religious individuals exhibit a high degree of self-control (McCullough & Willoughby, 2009), particularly in situations requiring sustained self-regulating efforts, which has led researchers to conclude, "When the going gets tough, the religious self-regulate" (Watterson & Giesler, 2012, p. 202). It is hypothesized that religion contributes to self-control through providing clear moral standards, motivation, and resources for managing "sinful urges" (Baumeister & Zell, 2013). However, psychological motivation for self-control and religious motivation differ significantly when it comes to telos. Bland (2008) describes the difference in this way:

Consequently, while psychologists may talk of self-control being a master virtue, the psychological definition of virtue is only distantly related to religious conceptualizations of self-control which are embedded within deontological or virtue ethics. Simply put, one can practice self-control without attaining the virtue of temperance. In religious worldviews self-control acts can be virtuous in and of themselves (deontological ethics) or because they lead to a good and meaningful life (virtue ethics). (pp. 11-12)

From a religious worldview, Bland makes the important point that self-control is pursued for the love of God and neighbor and not as an end it itself.

How does the development of self-regulation and self-control occur? Similar to other virtues, the development of self-regulation skills and abilities is influenced by multiple factors including the interaction between biological factors, early attachment experiences, temperament, modeling, and parenting practices (Cook & Cook, 2009). Social scientists have proposed a *muscle model* to understand the development of self-control as a personality characteristic and virtue (Baumeister & Exline, 1999; Baumeister, Vohs, & Tice, 2007). Much like the development of physical strength through exercise, this model proposes that self-control is a resource that becomes depleted with short-term use but can be developed through regular practice, which strengthens the capacity for self-restraint in future events. Research has demonstrated that higher self-control as a character trait correlates with a number of markers of life success including better relationships and social skills, less psychopathology, and better grade point average (Tangney, Baumeister, & Boone, 2004).

The virtue of humility has been widely researched in the social sciences and has important implications for supervision and clinical effectiveness. Humility is defined as "the willingness to see the self accurately and propensity to put oneself in perspective" (Bollinger & Hill, 2012, p. 32). As a character trait, it also includes the willingness to recognize one's errors and limits, nondefensiveness, and low self-focus (Tangney, 2000). However, a low self-focus alone is insufficient for the virtue of humility, which also requires a *high other-focus* on the needs, concerns, and well-being of others (Nadelhoffer & Wright, 2017). Research has found humility to be associated with several other prosocial traits including empathy, forgiveness, and warmth (Davis et al., 2011), cultural humility (Hook, Davis, Owen, Worthington, & Utsey, 2013), and strong relationship bonds and social acceptance (Davis et al., 2013). The important role of humility in facilitating a more accurate view of ourselves in relationship to others has led researchers to conclude that "humility is necessary in order for the full development of other virtues to occur" (Nadelhoffer & Wright, 2017, p. 329).

In counseling, psychology, and marriage and family therapy, there has been a growing interest in the study of humility as a character strength linked to professional competence and effectiveness. A meta-analysis of studies of master therapists from multiple countries identified humility as a characteristic of clinicians who were thought to be especially effective in their practice of counseling and psychotherapy (Jennings et al., 2016). Therapists evidencing this character trait were described as self-aware of their limitations and mistakes and willing to use this awareness as a stimulus for growth. Humility in clinical practice was observed as an "other-oriented" attitude. For example, therapists evidencing this character trait viewed the client as the "hero" in the change process, rather than the therapist's own skill and effectiveness. *Clinical humility* is a term used to describe the virtue of humility in a therapeutic context. Paine, Sandage, Rupert, Devor, and Bronstein (2015) offer the following definition:

> It is the evolving inclination toward accurate self-assessment, recognition of limits, the regulation of self-centered emotions, and the cultivation of other-centered emotions in a clinical setting. Like other virtues, humility is a term in reference to what sort of person the clinician is becoming rather than what skills they are proficient in. Becoming encompasses who the clinician already is, on-going organic developmental processes, and the intentional orientation toward growth. (p. 11)

The authors propose cultivating clinical humility as a potential protective factor against professional burnout, as humble and aware clinicians are more likely to recognize their limits and seek supervision and support.

Humility is as an essential trait for supervisors and particularly important for repairing the inevitable relationship ruptures that occur in the supervision process related to differing expectations and role conflicts (Watkins, Hook, Ramacker, & Ramos, 2016). Supervisors who practice humility demonstrate openness to self-reflection on the supervisory experience, recognize their mistakes, and are motivated to initiate relational repairs, all because they value the supervisory relationship and even privilege the perspectives and experiences of the supervisee through adopting an other-orientation (Watkins et al., pp. 28-30). It is no surprise that greater clinical experience leads to a larger measure of humility, as clinicians develop a deeper sense of how little we know and how much there is still to learn.

TEMPERANCE, NONMALEFICENCE, AND REFLECTIVE PRACTICE: DO NO HARM

Developing the virtue of temperance, as evidenced by self-regulation, self-awareness, and humility, is essential for upholding the ethical mandate of nonmaleficence. This ethical commitment requires awareness and monitoring of the clinician's own emotional and physical health for potential impact on professional competence. The APA ethical code states, "Psychologists strive to be aware of the possible effect of their own physical and mental health on their ability to help those with whom they work" (American Psychological Association [APA], 2010). The code later specifies that psychologists are ethically responsible for maintaining awareness of personal problems and conflicts that may negatively affect the pro-vision of competent service and should suspend professional duties and seek consultation when such personal problems occur. Similarly, the ACA ethics code includes nonmaleficence as a core ethical principle and describes the counselor's responsibility to self-monitor for physical, emotional, or mental impairments (American Counseling Association [ACA], 2014). Counselors are required to refrain from providing services in the event of impairment that could cause harm, and also to seek consultation and assistance. The ACA ethics code also includes the admonition for counselors to assist colleagues in recognition of areas of impairment. The ethical codes recognize that self-awareness, self-monitoring, and self-control are essential to protecting the public from harm and ensuring the integrity and effectiveness of the mental health professional.

Counselors, psychologists, and MFTs demonstrate temperance and avoid harm to others through a commitment to *reflective practice*. The ability to reflect, assess, and monitor oneself is a prerequisite characteristic of clinicians and foundational for lifelong professional effectiveness. Reflective practice is also an approach to learning that encourages self-reflection on experiences as a primary means of professional learning and development. Originally developed in the field of education, reflective practice has found applications in education, business, and the health professions (Schön, 1987). In the training of mental health professionals, the development of self-reflection and self-awareness is identified as a benchmark competency. Psychologists in training are required to demonstrate reflective practice as a component of professionalism as defined in this way: "Practice conducted with personal and professional self-awareness and reflection; with awareness of competencies; with appropriate self-care" (APA, 2011). Benchmarks are considered developmentally with specific competencies for different levels of training. To demonstrate readiness to enter into independent practice, psychologists should demonstrate the following self-reflection/awareness competencies:

- Reflective Practice: Demonstrates reflectivity both during and after professional activity; acts upon reflection; uses self as a therapeutic tool
- Self-Assessment: Accurately self-assesses competence in all competency domains; integrates self-assessment in practice; recognizes limits of knowledge/skills and

acts to address them; has extended plan to enhance knowledge/skills

- Self-Care (attention to personal health and well-being to assure effective professional functioning): Self-monitors issues related to self-care and promptly intervenes when disruptions occur
- Participation in Supervision Process: Independently seeks supervision when needed (APA, 2011)

It is important to note that reflective practice competencies include a commitment from clinicians to practice self-care to ensure personal well-being. Ideally, self-awareness leads to better self-care and overall functioning, which in turn promotes self-regulation and minimizes harm to others.

MFT core competencies include the expectation that clinicians will "monitor personal reactions to clients and treatment process, especially in terms of therapeutic behavior, relationship with clients, process for explaining procedures, and outcomes"; in addition, MFTs in training must be able to "consult with peers and/or supervisors if personal issues, attitudes, or beliefs threaten to adversely impact clinical work" (American Association for Marriage and Family Therapy [AAMFT], 2004, p. 6). Likewise, CACREP standards require graduate programs to provide students with "strategies for personal and professional self-evaluation and implications for practice" and "self-care strategies appropriate to the counselor role" (Council for Accreditation of Counseling and Related Educational Programs, 2016). Across the ethical codes, we see a recognition of the importance of self-regulation and self-monitoring for optimal professional functioning.

Reflective practice is particularly important to foster through the supervision process as students enter into their practicum experiences with real clients. Supervisees need to develop the ability to self-reflect during their clinical interactions and to be aware of their thoughts and emotional reactions to clients to avoid doing harm. Supervision also facilitates trainee self-reflection on clinical activities already performed through review of taped sessions and consideration of client outcome data. Supervision is a critically important modality for helping supervisees reflect on their clinical experiences, accurately assess their skills and areas of needed growth, and monitor their re-

actions to clients. In fact, Bernard and Goodyear (2014) assert that "encouraging reflective practice is an overriding supervision goal" (p. 166). Supervisees need to develop professional habits consistent with reflective practice to ensure that they will do no harm as they become increasingly independent in their professional work. We develop the virtue of temperance in supervisees when we utilize supervision models and methods to foster greater capacities for self-evaluation and self-awareness, which lead to professional humility and recognition of one's limits.

SUPERVISION MODELS AND METHODS FOR FOSTERING REFLECTIVE PRACTICE

Clinical supervision at its best provides supervisees with multiple opportunities to assess, reflect, and monitor their thoughts, feelings, and behaviors in the context of clinical practice. Through formative and summative evaluation, supervisees gain a realistic assessment of areas of needed growth and also their developing competencies. Clinical supervision provides a context for developing self-observation and self-supervision skills through live observation, review of audio or videotaped sessions, and process notes. Supervision promotes the development of habits and skills related to "reflection in action" (Schön, 1987) as supervisees develop capacities for mindfulness of their feelings and reactions to clients during sessions so they can respond appropriately in ways that are facilitative of the therapeutic process. Through the development of self-reflective capacities, supervisees also have the opportunity to develop character strengths of humility and modesty as they recognize their need for supervision and consultation and learn to openly seek help for their areas of

needed growth. Within the context of a safe and secure supervision alliance, supervisees can learn to offer themselves self-compassion and the same patience, hope, and empathy that they offer to clients.

Reflective practice can be incorporated into all aspects of the supervision process. Curtis, Elkins, Duran, and Venta (2016) recommend a developmental approach that provides scaffolding for the clinician in training as they grow in reflective capabilities utilizing various supervision modalities including individual, group, co-therapy, and live supervision. In contrast to the medical model that focuses on precision of technique in fostering reflective practice, mental health professionals also need to develop capacities to reflect on process: "Moving away from the medical model, there is a need to establish a climate of reflective practices via supervisor modeling, provision of observational and/or direct feedback, encouragement, and prompting of critical thinking, and self-reflection of learning clinicians" (Curtis et al., 2016, p. 134). Reflective practices are facilitated in all stages of the learning process as supervisors incorporate questions designed to promote self-awareness, critical thinking, and self-evaluation.

In a similar way, the Integrative Developmental Model (IDM) discussed in chapter four includes explicit attention to self-other awareness in supervisee development (Stoltenberg, Bailey, Cruzan, Hart, & Ukuku, 2014). The IDM describes supervisee progression from a primary focus on self and one's own performance during the first level of professional development toward an increased focus on the client and a capacity for reflection and self-assessment as the supervisee progresses (Stoltenberg et al., 2014). Supervision models and methods that develop reflective practice should be implemented with these developmental sensitivities in mind.

In this section, we examine models of supervision and supervision best practices that foster the development of essential reflective capacities in supervisees.

"Person of the Therapist" Supervision in MFT

MFTs have long advocated for the importance of self-of-the-therapist work as part of the clinical process. Perhaps no other MFT has been a stronger advocate of this approach than Harry Aponte, who asserts, "All therapy is a marriage of the technical with the personal" (Aponte et al., 2009, p. 395). Aponte proposes an approach to the use of self in therapy that aims to foster the ability of the therapist to be a "wounded healer" who is aware of personal issues and themes that may affect clinical work. In contrast to models that hold that clinicians must first resolve personal issues before they can be effective, Aponte's Person of the Therapist Training (POTT) model encourages clini-

cians to identify and address personal issues as "signature themes" that likely affect their clinical work and professional practice. Training and supervision facilitate the therapist's ability to recognize and make use of the signature theme as a valuable and integrated component of their clinical work. Aponte writes:

> We are speaking here of the pursuit of a sophisticated level of mastery of self within the therapeutic relationship and technical process. Yes, this mastery aspires for greater freedom from the restrictiveness of our personal issues; yes, greater emotional and cultural/spiritual self-awareness; but also an elevated level of skill in the conscious and intentional use of the self within the philosophy and technical toolbox of our models. Training and supervision in this use of self, both from emotional and cultural/spiritual perspectives, are lagging. How to use the self in therapy needs conceptual clarity and systematic methodology. (Aponte, 2009, p. 397)

The POTT model includes three components. First, clinicians in training are encouraged to engage in a process of self-assessment and identification of their signature theme(s). Second, therapists learn to engage in self-reflection and observation during clinical encounters. Third, therapists are trained to use self-of-the-therapist knowledge and experience in all aspects of clinical practice including developing a therapeutic alliance, assessment, case conceptualization, and intervention. The Person-of-the-Therapist Supervision Instrument can be utilized in the supervision and training process. It poses a series of questions about the interaction between clinical material and supervisees' personal reactions, values, and meanings (Aponte & Carlsen, 2009). The POTT model is intended for use with all theoretical orientations as a way of improving self-of-the-therapist competency in clinical practice.

As supervisees grow in their ability to self-assess, they are one step closer to developing *self-supervision* competencies, which, according to Todd and Storm (2014), is the "universal goal of supervision" (p. 152). Self-supervision competencies include the ability to self-monitor, then to evaluate one's skill in light of an "idealized norm" (Todd & Storm, 2014, p. 152), and finally to implement changes toward achieving this idealized norm in regard to a therapeutic skill or ability. Todd and Storm suggest that supervisors should be constantly focused on facilitating self-efficacy through fostering self-assessment, helping supervisees develop a solid theoretical orientation, and teaching supervisees how to access needed resources for continued development. Supervisors can encourage the practice of "positive self-monitoring" (Storm, 1997) to combat the often self-critical focus of assessing one's work. Through positive self-monitoring, supervisees learn to identify areas of strength resulting in successful therapeutic habits and skills that bear repeating.

Reflective Practice in CBT Supervision: Incorporating Mindfulness Meditation

The cognitive-behavioral therapy (CBT) tradition places a high value on assessment of effectiveness in clinical practice. Although *reflective practice* is a relatively recent term used in CBT training and supervision, it can be argued that "for CBT therapists, the very act of evaluative research, and use of measurement in individual therapy, is an intrinsically reflective practice" (Bennett-Levy, Thwaites, Chaddock, & Davis, 2009, p. 117). One reflective practice commonly used in CBT training is termed "self-practice/self-reflection" (SP/SR). SP/SR involves practicing a CBT in-tervention on oneself, either individually or in training dyads, and then engaging in structured reflection of the impact and personal experience of the intervention (Bennett-Levy et al., 2009). This training tool is "designed to give CBT therapists a personal therapy-like experience through the practicing of CBT techniques on the self, along with the experience of reflecting on and integrating what has been learnt during the self-practice" (Bennett-Levy et al., 2009, p. 122). Through use of SP/SR, trainees have the opportunity to engage in experiential learning and self-reflection on specific CBT techniques and consider implications for clinical practice.

The use of self-practice has been particularly evident in training supervisees to use third-wave CBT techniques that incorporate mindfulness-based practices to aid in the development of self-awareness and self-regulatory capacities. A growing body of research supports the benefits of incorporating mindfulness meditation practices into therapist training and supervision. Davis and Hayes (2011) define mindfulness as "a moment-to-moment awareness of one's experience without judgment" (p. 198). The authors suggest four outcomes of mindfulness-based practices with therapist trainees: increased empathy, increased self-compassion, improved clinical skills, and improved coping with anxiety and stress. Davis and Hayes recommend specific strategies for incorporating mindfulness-based practices to improve therapist functioning in each of these areas. For example, one exercise encourages trainees to practice sitting in silence in dyads, focusing their attention on being present with the other person, and paying attention to their breathing when attention begins to wander (Davis & Hayes, 2011, p. 202).

Mindfulness meditation has been identified as an important practice in training MFTs to develop the important skill of "therapeutic presence" that is essential to the development of a strong therapeutic alliance (McCollum & Gehart, 2010). The authors describe specific strategies for incorporating mindfulness training into the curriculum in their MFT program. For example, therapists in training are encouraged to practice 5-10 minutes of daily mindfulness meditation practices of their choice (spiritual or nonspiritual) during their graduate training and then participate in guided reflection on the personal and professional impact through journaling. Suggestions for incorporating mindfulness meditation into clinical supervision include adopting a "down to earth" style that embraces imperfections and humor in the learning process. In addition, it is important for supervisors and educators to link the practice of mindfulness meditation to specific educational outcomes—for example, improving therapeutic presence and in-session reflective capacities (McCollum & Gehart, 2010).

Mindfulness meditation can be beneficially practiced in the context of group supervision. Safran, Muran, Stevens, and Rothman (2008) recommend starting group supervision sessions with a mindfulness exercise, as this "can help supervisees to develop an awareness of, and openness to, their own experience rather than focus on their intellectual understanding" (p. 144). Using breathing exercises, attending to bodily sensations, and so on "set the tone for each session by focusing trainees' awareness on the present and helping them adopt a sense of nonjudgmental awareness of their own sensory and emotional states" (Safran et al.,

2008, p. 145). Group supervision provides a helpful context for supervisees to raise questions, personal reactions, and challenges they experience with the practice of mindfulness, and supervisors can normalize the difficulties that some trainees will encounter as they attempt a practice that may be new and unfamiliar to them (and one that may be especially challenging for multitasking graduate students).

Psychodynamic Supervision and Reflective Capabilities

Relational psychodynamic supervision approaches emphasize self-reflective capacities as a core competency and encourage the development of a "participant-observational" stance in the therapeutic process. Sarnat (2010) defines this capacity as follows: "Self-reflection competence requires a highly-developed capacity to bear, observe, think about, and make psychotherapeutic use of one's own emotional, bodily, and fantasy experiences when in interaction with a client" (p. 23). The psychodynamic clinician develops the important capacity to remain emotionally engaged with the client while at the same time observing and reflecting on the relational dynamics between client and therapist, what these dynamics might mean, and how to best respond therapeutically. Because the relationship is the central vehicle for healing in psychodynamic psychotherapy, self-assessment and reflective capacities are fundamental competencies. Similarly, the supervisory relationship becomes an integral component of the learning process as supervisor and supervisee pay attention to the needs, feelings, and thoughts that arise in the interaction. Supervisors provide a safe holding environment for the containment of the supervisee's emotional states and responses to clients, and this provides the context for facilitating self-assessment and reflection:

> The implication of this research is that the atmosphere one creates in the supervisory hour—an atmosphere of spaciousness, emotional receptivity, and calmness—can have a profound impact on the supervisee's ability to feel secure in supervision, to settle down emotionally, and to think and feel deeply and creatively. This then translates into the supervisee's increased ability to offer both secure attachment and a containing, analytic attitude to his patients, essential capacities for sustaining the participant observational frame that Tuckett (2005) described as a primary psychoanalytic competency. (Sarnat, 2012, p. 157)

In psychodynamic supervision, then, the supervisor adopts an analytic stance parallel to the attitude that the supervisee is being encouraged to learn: "The relational supervisor uses tensions in the supervisory relationship as opportunities to give the supervisee a first-hand experience of how one works in treatment" (Sarnat, 2012, p. 154). Sarnat (2012) provides an example of offering an interpretation to a supervisee to get her unstuck from a critical and negative transference with the supervisor (similar to her parents), which then allowed the supervisee to manage self-critical attitudes that would arise during interactions with the client. She underscores that the use of analytic interventions in supervision must always be done with the supervisory task in mind (i.e., the client and training goals), rather than pursuing details about the supervisee's personal history and underlying issues, consistent with ethical guidelines for supervision.

Facilitating Reflective Practice Through Supervision Formats

Supervision best practices require a review of the supervisee's actual clinical work. The following three formats are commonly utilized to facilitate reflective practice.

Review of recorded sessions. Thoughtful use of audio or videotaped sessions in supervision is an essential practice for the development of an accurate assessment of the clinician's developing skills, abilities, and the impact of clinical interventions on the client. In reviewing their own recorded sessions, supervisees are encouraged to develop an "observational stance" toward their clinical work where they can assess their clinical effectiveness, behaviors, reactions, and interpersonal dynamics in a given therapeutic interaction (Kagan, 1984). Although review of recorded sessions can be initially anxiety provoking for supervisees, the practice is ranked as one of the most preferred and valuable formats for supervision (Goodyear & Nelson, 1997), with live supervision and co-therapy with supervisors as close seconds.

Providing structure for video review helps maximize learning and can reduce supervisee anxiety. Supervisors should always have a teaching goal in mind to guide their choice of how to use segments of recorded sessions (Bernard & Goodyear, 2014). Consider the following practices for use of recordings in supervision to facilitate reflective practice:

- The supervisor provides guidance on approaching clients about recording sessions, obtaining informed consent, and protecting confidentiality of recordings. It may be helpful to practice this by role-playing in individual or group supervision.

- Supervisees review their recording before supervision and provide a self-assessment of strengths and areas for growth. Research suggests this practice of self-critique before supervisor review can decrease defensiveness to feedback (Sobell, Manor, Sobell, & Dum, 2008). Supervisees can use a structured evaluation tool such as the Counseling Skills Scale (CSS) to evaluate the session and review their assessment in supervision.

- Supervisees are asked to choose a segment of a recorded session to view together in supervision that is consistent with a supervision goal or theme (Bernard & Goodyear, 2014). For example, a supervisee may be instructed to choose a part of a session where they felt stuck or confused, where they implemented a specific technique, or where a particular interpersonal or process issue is illustrated.

- Recorded sessions are reviewed together in supervision, and the recording is paused at various points to allow exploration of the supervisee's thoughts, emotions, and reactions during the session. Supervisors adopt the role of facilitator rather than teacher by posing exploratory questions designed to encourage self-reflection. For example, a supervisor may ask the supervisee what they were thinking or feeling at a given moment in the session, what their experience was of the interpersonal dynamics with the client, or what they wish they had done or said in the session. Kagan's (1980) Interpersonal Process Recall provides a structured supervision approach with supervisor leads and questions to facilitate exploration of the relational component of the session.

- Supervisors may also find it beneficial to periodically review an entire assessment or therapy session to gain an overall sense of the supervisee's development of clinical skills and their use of the therapy hour.

Co-therapy with supervisor. One supervision method sometimes used to gradually introduce supervisees to clinical experience is pairing a supervisee as a co-therapist with the supervisor or another experienced clinician. Supervisees are invited to pay attention to the clinical process as well as their own reactions and experience, and then gradually participate as they develop comfort and greater expertise. Reflecting on the shared experience of the session can provide rich opportunities for the supervisor to "think out loud" about their own internal process during the session, to model reflection in action, and to demonstrate self-evaluation of effectiveness of therapeutic interventions.

Live supervision. A common practice in MFT supervision, live supervision involves trainees conducting assessment or therapy with a supervisor and team observing via video or one-way mirror. Traditionally, supervisors have the option to call in with input during the session, or to speak to the supervisee using a "bug in the ear" method to provide coaching during the session. Alternatively, supervisees can take a break mid-session to check in with the reflecting team for feedback. To promote optimal self-reflection and efficacy, a supervisor might opt for a less directive approach ("do this") and pose questions to stimulate critical thinking and self-reflection ("What did you notice about the client's reaction to your intervention?"). An explicit focus on the development of reflective practice skills will ultimately lead to greater self-efficacy and self-supervision skills toward lifelong learning.

Developing Accurate Self-Appraisal Through Formative and Summative Evaluation

Evaluation has been called the "nucleus" of clinical supervision (Bernard & Goodyear, 2014, p. 222); however, it is the component of the supervision experience that creates the most anxiety and avoidance for both supervisors and supervisees. Without accurate and well-delivered feedback, however, supervisees are left without a realistic assessment of their competence, emerging strengths, and areas for growth. Chapter three discussed the importance of informed consent and including the evaluation tools and procedures as part of the supervision contract with the goal of transparent power. Supervisees should know ahead of time the areas that will be evaluated, criteria for evaluation, how often evaluation will occur, and who will see the evaluation.

Formative feedback occurs throughout the supervision process to "assist in skill refinement and identification of personal issues that may be impeding clinical practice" (Falender & Shafranske, 2004, p. 204). It includes ongoing feedback on the supervisee's progress toward goals and competencies and ideally should be tied to the training contract. Formative feedback can be reflective, corrective, and evaluative and can identify areas of emerging strength as well as areas of concern to the supervisor. Learning the art of giving accurate and direct feedback in a formative way that supervisees can receive is a critical task for supervisors. Consider the following evaluation tips:

- Consider starting and ending your evaluation with an affirmation of strengths. Titrate amount and type of feedback so your supervisee is able to process effectively.

- Develop a structure for your feedback. For example, after every video review, both supervisor and supervisee identify one strength and one area for growth.

- Use a rating form or standardized assessment tool for each session, and track progress over time.

- Make use of multiple sources of feedback and assessment of clinical effectiveness including client outcomes, video review, live observation, and process notes.

Summative feedback involves a more formal evaluation of the major areas of clinical competence. For supervision in an academic setting, programs usually provide a specific evaluation form tied to program goals and desired competencies as some competencies may be discipline specific (e.g., in MFT, the evaluation of supervisees' ability to formulate cases from a systemic and relational theoretical foundation). A number of excellent evaluation tools are available for use by supervisors and can be found in the appendixes of the major textbooks on clinical supervision (for a good review of evaluation tools, see Watkins & Milne, 2014, chapters 16–22). One rule of thumb that can be helpful is to avoid rating a supervisee as subpar on any competency area that has not already been discussed in supervision. In other words, the evaluation should not be used as a time to overwhelm the supervisee with feedback the supervisor has neglected to raise. This does a disservice to the supervisee and will likely put a strain on the supervision alliance.

Supervisees should also have the opportunity to evaluate the supervision experience and provide feedback to the supervisor about areas for improvement. Helpful evaluation forms have been developed for this purpose, for example, the Supervisee Satisfaction Questionnaire (Ladany, Hill, Corbett, & Nutt, 1996). Ideally, supervisors will model non-defensive and gracious acceptance of feedback that is used to develop greater self-awareness and effectiveness.

Using Outcome Assessment with Clients in Supervision

The collection and utilization of outcome assessment data from clients is important in assessing clinical effectiveness and therapeutic alliance and contributes to accurate self-evaluation and improved treatment. A number of well-researched, brief measures are available to use with clients, and supervisees should first check with their agencies to see if a format is preferred. MFT educators Sparks, Kisler, Adams, and Blumen (2011) recommend that supervisors should create a "feedback-rich" environment throughout the clinical training process from pre-practicum role-playing to actual clinical work where outcome assessment tools are utilized and incorporated into the therapeutic process. In this way, clinicians in training become increasingly comfortable and confident with use of client feedback to strengthen therapeutic alliance and improve clinical effectiveness. Incorporating outcome assessment into the supervision process ensures that clinicians develop good professional habits of not relying solely on their own self-evaluation but routinely seeking feedback from clients regarding clinical effectiveness. This goes a long way toward effective self-supervision as a lifelong practice.

Conclusion

Clinical supervision encourages supervisees to develop the character strength of temperance through implementing models and interventions that develop a greater awareness of self-of-the-therapist issues and a more accurate assessment of their personal and professional functioning through a variety of supervision formats and evaluation practices. Supervision fosters a commitment to reflective practices as a necessary and valuable professional endeavor throughout the career of a mental health professional.

A CHRISTIAN INTEGRATIVE APPROACH: ORDERING OUR PROFESSIONAL LIVES FOR SERVICE OF GOD AND OTHERS

A Christian integrative approach to clinical supervision embraces the opportunity to utilize supervision practices that foster temperance through reflective practice, attention to the person of the therapist, self-control, and accurate self-assessment. This approach adds "something more" to the supervision process in two important ways. First, it considers the ultimate aims of such endeavors less as an end in themselves (i.e., becoming a self-disciplined and reflective clinician) and more as an ethic for Christian life and vocation with the aim of loving God and neighbor. Second, a Christian integrative supervision approach views growth in temperance as both an act of the will and also a fruit of the Spirit, as God transforms us into Christlikeness through the power of his Spirit. From a theological perspective, our efforts toward self-control are both motivated and empowered by God as we practice obedience to him out of love and for love. Practicing self-control as a virtue is made possible through the power of the Holy Spirit and also as an act of our will. A Christian integrative perspective asserts, "Christianity sees the power of God operating in and through behavioral and psychological processes; to talk about self-control apart from divine influence is to sector the person from his or her inescapable spiritual union with God and his redemptive purposes" (Bland, 2008, p. 13).

Clinical supervisors have a spiritual mentoring responsibility as we view our responsibilities as an opportunity to be a part of God's formational work in the life of our supervisees. For example, we can approach the evaluation process as a time for the Spirit to shed light on areas of personal and professional formation where God may already be at work. We can do this with a deep humility and awareness of our own areas of weakness and need for God's transforming work in our own lives.

Integrating Personal, Professional, and Spiritual Self-Assessment and Growth

As supervisees become aware of the personal issues that limit their effectiveness as clinicians, a Christian integrative perspective on professional development can incorporate personal, spiritual, and professional pathways to growth. Here we have the opportunity to incorporate the Christian traditions of self-examination, contemplative prayer, and spiritual disciplines into clinical supervision as "graced habits" that will lead to personal and professional growth. We remind our supervisees that as Christians we are not left on our own to form our character, but rather we rely on God's transforming power as he sanctifies us in love for more effective service to his kingdom. While supervisors are not spiritual directors, we can listen prayerfully for areas of needed growth and assist supervisees in constructing a professional development plan that incorporates personal, professional, and spiritual strategies

for change. We can help supervisees recognize the importance of self-understanding and discipline both as fruits of the Spirit and as professional core values.

The clinical supervision approaches discussed above can be integrated with a Christian worldview and practices to incorporate the spiritual aspect of the person of the therapist into the process of self-assessment and growth. The use of mindfulness meditation practices in clinical supervision can be integrated with Christian spiritual disciplines to help clinicians be present to clients, themselves, and God during clinical work. Supervisors can offer an appraisal of mindfulness from a Christian worldview. Tan (2011a) emphasizes that the here-and-now emphasis of mindfulness must be balanced with the Christian hope of our future with Christ in eternity. Tan writes, "A Christian approach to mindfulness and acceptance-based CBT can use some of these techniques but will contextualize them within a Christian contemplative tradition of learning to be mindful of the sacrament or sacredness of the present moment, and surrendering to God and His will" (p. 246). Students anxious about using meditation can benefit from exploring the ancient contemplative prayer practices of the Christian church, as we considered in chapter three. The purpose of a meditative practice for the Christian is prayerful, moment-by-moment connection with the living God, through faith, as a real and vibrant presence in our lives.

Transformational Psychology

Christian integrative approaches to counseling, psychology, and marriage and family therapy emphasize the person of the therapist as an important component of a faith-informed approach to clinical work. In fact, the clinician's personal spirituality is considered a core integration competency for Christian clinicians as well as a developmental integration task (Gingrich & Worthington, 2007). This is perhaps nowhere better articulated than in Coe and Hall's (2010) transformational psychology approach to integrating faith and psychology. This approach to integration moves beyond theoretical conceptualizations and seeks to anchor the process of integrative psychology, both clinical and research, in the person of the psychologist:

> We want to build a whole theory of relating psychology to Christianity that is grounded in the person and process of doing a holistic psychology in the Spirit. In the first place, we will argue that the character of the person or psychologist grounds, preserves and guards the process and product of science and psychology insofar as the quality of the character determines the degree to which one will be honest and open to what is real and true, without need for distortion. This honesty and courage are crucial to the scientific enterprise. This focus on the person will also keep the Christian psychologist honest to do psychology anew in God, and not merely rely upon prior traditions. . . . We believe the *whole* enterprise of psychology and science is built on this principle. (Coe & Hall, 2010, pp. 71-72)

The authors assert that for the Christian psychologist, practicing the spiritual disciplines and being transformed by the Spirit toward the ultimate purpose of loving God and neighbor are "essential to doing good science and psychology" (p. 91) because this allows the psychologist to apprehend reality more accurately, honestly, and openly.

While Coe and Hall's integrative approach focuses primarily on scientific inquiry, it follows that clinical supervision informed by transformational psychology would place the character of the supervisor and supervisee (and the relationship) at the heart of the supervision endeavor as essential to the methodology and outcome. Being transformed by the Spirit is vital for supervisors seeking to accurately discern supervisee personal and professional needs and for the provision of wise guidance. The supervision experience is transformed when both supervisor and supervisee are seeking to ground themselves in Christlike character qualities of faith, hope, and love.

Humility as a Desired Outcome

A Christian integrative approach views true humility as one of the desired outcomes of practicing the virtue of temperance. As we see ourselves and others more honestly and accurately, we become more aware of our deep need for God and for Christian community. This becomes the foundation for a commitment to lifelong habits of temperance that require constant recognition of our need for growth and change.

One way to provide supervisees with a hopeful vision for humility is through examining Jesus' model of servant leadership and its relevance for Christian vocation in the mental health professions. Nowhere is this better articulated than in Henri Nouwen's thoughtful book *In the Name of Jesus* (1989). Nouwen describes the three great spiritual risks of leadership as they are reflected in the temptations of Jesus: the desire to be relevant, the need to be popular, and the enticement of power. He challenges Christians in leadership positions to commit to the spiritual disciplines of contemplative prayer, confession and forgiveness, and theological study as practices that underscore our humble dependence on God and on Christian community for life and hope.

Nouwen summarizes this radically different view of Christian leadership in this way:

> Jesus sends us out to be shepherds, and Jesus promises a life in which we increasingly have to stretch out our hands and be led to places where we would rather not go. He asks us to move from a concern for relevance to a life of prayer, from worries about popularity to communal and mutual ministry and from a leadership built on power to a leadership in which we critically discern where God is leading us and our people. . . . I leave you with the image of the leader with outstretched hands, who chooses a life of downward mobility. It is the image of the praying leader, the vulnerable leader, and the trusting leader. (pp. 91-93)

Reading Nouwen's book together as a devotional practice with supervisees can provide a springboard for discussions about humility and Christian vocation. As supervisors, we have an important role to play in helping the next generation of supervisors and Christian mental health leaders pursue humility as a desired outcome for life and vocation.

SPIRITUAL DISCIPLINES FOR THE FORMATION OF TEMPERANCE: INDIVIDUAL AND COMMUNITY PRACTICES

Essentially, all individual and community spiritual practices contribute to the development of the personal and professional life that is ordered for the service of God and neighbor. Regular church attendance, disciplines of prayer, and Scripture study plans all contribute to the strengthening of the "moral muscle" of self-control and self-discipline. However, two spiritual disciplines in particular are especially relevant for inviting God's transforming work in the areas of self-awareness and self-control toward the goal of godly humility. Both can be integrated well into the clinical supervision process as a means of personal and professional character formation.

The Examen

The prayer of the examen is a spiritual practice that involves disciplined and prayerful reflection on the events of the day to consider how God is at work within us. Saint Ignatius proposed this as an essential spiritual exercise and admonished believers to pay attention to experiences of *consolation*, where one feels alive to the love of God and others, as well as *desolation*, where the experience is one of distance from God, self, and others (Gallagher, 2006). Through regular practice of the examen, we can begin to see the patterns of our lives that lead us toward life and spiritual health, as well as those patterns that lead us away. Manney (2011) offers the examen prayer in a nutshell:

1. Ask God for light.
I want to look at my day with God's eyes, not merely my own.

2. Give thanks.
The day I have just lived is a gift from God. Be grateful for it.

3. Review the day.
I carefully look back on the day just completed, being guided by the Holy Spirit.

4. Face your shortcomings.
I face up to what is wrong—in my life and in me.

5. Look toward the day to come.
I ask where I need God in the day to come. (p. 1)

Foster (1992) suggests that the prayer of the examen involves two parts: an examen of consciousness and an examen of conscience. Foster writes, "In the examen of consciousness we prayerfully reflect on the thoughts, feelings, and actions of our days to see how God has been at work among us and how we responded" (p. 29). Through a prayerful recollection of the events of our day-to-day lives, we begin to see patterns emerge that invite further reflection. Calhoun (2015) describes this practice as a way to "listen deeply to the data of our lives" (p. 59) to better understand our needs, desires, areas of gratitude, and directions for growth. She proposes the following questions for prayerful examen:

- When did I give and receive the most love today? When did I give and receive the least love today?

- What was the most life-giving part of my day? What was the most life-thwarting part of my day?

- When today did I have the deepest sense of connection with God, others, and myself? When today did I have the least sense of connection? (p. 59)

Through making the examen a regular practice, we begin to notice patterns in the way God is at work in our feelings, needs, and responses that can guide our choices and actions. We will also begin to notice patterns of sinful or harmful behaviors that need to be addressed. This awareness leads to the second part of the examen, the examination of conscience. Foster (1992) describes the prayerful reflection in this way:

> In the examen of conscience we are inviting the Lord to search our hearts to the depths. Far from being dreadful, it is a scrutiny of love. We boldly speak the words of the psalmist, "Search me, O God, and know my heart; test me and know my thoughts. See if there is any wicked way in me, and lead me in the way everlasting" (Ps. 139:23-24). Without apology and without defense we ask to see what is truly in us. It is for our own sake that we ask these things. It is for our good, for our healing, for our happiness. I want you to know that God goes with us in the examen of conscience. . . . He will never allow us to see more than we are able to handle. He knows that too much introspection can harm more than help. (p. 29)

Foster (1992) encourages us to see that the outcome of this process of self-examination is a "priceless grace of self-knowledge" (p. 30) that is the foundation for true humility and acceptance of who we are before God, including our brokenness and sinfulness. Examination of conscience often leads to confession before God and others as we recognize areas of our own sinfulness and brokenness. It helps us realize desires and behaviors in our lives that need to be ordered, disciplined, and moderated. It moves us to humbly seek the help of mentors and Christian community for needed change.

Supervisees can be invited to practice the examen as a spiritual discipline that invites God's presence and involvement in the journey of self-knowledge and spiritual transformation. The prayer of examen can also be a community or group practice where participants share their insights and provide feedback to each other. The examen is often practiced as a daily spiritual exercise, but also as part of weekly, monthly, or annual retreats where we have the opportunity to review our lives and "take stock." The prayer of the examen can be combined with formulating a professional development plan toward holistic personal, professional, and spiritual growth for the supervisee.

Fasting

Throughout the history of the people of God, fasting and prayer have served as a spiritual practice of self-discipline and self-control where believers seek to subdue appetites to focus more intently on prayerful connection with God. As we abstain from fulfilling our desires for food, technology, and consumerism, for example, we recognize how we can use our appetites in unhealthy ways to attempt to satisfy the deep spiritual needs that only God can address. Fasting is a common individual and community practice during seasons of the church calendar, such as Lent, when church communities abstain from food or activities for the purpose of prayer and drawing closer to God.

Willard (1998) describes fasting as a spiritual discipline of "abstinence" that has as its goal the right ordering of the human desires that are not sinful in themselves but can become a source of sin if they are indulged in excess or used to distract us from our deeper spiritual needs. Fasting requires us to turn to God as the source of all comfort and nourishment. Willard writes:

> Fasting teaches temperance or self-control and therefore teaches moderation and restraint with regard to *all* our fundamental drives. Since food has the pervasive place it does in our lives, the effects of fasting will be diffused throughout our personality. In the midst of all our needs and wants, we experience the contentment of the child that has been weaned from its mother's breast (Ps. 131:2). And "Godliness with contentment is great gain" (1 Tim. 6:6). (pp. 167-68)

Inviting supervisees to consider the Christian spiritual practice of fasting can aid in the development of godly character as we become aware of areas of excess in our lives that can be a barrier to spiritual, personal, and professional maturity. Strengthening the development of the "moral muscle" through spiritual disciplines draws us closer to our Creator, who is the source of all sustenance and meaning, and who gives us the strength and courage to order our desires in service to his kingdom.

CONCLUSION

For the Christian, the motivation for temperance is less about character formation as an end in itself, but rather we aspire to the development of "graced habits" that lead to moderation, balance, and humility as part of the sanctification process and being remade in the likeness of Christ. Our love for God compels us to pursue obedience in all things, exercising our will and also depending on the Holy Spirit to empower and guide us in wise discernment of prudent actions. We cultivate habits of temperance in supervision to provide supervisees with practices that will foster the development of humble and self-reflective clinicians who do no harm through ordering their lives for the service of God and neighbor, engaging in regular practices of self-examination, self-supervision, and reflective practice.

Let us return to the skilled but professionally faltering supervisee we discussed in the introduction. How does a deeper understanding of the character strength of temperance help us guide him in developing personal and professional habits that will lead to long-term effectiveness and flourishing? First, in the context of a strong supervision alliance, we begin to explore his reactions and experiences with clients (and in supervision) that trigger his distraction and impulsive behaviors. We help him develop reflective skills through reviewing recorded sessions and initiating use of assessment tools such as the client outcome assessment. Use of the "self of the therapist" supervision model and assessment tool could help him identify signature themes that may emerge in his interactions with clients and in the supervision relationship. Through teaching a mindfulness meditation exercise, we help him stay present and attentive in supervision and discuss how he can also implement these skills in sessions with clients. As supervisors fully aware of our own shortcomings, we approach our conversations with deep humility and potentially some honest disclosure about our own professional journey to greater self-discipline. We invite the supervisee to consider the spiritual practice of daily examen as a way to cultivate a deeper experience of God's loving presence and encourage him to seek God's help and empowerment in transforming his character toward Christlikeness and more effective service for the kingdom. He may also benefit from a periodic technology fast—that is, putting his phone away during interpersonal engagements such as counseling, supervision, and individual and corporate worship. We help him reconnect to his faith community and find a spiritual mentor for accountability.

It is ironic in a chapter on temperance and humility that the word *self* is mentioned well over a hundred times. As Pieper aptly described, temperance is paradoxically "selfless self-preservation" in that it requires an engagement in self-reflection for the purpose of ordering our lives, yielding the fruit of awareness, humility, and freedom. In contrast, unreflective living and lack of awareness of our impact on others can lead to doing harm. As a wise mentor used to say, "What we don't know about ourselves controls us" (F. White, personal communication). Truly, this is a paradox. Maybe this is why Jesus, in his divine wisdom, admonishes us to love others as ourselves.

"Precious Savior, why do I fear your scrutiny? Yours is an examen of love. Still I am afraid . . . afraid of what may surface. Even so, I invite you to search me to the depths so that I may know myself—and you—in fuller measure" (Foster, 1992, p. 35).

CHAPTER SUMMARY / SUPERVISION GUIDE

Virtue	• **Temperance:** chastity, self-control, humility, fasting, sobriety
Description	• "Temperance is: the discipline of oneself to live a more ordered life for the glory of God and the service of others" (Jones, 1994, p. 99).
Scripture	• "For the Spirit God gave us does not make us timid, but gives us power, love and self-discipline" (2 Tim 1:7).
Ethical principle	• **Nonmaleficence:** doing no harm through awareness of own health on practice, self-care and regulation, humility
Supervision focus	• Person-of-the-therapist supervision • CBT supervision and mindfulness practices • Psychodynamic supervision and reflective capabilities • Facilitating reflective practice through various supervision formats • Formative and summative evaluation • Using outcome assessment

Christian integration focus	• Integration of personal, professional, and spiritual development • Transformational psychology • Humility as a desired outcome
Spiritual practices	• Self-examination • Fasting
Desired outcome	• Self-controlled clinicians who do no harm and can self-regulate and self-supervise, who in all humility are aware of strengths and limitations, and who are other-centered

CHAPTER 9

COURAGE

Professional Endurance and Integrity

By your endurance you will gain your lives.

LUKE 21:19 NASB

JESUS SPOKE THESE WORDS of encouragement to his disciples to offer them strength and hope as they faced persecution, doubt, and even death as his followers. While our supervisees do not face quite the same level of peril in their work as mental health professionals, they are often ill prepared for the personal toll that occurs when dealing with suffering, relational brokenness, and the effects of sin on a daily basis in clinical practice. As supervisors, we must follow Jesus' example and foster the development of the character strength of courage as an explicit aim of the supervision process. We do this through cultivating the personal and professional habits that lead to long-term resilience, integrity, and purpose.

How is the character strength of courage relevant to clinical supervision and practice? Consider the following example. Students in a weekly supervision group begin to share how weary, discouraged, and helpless they feel as they work with individuals and families. One student talks about his work with a suicidal client and his constant worry about the client's safety and well-being. Another student shares about her recent experience of making a report

of child abuse and her anxiety about seeing the family for their next session. A third student mentions that he is struggling with his trust in God's goodness and care as a result of hearing the stories of trauma and abuse that his clients have suffered. Students wonder if it is possible to refrain from bringing their work home and describe the emotional burden of caring for their clients. They acknowledge how difficult it is to do good work when they are tired, discouraged, and disillusioned. Clearly, these supervisees are in need of a hopeful vision from their supervisor of long-term personal and professional flourishing, with specific practices that cultivate endurance and integrity.

This chapter provides an overview of the character strength of courage and the importance of fortitude, integrity, and resilience for long-term personal and professional flourishing. Courage includes the professional value of integrity, and professional ethics affirm honesty, accuracy, and commitment as essential qualities for teaching, research, and clinical practice. Clinical supervision models and methods for fostering resilience are described in detail and address clinician wellness, prevention of vicarious trauma, and self-compassion strategies. A Christian integrative approach for cultivating courageous clinicians incorporates a theologically grounded under-standing of suffering and invites spiritual prac-tices that promote courage and resilience through spiritual rhythms of retreat, rest, si-lence, and solitude.

COURAGE: BIBLICAL AND THEOLOGICAL PERSPECTIVES

The New Testament is rich with lessons on courage for the young church. Hebrews 12 uses the image of the race to remind believers to "run with perseverance" through keeping our eyes on Jesus and his example of strength in suffering. We are taught in verse 7 to "endure hardship as discipline" and as an act by a loving Father. Romans 12 admonishes us to "never be lacking in zeal, but keep your spiritual fervor, serving the Lord. Be joyful in hope, patient in affliction, faithful in prayer" (vv. 11-12). Romans 5:3-5 encourages believers to "glory in our sufferings, because we know that suffering produces perseverance; perseverance, char-acter; and character, hope. And hope does not put us to shame, because God's love has been poured out into our hearts through the Holy Spirit, who has been given to us."

In fact, Wright (2010) asserts that Paul's letter to the Romans provides "a theory of how character is formed" (p. 175), which involves the endurance of suffering in anticipation of a future hope of eternity with God:

> What we find here in Romans 5 is that Paul incorporates suffering, not only into a general statement about suffering with Christ in order to be glorified with him . . . but into a remarkable, almost unique statement about character formation. Suf-fering produces endurance or patience, en-durance produces character (not just any sort of character, but one that has been tried and tested and has proved its worth), and character gives birth to hope, a hope that does not disappoint. . . . Paul did indeed en-visage the whole question of Christian living on the model of the classical virtue tradition, but . . . he had radically rethought this tra-dition around Jesus and the Spirit, changing both its content and its shape but retaining the key elements, the sense of an ultimate *telos* and the insistence on working toward that goal by character-building, habit-forming steps. (Wright, 2010, p. 178)

A biblical understanding of courage and en-durance, then, encourages believers to under-stand suffering in the present in light of our future hope of Christ's kingdom, trusting that endurance of suffering is essential to the char-acter formation work that God has begun in us.

In the Gospel narrative, we see Jesus calling his disciples to courage, endurance, and con-stancy. Farley (1995) examines the virtue of courage in Jesus' teaching in the Beatitudes and the Gospel of John. He writes:

> A life rooted in Christ's love, presence, and Spirit (the Comforter) not only invites con-stancy, but requires endurance and courage. At the same time, it engenders the same. Ar-istotle assayed rightly that one becomes cou-rageous only by acting courageously. Oth-erwise one is swallowed up by its defect: cowardice. So too Jesus teaches that the Christian life requires a courageous kind of endurance, a determination that unpreten-tiously scorns one's own values and one's own goals in order that God might be foremost, that God might prevail. . . . For Jesus such a life cannot be pursued without cost, without

having to reassess priorities and goals. That is why endurance is required. . . . It is a courage that is made possible because Christ has chosen the disciple, because God in Christ accompanies each in the power of the Spirit. (pp. 123-24)

From a theological perspective, the virtue of courage is also called "fortitude," from the Latin word *fortitudo* (the words will be used interchangeably in this chapter, consistent with the word usage by each author). Thomas Aquinas's original work has been translated using both terms (Titus, 2006, p. 145). According to Westberg (2015), "Fortitude can be defined in general as firmness of mind, and more specifically firmness in the face of threat or anger. It is the quality of character that enables a person not to be diverted by difficulty or danger from carrying out an action or plan for achieving some good purpose" (p. 199). The Catholic catechism defines the Christian virtue of fortitude as follows:

> *Fortitude* is the moral virtue that ensures firmness in difficulties and constancy in the pursuit of the good. It strengthens the resolve to resist temptations and to overcome obstacles in the moral life. The virtue of fortitude enables one to conquer fear, even fear of death, and to face trials and persecutions. It disposes one even to renounce and sacrifice his life in defense of a just cause. "The Lord is my strength and my song." "In the world you have tribulation; but be of good cheer, I have overcome the world." (*Catechism of the Catholic Church*, 2003, para. 1808)

In *Summa Theologica*, Aquinas describes courage as made up of four subvirtues: *magnanimity*, or the confidence to develop our abilities and talents as gifts from God; *magnificence*, or the courage to take on great tasks for God; *patience* or longsuffering; and *perseverance* or constancy (Kaczor & Sherman, 2009). Certainly, the inclusion of magnanimity and magnificence as Christian virtues may appear to be a philosophical and historical artifact of ancient Greek and Roman characterization of the courage of the warrior in battle. While on the surface this seems to contradict Christian teaching on humility, in actuality "great mindedness" and "initiative" are characteristic of Christians throughout the centuries—such as John Wesley, Hudson Taylor, and Mother Teresa of Calcutta—who have overcome hardship to achieve great things in service to God (Westberg, 2015, p. 206).

Westberg (2015) also elaborates on the two seemingly contradictory ways that Aquinas conceptualizes fortitude. First, courage is "patient endurance" of hardship and suffering, and Christians look to the example of Jesus in his death and resurrection, as well as the courageous actions of the disciples and early church martyrs to endure hardship for the sake of the gospel. A second form of fortitude is action-oriented and may even make use of aggression in the service of a godly purpose, guided by wisdom: "There are also situations that call for resistance, righteous wrath and forceful defense or intervention" (Westberg, 2015, p. 204). We see this courage modeled in the life of Jesus and his active response to his accusers, moneylenders, and injustices. For Aquinas, the ultimate act of courage is martyrdom, where one is willing to lay down one's very life for the sake of Christ.

Pieper (1996) emphasizes that at the heart of the virtue of fortitude is a readiness to let go of one's life, even to the point of death, in service of God's purposes. Pieper asserts that both prudence and justice are necessary for true fortitude—prudence to guide the exercise of fortitude for the purpose of justice: "The virtue of fortitude keeps man from so loving his life that he loses it" (p. 134). The spiritual path to letting go of one's life and thus pursuing a higher degree of fortitude involves purgation, the dark night of the soul: "The Christian who dares to take the leap into this darkness and relinquishes the hold of his anxiously grasping hand, totally abandoning himself to God's absolute control, thus realizes in a very strict sense the nature of fortitude; for the sake of love's perfection he walks straight up to the dreadfulness; he is not afraid to lose his life for Life's sake" (Pieper, 1996, p. 137). Only the Holy Spirit, emphasizes Pieper, can bestow this supernatural gift of fortitude, what Pieper calls "mystical" fortitude, as sheer human effort is insufficient to provide the confidence and courage necessary to let go of one's life for God's purposes. Through the Spirit, fortitude is "nourished by hope" of eternal life; according to Pieper, the more certain the hope, the more the risk (p. 141). By letting go of control and losing one's life and all the attachments therein through the power of the Spirit, one gains the world through God's gift of spiritual fortitude. This perspective brings to mind Jesus' teaching in Matthew 16:25: "For whoever wants to save their life will lose it, but whoever loses their life for me will find it."

Finally, fortitude is a necessary component of all the virtues, which require patience, endurance, and constancy to develop over one's lifetime. Lewis (1977) put it this way: "Courage is not simply one of the virtues, but the form of every virtue at the testing point, which means, at the point of highest reality. A chastity or honesty, or mercy, which yields to danger will be chaste or honest or merciful only on conditions. Pilate was merciful till it became risky" (pp. 137-38). Titus (2006) likens fortitude to "the cement that, when added to the other ingredients (a specific matter, action, or faculty), becomes a solid foundation for the life of excellence" (p. 148). Indeed, patient endurance of suffering through the power of the Holy Spirit and for the sake of God's purposes is essential to Christian character formation. Biblical and theological definitions of courage demonstrate that courage is somewhat of a paradox. It involves active elements as we recognize our God-given gifts and act on them with confidence and vitality in pursuit of the goals and causes God has laid before us. Courage also involves the patience and longsuffering to endure sufferings as we "lose our lives" for the sake of God's kingdom.

COURAGE: PSYCHOLOGICAL PERSPECTIVES

Christian theologians have linked the virtue of courage with the psychological construct of resilience. Titus (2006) suggests the social sciences deepen our understanding of the Christian virtue of courage by the study of the factors that contribute to the development of *resilient fortitude*. Moral theology, in turn, provides the theological and philosophical foundation for the moral dimensions of resilience that in the sciences are often underdeveloped.

Titus examines the subtypes of fortitude given by Aquinas and proposes that the "virtues of initiative" (magnanimity and magnificence) are consistent with a type of "constructive resilience," where individuals activate hope, daring, and social support to rebuild and rebound in the face of challenges and adversity (p. 239). The "virtues of endurance" (longsuffering, perseverance) are "resistant resilience" and pertain to how individuals and communities cope, endure, and persevere in the face of suffering and struggle (p. 261). Westberg (2015) also identifies parallels between classical Christian definitions of courage and contemporary psychological understandings of coping and resilience. Science, he suggests, can inform and expand our understanding of the nature of courage as resilient coping that involves cognitive appraisal (prudence) and meaning making through accessing hope and optimism.

Indeed, the research on religion, coping, and resilience provides important findings to consider for our understanding of courage. Pargament defines research on religious coping as the comprehensive study of how, why, when, and how much "religion is part of the process of understanding and dealing with critical life events" (Pargament, Falb, Ano, & Wachholtz, 2013, p. 562). Religious coping has been conceptualized as an attempt to gain some degree of control in solving problem situations, and Pargament suggests three primary approaches: *deferring* to God, *self-directing* through believing oneself to be equipped by God to deal with problems, and *collaborating* with God as a companion in the problem-solving process (Pargament et al., 1988). The many methods of religious coping consist of two general approaches: *positive religious coping*, which manifests in strong connections to God and others (e.g., seeking comfort from God, support from others in congregation, forgiveness), and *negative religious coping*, which is associated with spiritual struggles and disconnection with God, self, and others (e.g., feeling punished by God, discontent with God's or others' response to a crisis situation). Research has found strong relationships between positive religious coping and physical health benefits (Koenig, 2012), good psychological outcomes (Ano & Vasconcelles, 2005), and posttraumatic growth (Harris et al.,

2008). Conversely, negative religious coping has been associated with psychopathology and maladaptive behaviors (Ano & Vasoncelles, 2005; McConnell, Pargament, Ellison, & Flannelly, 2006). Thus, religious coping can affect resilience in both positive and negative ways. Religion and spirituality can contribute positively to resilience through providing connections to God and others, through facilitating positive emotions such as hope and gratitude, and especially through a system of beliefs and practices that foster positive meaning making (as we discussed in chapter four).

Peterson and Seligman (2004) identify courage as "emotional strengths that involve the exercise of will to accomplish goals in the face of opposition, external or internal" (p. 29). According to the authors, this strength of character consists of four related qualities. *Bravery* involves how one responds to danger or threat and "can be promoted by practice (moral habit), by example (modeling), and by developing certain attributes of the individual (self-confidence) or group (cohesion)" (p. 221). *Persistence* involves "voluntary continuation of a goal-directed action in spite of obstacles, difficulties, or discouragement" (p. 229) and is enabled by a variety of factors including positive reinforcement, social support, and self-control. *Integrity* involves both public and private actions in which people are "true to themselves." Finally, *vitality* or *zest* is a "dynamic aspect of well-being marked by the subjective experience of energy and aliveness" (p. 273) that is closely linked to one's health and lifestyle routines. Let us examine the relevant empirical research in these areas that can guide our understanding of this important virtue for clinicians.

Research in psychology suggests that the character strength of courage can be cultivated and developed. Hannah, Sweeney, and Lester (2010) propose a "courageous mind-set" as a "dynamic versus dispositional personality processing system" (p. 132) that is activated in the face of fearful stimuli and stimulates coping resources and brave actions. This courageous mind-set involves a dynamic interaction between positive states, positive traits, values and beliefs, and social influences. Fears and threats activate both internal and external resources, which then lead to courageous actions. The researchers propose a feedback loop of self-reflection and self-attribution of courage, which then reinforces positive states and traits, leading to more courageous acts in the future (Hannah et al., 2010, p. 128).

Social cognitive theories of the development of courage suggest that observational learning, guided mastery experiences, mental rehearsal, vicarious learning, and social persuasion can all contribute to the cultivation of courage in individuals and groups (Lester, Vogelgesang, Hannah, & Kimmey, 2010). Mentoring in general, and transformational leadership practices in particular, can be especially impactful in guiding the development of courageous qualities and behaviors in others, according to the authors. Mentors teach and train others to develop skills related to courage through elucidating the deeper principles relevant to a particular situation or context, through encouraging thoughtful risk-taking, through encouragement and affirmation, and through offering feedback on the development of courageous skills and traits (Lester et al., 2010). This research underscores the importance of clinical supervisors as models and mentors for courage in the face of clinical and professional challenges.

The literature on positive affect, well-being, and resilience is also relevant to our understanding of developing and maintaining

courage. This is a vast literature and only a brief summary is offered here for our purposes. Characteristic of the positive psychology movement has been a wealth of research on positive emotions and character traits that contribute to well-being, life satisfaction, and happiness (Niemiec, 2013). Generally, research suggests that positive affect is strongly related to human flourishing (Fredrickson & Losada, 2005). Character strengths—particularly the traits of hopefulness, vitality, gratitude, curiosity, and love—demonstrate a significant relationship with positive life satisfaction and happiness (Ruch, Huber, Beermann, & Proyer, 2007; Park, Peterson, & Seligman, 2004). Seligman (2011) proposes *well-being theory* as an encompassing approach to human flourishing and offers PERMA as an acronym to describe the five factors necessary for life satisfaction and happiness: positive emotion, engagement, relationships, meaning, and achievement. Reviews of research on the contribution of religion and spirituality to well-being suggest that a significant percentage of empirical studies demonstrate a positive relationship between religiousness and physical and psychological health, and this relationship appears to be strong across cultures and people groups (Koenig, 2012; Fave, Brdar, Vella-Brodrick, & Wissing, 2013). Smith, Ortiz, Wiggins, Berhard, and Dalen (2012) propose that healthy spirituality contributes to the development of positive emotions, positive meaning, and resilience. The authors write:

> We suspect that spirituality is most often the cause rather than the result of resilience and positive emotions. . . . Spirituality may increase resilience in at least four ways, including through relationships, life values, personal meaning, and coping. . . . Spirituality and religion may increase positive emotions

such as love, joy, and contentment through ethical guidelines and various religious and spiritual beliefs and practices. (p. 450)

Understanding the contribution of religion and spirituality to well-being is important for fostering resilience and endurance as part of the character strength of courage.

Finally, existential perspectives equate courage with authenticity and personal meaning making (Tillich, 1952). Authenticity as an act of courage is the willingness to endure hardship, challenge, and suffering to live in a way that is true to one's deepest hopes, dreams, and longings. McInerny (2014) suggests that cultural icon Steve Jobs epitomizes this perspective. In a commencement address in 2005, Jobs admonished Stanford graduates to not let anything drown out their "inner voice" as the trustworthy guide to living. McInerny writes:

> At the heart of courage, as Taylor might put it, is "contact with myself, with my own inner nature," or what Jobs calls the "inner voice." It is this contact that helps us overcome fear, above all the fear of death, by the deep satisfaction of realizing who we are truly meant to be. This doesn't mean that courage is no longer focused on patriotism, care of the family and others communities, or even God. It means, rather, that these horizons of significance have become internalized in a way that is specific to contemporary culture. (pp. 88-89)

McInerny cautions that this approach to courage, without an external or divine measure of the value and meaning of the personal choices, can lead to shallow "self-assertion" (p. 91). In contrast, Aquinas's and other classical views of courage ground authenticity and human choice in an eternal telos—that is, authenticity tempered by moral, rational, and divine measures of one's actions.

From a psychological perspective, we see that the virtue of courage can be understood as a character strength related to responding to threatening situations with brave actions, resilience, endurance, and integrity. In addition, courage manifests in long-term resilience, endurance, and maintenance of well-being in the face of personal and professional challenges. Courage can be fostered through a variety of learning experiences and practices. As we engage in courageous actions, we experience ourselves as courageous, which increases the potential for future bravery. In this way, research in modern psychology is in agreement with Aquinas, who proposed that human beings become courageous by acting courageously (Farley, 1995). Let us explore further how to apply these important psychological perspectives to the development of courage and resilience through the clinical supervision process.

PROFESSIONAL ETHICAL PRINCIPLES: INTEGRITY AND CLINICIAN WELLNESS

Across the ethical codes for counselors, psychologists, and MFTs is the admonition for mental health professionals to be people of integrity who embody the virtues of veracity, honesty, and constancy in our interactions with students, clients, and colleagues. To act honestly and ethically requires courage and the endurance to faithfully engage in ethical practices even when no one is looking, the very definition of integrity. The mandated reporter, the researcher who reports findings truthfully and accurately, and even the supervisor who gives hard but honest feedback to a therapist in training are all demonstrating acts of integrity and courage.

The supervision process fosters integrity in a myriad of ways. As we discussed in chapter six, supervision ensures integrity in clinical practice through competency-based supervision aimed to teach students consistency, accuracy, and effectiveness in their use of clinical assessment and intervention techniques. Faculty supervisors promote integrity in research by ensuring competent use of experimental design and accurate reporting of results. Professional integrity involves "practicing what we preach" through developing lifestyle habits that foster psychological, physical, and relational health toward personal wholeness.

Integrity is fostered by maintaining good boundaries and avoiding multiple relationships that could potentially be harmful to students, supervisees, or clients. Most international codes of ethics recognize the power differential inherent in the supervisory relationship and articulate strict ethical guidelines for supervisors to refrain from harm or exploitation of supervisees (Thomas, 2104). Falender and Shafranske (2004) assert that "integrity in relationship" is one of the superordinate values of clinical supervision. Supervisors with integrity refuse to engage in activities that lead to exploitation of students or clients. And integrity compels supervisors to have the courage to call out peers or colleagues who do. One leading supervision researcher writes that in his 28 years of doing clinical supervision, one of the greatest lessons he has learned is the importance of courage for "doing the right thing," which is often the "hard thing" (Ellis, 2010). This includes the gatekeeping and evaluation functions of supervision, as well as challenging colleagues who are providing inadequate or harmful supervision.

Integrity can be compromised when the clinician's needs and personal issues are not well managed, which can result in personal impairment and ethical violations. Most ethics textbooks include attention to clinician self-care, as this is an occupational hazard. Prevention of clinician impairment requires self-reflection and self-control, as we discussed in the previous chapter, but also necessitates disciplines related to endurance and resilience that ensure management of personal and professional stressors as a lifestyle commitment.

The unique challenges of the mental health professions put practitioners at risk for stress and burnout. *Burnout* is a more general term referring to the physical and psychological symptoms related to job stress, whereas *vicarious trauma* or *secondary trauma* is more specific to the helping professions and occurs when helpers begin to exhibit symptoms of trauma similar to their clients as a result of exposure to traumatic stories (Sadler-Gerhardt & Stevenson, 2011; Figley, 1995; McCann & Pearlman, 1990). Professional challenges include caring for the emotional needs of clients, managing high-risk behaviors (including suicidality) and acting-out behaviors, and experiencing professional isolation. In addition, our orientation to care for the needs of others may blind us to our own needs and symptoms. Research suggests that a majority of psychologists have continued to practice even when they have known that personal issues are affecting their competency and effectiveness (Pope, Tabachnik, & Keith-Spiegel, 1987; Sherman, 1996).

Barnett, Baker, Elman, and Schoener (2007) assert that it is an "ethical imperative" for psychologists to attend to their own self and wellness as stress, burnout, isolation, and vicarious trauma can make clinicians vulnerable to ethical misconduct and incompetence and result in harm to others (and to self). They write, "Psychologists are aware of the possible impact of their own physical and mental health on their ability to help those with whom they work, and they engage in ongoing efforts to minimize the impact of these factors on their clinical competence and professional functioning" (p. 208). The authors make a strong case for the fact that professional self-care and resilience should begin at the graduate-school level, with faculty and supervisors providing modeling, training, and explicit attention to healthy practices that sustain long-term flourishing. Long-term endurance and vitality as mental health professionals require the development of healthy lifestyle practices that promote physical, emotional, and spiritual health as a buffer against the stress of working with hurting people. Thus, the promotion of supervisee wellness and attention to secondary trauma prevention is a necessary responsibility for the clinical supervisor.

SUPERVISION MODELS AND METHODS FOR CULTIVATING INTEGRITY AND RESILIENCE

Supervisors are instrumental in helping to set a supervisee's professional trajectory toward the development of professional integrity and resilience. Given what we know about the risk factors for mental health professionals, it is of critical importance that supervisors engage in intentional supervision practices to foster supervisees' development of healthy practices that buffer vocational stress, isolation, and vicarious trauma toward the goal of professional endurance and vitality. The good news is that supervision research suggests that the supervision alliance itself is a protective factor. In a review of contemporary research on clinical supervision, Ellis (2010) concluded that "the supervisory working alliance mediates burnout and enhances vigor as well as mediates the effects of vicarious traumatization" (p. 106). Providing supervisees with a safe place to process their thoughts, reactions, and negative emotional experiences related to clinical work offers protection against burnout. Supervision models that are wellness-oriented, trauma-informed, and self-compassion-focused are particularly helpful in fostering habits and practices toward long-term endurance, integrity, and ultimately courage.

Wellness-Oriented Supervision

The counseling profession in particular has transitioned from a focus on counselor impairment to counselor wellness, integrating wellness strategies into counselor education, clinical supervision, and standards for ongoing professional practice. Myers, Sweeney, and Witmer (2000) define wellness as "a way of life oriented towards optimal health and well-being in which body, mind, and spirit are integrated by the individual to live life more fully within the human and natural community. Ideally, it is the optimum state of health and well-being that each individual is capable of achieving" (p. 252). Wellness-oriented supervision models incorporate research on health, wellness, and coping into the clinical supervision process to facilitate the holistic health and well-being of supervisees. Supervisors can make clinician wellness an explicit focus of the supervision process with the goal of fostering supervisee awareness and attention to the importance of personal health for sustainable professional engagement.

The Wellness Model of Clinical Supervision (WELMS) developed by Lenz and Smith (2010) applies strategies from wellness-oriented counseling to the supervision process. WELMS is based on a five-factor model of wellness developed by Myers and Sweeney (2005), which proposes wellness as a combination of the creative self, the coping self, the social self, the essential self, and the physical self (Lenz & Smith, 2010, p. 232). Supervisors facilitate a four-stage process to encourage supervisee wellness:

1. Educating supervisees about wellness and providing resources

2. Fostering self-assessment of holistic wellness across domains of functioning through use of informal discussion, scaling questions (i.e., "How would you rate your satisfaction with your spiritual health on a scale of 1 to 10?"), or more formal self-assessment measures of wellness such as the 5F-WEL (Myers & Sweeney, 2005)

3. Facilitating planning and goal setting where the supervisee selects areas for improvement and devises a written wellness plan with specific goals, interventions, and ways of measuring progress

4. Encouraging ongoing, systemic evaluation of progress through behavioral tracking, journal keeping, accountability, etc.

Lenz and Smith (2010) encourage a collaborative approach to wellness discussions with supervisees and recommend that wellness-oriented discussions account for approximately 40 percent of the supervision time. This approach also emphasizes the importance of supervisors' commitment to wellness and holistic health in their own lives and in their clinical work with clients. Research on wellness-oriented models of supervision has demonstrated good effects on improving the holistic health of counselors (Lenz, Sangganjanavanich, Balkin, Oliver, & Smith, 2012). Wellness-oriented supervision may indeed be a preventative intervention that decreases the incidence of professional burnout and vicarious trauma.

Promoting Wellness and Endurance Through Trauma-Informed Supervision

Trauma-informed supervision focuses explicitly on the prevention of secondary trauma in supervisees and is critical for supervisee wellness and endurance (Berger & Quiros, 2014). This approach applies the principles of trauma-informed treatment to clinical supervision to support the personal and professional functioning of supervisees as they work with traumatized clients. Berger and Quiros (2014) integrate the educational, supportive, and administrative aims of clinical supervision with trauma-informed practices. First, supervisees should be educated about evidence-based treatment approaches for trauma as well as the risks and challenges to clinicians working with trauma, including the signs and symptoms of vicarious trauma. Next, supportive practices in supervision include facilitating the supervisee's personal and professional growth through encouraging reflective practice, monitoring well-being and symptoms of stress, and encouraging healthy personal practices and work-life balance. Finally, the administrative functions of supervision include oversight of the supervisee's caseload and work environment to reduce risk of vicarious trauma and improve functioning. For example, a supervisor may want to ensure that the number, type, and pacing of clinical contact hours are reasonable for a supervisee's health and optimal functioning.

Berger and Quiros (2014) recommend the following principles as integral to a trauma-informed approach to supervision:

- A strong supervision alliance marked by safety and trust is important for this approach, as supervisees are invited to explore their experiences and reactions as they work with traumatized clients.

- Self-assessment and identification of supervisees' personal history and risk factors are key components of reflective practice.

- Supervisors adopt a collaborative supervision style in which fostering supervisees' choice and self-efficacy can decrease the sense of helplessness and powerlessness that trauma treatment can evoke.

- Empowering supervisees through education, skill development, and regular feedback on both successes and challenges provides a sense of self-efficacy and effectiveness and combats the loss of meaning and purpose that can be a symptom of vicarious trauma.

The authors conclude that because of the risk of burnout and secondary traumatization, supervision should be considered a required component of the professional lives of clinicians who specialize in this area.

Another valuable resource for professionals working with trauma is the Headington Institute (www.headington-institute.org), which provides web-based resources and free online training for caregivers involved in humanitarian work to support professional resilience and professional well-being. Particularly helpful for counselors, psychologists, and MFTs are the resources on compassion fatigue and vicarious trauma, which provide education, self-assessment tools, and practical strategies for prevention and intervention with vicarious trauma symptoms for individuals and groups.

Supervision and Self-Compassion

A significant challenge to clinician wellness and endurance is the mental toll of self-criticism, doubt, and worry that can elicit feelings of shame, professional withdraw, and burnout. One preventative approach used by clinicians is the practice of self-compassion, defined in the following way:

> When faced with experiences of suffering or personal failure, self-compassion entails three basic components: (a) self-kindness—extending kindness and understanding to oneself rather than harsh judgment and self-criticism, (b) common humanity—seeing one's experiences as part of the larger human experience rather than seeing them as separating and isolating, and (c) mindfulness—holding one's painful thoughts and feelings in balanced awareness rather than over-identifying with them. (Neff, p. 89, 2003)

In a narrative study exploring experienced counselors' practice of self-compassion, Patsiopoulos and Buchanan (2011) found that clinicians reported significant benefits from self-compassion practices for their therapeutic presence in sessions with clients, their relationships in the workplace, and their work-life balance. The authors concluded that "the overall resounding message was that practicing self-compassion served to enhance counselor well-being, counselor effectiveness in the workplace, and therapeutic relationships with clients" (p. 306).

Bell, Dixon, and Kolts (2016) adapted self-compassion-focused therapy to the process of clinical training and supervision where beginning supervisees learn to develop and internalize a "compassionate internal supervisor" that they bring to bear on their clinical work. In a guided imagery exercise, supervisees are directed to envision the characteristics and qualities of the "ideal compassionate supervisor" from their actual or imagined supervision experiences. Then supervisees imagine bringing a difficult professional issue to the compassionate internal supervisor. The authors found a decrease in feelings of shame and self-criticism and increased positive experiences of resilience when supervisees used the compassionate supervisor imagery. As supervisees adopt a more supportive and compassionate mindset toward their clinical experiences and difficulties, they are able to engage in honest and courageous self-reflection without debilitating shame and worry.

CULTIVATING COURAGE: CHRISTIAN INTEGRATIVE APPROACHES

Christian integrative approaches to fostering courage, endurance, and perseverance in clinical supervision invite supervisees to bring a Christian worldview to bear on their approach to vocational challenges, human suffering, and personal well-being. This involves teaching supervisees to access spiritual resources for Spirit-infused fortitude to "run the race with endurance" for the sake of Christ, the author of our faith. It involves both "active courage," where we seek to encourage supervisees to develop their God-given gifts and talents, and "enduring courage," where we encourage them to maintain Christian hope in the face of their clients' (and their own) suffering. It involves the development of spiritual practices that give us courage and endurance in our call to lay down our lives for God and neighbor. In this section, we examine three approaches to foster the character strength of courage in the supervision process.

Magnanimity and Magnificence: Encouraging Personal Mission and Vision

In chapter four, we discussed the importance of a Christian view of vocation for fostering hope. Supervision encourages trainees to consider their vocation as counselors, psychologists, and marriage and family therapists as part of a larger call to use their gifts and skills to serve Christ's kingdom. Through cultivating the virtues of magnanimity and magnificence (purpose and confidence), supervisees access the drive, motivation, and confidence to develop their knowledge, competencies, and passions for working with specific populations and clinical specialties. Supervisors look for opportunities to call out strengths and unique competencies to "en-courage" supervisees to persevere in their professional and personal development toward fulfilling God-given vocational tasks. Not unlike the military general inspiring confidence in their troops on the eve of battle, the empowering supervisor communicates: "I believe in who God has made you to be. Have the courage to develop your gifts."

Writing to supervisors of pastoral candidates, Fullam (2014) encourages supervisors to cultivate character strengths of both humility and magnanimity as important "companion virtues" for the work of the spiritual director and counselor. She offers the following definition of magnanimity:

Magnanimity's mode is encouragement. Magnanimity urges us to make the best of the gifts God has given us. Beyond mere self-understanding, this requires devotion and effort. Consider the countless hours of practice that contributes to a virtuoso musical performance, or the miles and miles run by a marathoner in training. While some of us naturally overreach, most of us need a little push to work hard to "be all we can be." To practice magnanimity, then, is to work to recognize the gifts we have; to see how we need to work to perfect them for the good of all. If humility invites us to see and value others' gifts, magnanimity requires that we see, and value, our own intrinsic worth as human beings, and to act from a position of healthy self-love. To fail in magnanimity is to be pusillanimous, "small-souled," which implies a timid, lazy, or socially-imposed reluctance to "be all we can be." (pp. 41-42)

Fullam encourages supervisors to be magnanimous through not holding back from sharing our own wisdom, our own vulnerabilities, and our honest feedback about areas of needed growth for our supervisees. Practical recommendations for developing the virtue of magnanimity include taking the risk to try those things we have always wanted to do, equipping ourselves with what we need to get there, and finding "adventurous companions" for mutual encouragement along the way.

One way to foster courage and confidence in personal mission in graduate training and supervision is to regularly inquire about students' emerging sense of calling and unique interests and competencies to promote self-reflection. Supervisors can encourage involvement in professional organizations, training opportunities, and experiences to foster the development of supervisees' gifts and interests. In group supervision, faculty can foster active courage through offering stories and examples, bringing in guest lecturers to share their vocational journeys, and watching videos of exemplars.

Another suggestion is to have students in a supervision group or class write their personal missions in one phrase or statement on slips of paper. Then the papers can be combined into a collage that is photocopied and distributed to the class to reflect on together. The collective mission statements can serve as an inspiring picture that reflects the collective calling of the group of soon-to-be graduates. Active courage is fostered through encouraging supervisees to develop and maintain a sense of personal calling that links their own stories of suffering with God's call to serve suffering people.

Spiritually Informed Trauma Treatment

The emerging literature on trauma and spirituality (Walker, Cortois, & Aten; 2015; Gingrich & Gingrich, 2017) provides an important resource for supervision as supervisees seek to integrate their faith with clinical practice in the treatment of trauma. Spiritual practices including prayer, meaning making, and connection to a faith community can be incorporated into the clinical supervision process as a resource for supervisees and clients.

As supervisees confront the realities of human suffering, their cherished beliefs and ideals can be profoundly challenged. It is not uncommon for supervisees exposed to their clients' traumatic experiences to begin to question their own beliefs about God, the world, and people. Spiritual questions about theodicy—that is, how a good and loving God can allow such suffering—may emerge, along with a sense of helplessness and hopelessness about one's own ability to make a difference. Wang, Strosky, and Fletes (2014) draw from the vicarious trauma literature to provide several helpful suggestions for supervisors to attend to the impact of trauma work on the Christian therapist:

- Educate supervisees about the multiple ways that trauma can affect one's faith, as these are also relevant to vicarious trauma (i.e., trauma can strengthen, challenge, and disrupt one's trust in God's providence and goodness).

- Invite open exploration of the way clients' trauma stories may challenge the supervisee's beliefs and assumptions.

- Create a safe space for supervisees that can minimize the impact of guilt and shame for religious questions and doubts.

- Invite expression of negative emotions consistent with biblical lament for the sinfulness and brokenness of the present world.

- Encourage eschatological hope in Christ's kingdom.

Supervisors can encourage supervisees to engage in spiritual practices that reconnect them with their faith communities and encourage them to wrestle with emerging doubts in their relationships with mentors and peers.

Developing a Biblical and Theologically Grounded Perspective on Suffering

As supervisors, we do our trainees a great service when we send them out into the "battle" armed with theological and biblical resources to help them make sense of the suffering and pain they encounter as part of their clinical work. Most Christian mental health professionals inevitably must grapple with spiritual and existential questions related to theodicy. Inviting supervisees to bring their questions, doubts, and disillusionment into the context of supervision provides the opportunity to stimulate thoughtful reflection. To aid in this meaning making, supervisors can provide resources from Scripture, experience, and the integration literature.

The Christian integrative literature offers important resources for the development of a meaningful and robust view of theodicy. Hall, Langer, and McMartin (2010) raise the question, Should easing suffering always be the primary objective of counseling? The authors integrate perspectives from virtue ethics, theology, and positive psychology to propose three benefits of suffering for human flourishing. First, pain and suffering can be an indication of our own sinfulness and faulty living and our need for confession and repentance. At times, suffering is a wake-up call that we have brought hardship on ourselves when we move away from God's design for right living. Second, suffering is necessary to produce character and virtue with the goal of Christlikeness. This is consistent with the theological perspectives of Wright and Pieper discussed above. Finally, pain and suffering can serve as a "worldview modifier" (Hall et al., 2010, p. 118) that leads to a reevaluation of goals, priorities, and aims. For the Christian, this ultimately points us to God. Through the "dark night of the soul," we are again invited to lay down our lives to seek first God and his kingdom.

Supervisors can encourage a biblical and theologically grounded view of suffering to help supervisees maintain perspective and hope as they learn to "bear one another's burdens" in clinical practice. Clinical work, then, becomes an opportunity to help clients make meaning of suffering versus symptom relief only. This is not to discourage the use of psychological interventions to alleviate pain, as this must be balanced with the virtue of doing no harm and not withholding alleviation of suffering when it is within our power to help.

SPIRITUAL DISCIPLINES FOR THE FORMATION OF COURAGE: INDIVIDUAL AND COMMUNITY PRACTICES

Incorporating spiritual practices into the clinical supervision experience provides both supervisor and supervisee with the opportunity to utilize spiritual resources for the development of Christian fortitude, endurance, and integrity. Two spiritual practices are particularly germane to the character strength of courage: courageous narratives and a rule of life.

Courageous Narratives

For the development of courage and fortitude, stories and examples are particularly important as a source of inspiration and a model for faithful endurance. Wright (2010) encourages us to appreciate the wisdom about humanity and the virtues that can be found in stories both in Scripture and in the wider culture. Through story, we see ourselves in the narrative and find hope and encouragement that our own narrative is also purposefully being written in love by God for his purposes. Stories and examples are part of the "virtuous circle" that Wright proposes as the pathway to Christian character formation.

Similarly, looking to examples of the great "cloud of witnesses" that have braved adversity and courageously persevered in the face of hardship can nurture our courage. The liturgical calendar offers "feast days" when the lives of saints are held up as examples of both humanness and divine grace. Ultimately, we look to Jesus as our example of courage and endurance, as we are instructed to do in Hebrews 12. However, as Wright (2010) aptly states, looking to Jesus as a model of virtue for us is like looking to Tiger Woods as our model for how to play golf: the bar is set pretty high

(p. 126). Maybe this is why Scripture is full of stories and examples of men and women who suffer, sin, and make terrible mistakes, but still play an invaluable role in the larger biblical narrative. Wright puts it this way: "Bit by bit, we realize that scripture was not given so that we can comb it for saintly, virtuous lives that we can copy as they stand. It was written as the story of God, God's people and God's world; and God's people find themselves caught between God and the world again and again—in scripture as in today's life—in ambiguous and morally compromised situations" (p. 166). Still, we take courage from reading about the lives of Christian mothers and fathers of the faith who have gone before us and offer us their lives and wisdom, and the opportunity to learn from their failures.

Rule of Life

Progress in the cultivation of Christian character in general and the virtue of courage in particular requires a plan of action. The spiritual discipline for developing habits and rhythms for spiritual transformation is called a "rule of life." One of the earliest "rules" can be found in Acts 2 where the early Christians described their community commitments to prayer, worship, and breaking bread together (Calhoun, 2015). Originally developed by Saint Benedict to guide community life for monks and nuns, a rule of life outlines the specific spiritual practices for an individual or community to engage in on a daily, weekly, monthly, or annual basis that lead to spiritual growth and transformation. Through purposeful engagement in the spiritual rhythms of a rule of life, one "practices" the habits of prayer, thought, and behavior that will lead to long-term spiritual health and vitality and invites God's transformation of character.

The rule of life can be defined as "rhythms of spiritual practices" in response to the question "How do I want to live so I can be who I want to be?" (Barton, 2006, p. 147). Developing a rule of life begins with prayerful consideration of what we long for in our relationship with God, our areas of needed growth and sinfulness, our stage of life and what is realistic, and our need for community. Barton recommends approaching this task with flexibility versus legalism, and reevaluating our plan regularly. Rules of life commonly include a plan for drawing near to God in prayer, worship, Scripture study, and community, designating times during the day, week, month, and year to grow in our life with God. A rule of life can also include plans for regular personal or community retreats where one pulls away from normal life to listen to God more intensively. A rule of life can also incorporate healthy practices for body and mind as well as soul. It may include disciplines that block distractions (phones, email, even roommates and family).

For many mental health professionals, the spiritual disciplines of solitude and silence are particularly important for maintaining personal and professional equilibrium in the midst of an interpersonally demanding profession that involves other-centered speaking and listening. This rhythm of service and solitude is modeled for us in the life of Jesus, who took regular time away from the demands of ministry to be with his Father. Including in our spiritual rhythms regular times where we step away from the needs of others and the noise of our lives to listen to God in silence and solitude allows us to stay closely connected to God and to our deepest selves. Solitude and

silence are not always easy and enjoyable, as often the thoughts, feelings, worries, and areas of sin we have kept at bay during the busyness of the day will rise to the surface as we free ourselves from distractions. Dallas Willard (1988) describes solitude and silence as disciplines of *abstinence*, where we deny our legitimate desires and needs for spiritual purposes. He writes:

> Of all the disciplines of abstinence, solitude is generally the most fundamental in the beginning of the spiritual life, and it must be returned to again and again as that life develops. This factual priority of solitude is, I believe, a sound element in monastic asceticism. Locked into interaction with the human beings that make up our fallen world, it is all but impossible to grow in grace as one should. Just try fasting, prayer, service, giving, or even celebration without the preparation accomplished in withdrawal, and you will soon be thrown into despair by your efforts, very likely abandoning your attempt altogether. (pp. 161-62)

Willard's admonitions suggest that developing the virtues of courage and temperance may be closely intertwined, as the spiritual disciplines of silence and solitude are "factual priorities" necessary for spiritual reflection and growth.

Foster (1988) suggests that, historically, most spiritual writers see silence and solitude as disciplines that are best practiced together: "Without silence there is no solitude" (p. 98). He suggests paying attention to the opportunities in our day-to-day lives for "little solitudes," which might include the quiet of the morning or late evening, a walk, a commute to work, or even requesting a moment of silent contemplation or prayer when in a group. In addition, longer periods of solitude and silence are important for prayerful reflection and reevaluation of our desires and goals. Foster suggests seeking out a "quiet place" that provides space and sanctuary for these times of retreat: a church, retreat center, even creating a space in our homes. As our needs for sanctuary are met, Foster suggests we are better able to feel a renewed sense of compassion and love for others. He quotes Thomas Merton: "It is in deep solitude that I find the gentleness with which I can truly love my brothers. The more solitary I am the more affection I have for them. . . . Solitude and silence teach me to love my brothers for what they are, not for what they say" (as quoted in Foster, 1988, p. 108).

In clinical supervision, the development of a rule of life as a spiritual practice can go hand in hand with the development of a wellness plan as recommended by wellness-oriented supervision approaches. Forming the character strength of courage starts with small steps toward holistic spiritual, psychological, relational, and physical health, which can serve as the foundation for lifelong vitality, endurance, and professional engagement.

CONCLUSION

Let us return to the weary and discouraged supervision group from the beginning of the chapter. How can we apply the resources of this chapter to instill courage and resilience? We can start by encouraging our group to reflect together on how our work as mental health professionals requires courage and the will, determination, and persistence to follow through with difficult tasks for the sake of doing good and upholding our ethical integrity. Maybe this moment in supervision is a good opportunity to revisit our original calling to become counselors, psychologists, and MFTs. We can offer the supervision group as a time to process the upsetting and unsettling stories of trauma that our clients have experienced. We can bring biblical and theological resources to honest discussions about theodicy. And finally, we hold each other accountable for developing the spiritual rhythms and practices that cultivate endurance, patience, and meaning in the midst of our challenging clinical work. We take time in group supervision for individual reflection and take steps toward development of a rule of life.

As we share in each other's burdens and questions, we can hopefully catch a glimpse of God's plan for the redemption of suffering. We encourage each other to press on in the school of character formation, particularly when the best teacher is suffering. Let us be inspired to courage by a prayer written by the Scottish minister John Baillie:

> Let me stand to-day—
>> for whatever is pure and true and just and good:
>> for the advancement of science and education and true learning:
>> for the redemption of daily business from the blight of self-seeking:
>> for the rights of the weak and the oppressed:
>> for industrial co-operation and mutual help:
>> for the conservation of the rich traditions of the past:
>> for the recognition of new workings of Thy Spirit in the minds of the [people] of my own time:
>> for the hope of yet more glorious days to come.

To-Day, O Lord—
    let me put right before interest:
    let me put others before self:
    let me put the things of the spirit before
        the things of the body:
    let me put the attainment of noble ends
        above the enjoyment of present
        pleasures:

let me put principle above reputation:
let me put Thee before all else.

O Thou the reflection of whose transcendent glory did once appear unbroken in the face of Jesus Christ, give me to-day a heart like His—a brave heart, a true heart, a tender heart, a heart with great room in it, a heart fixed on Thyself; for His name's sake. Amen. (Baillie, 1949, p. 61)

CHAPTER SUMMARY / SUPERVISION GUIDE

Virtue	• **Courage:** fortitude, magnanimity, magnificence, patience, endurance
Description	• *"Fortitude* is the moral virtue that ensures firmness in difficulties and constancy in the pursuit of the good. It strengthens the resolve to resist temptations and to overcome obstacles in the moral life. The virtue of fortitude enables one to conquer fear, even fear of death, and to face trials and persecutions" (*Catechism of the Catholic Church*, 2003, para. 1808).
Scripture	• "By your endurance you will gain your lives" (Lk 21:19 NASB).
Ethical principle	• **Integrity:** accuracy, honesty, veracity in clinical and research practices
Supervision focus	• Wellness-oriented supervision • Trauma-informed supervision • Self-compassion and clinical supervision
Christian integration focus	• Encourage personal mission and vision • Spiritually informed trauma approaches • Foster biblically/theologically grounded perspectives on suffering
Spiritual practices	• Stories and examples of courage • Rule of life • Silence • Solitude
Desired outcome	• Courageous clinicians who demonstrate integrity, fortitude, honesty, commitment and veracity; who can demonstrate resilience and engagement in the profession for the long haul; who act on ethical principles and contribute to the profession and larger society with confidence and humility

CHAPTER 10

PERSONAL AND SPIRITUAL FORMATION IN COUNSELING, PSYCHOLOGY, AND MFT EDUCATION

The question to ask about education is not "What can I do with it?" That is the wrong question because it concentrates on instrumental values and reduces everything to a useful art. The right question is rather "What can it do to me?"

ARTHUR F. HOLMES

AS IMPORTANT AS THE clinical supervisor is to the graduate student's personal and professional development, supervision occurs in the context of a larger educational environment. MFT perspectives remind us that supervision takes place within the context of an interconnected web of relationships. For our supervisees, this includes their cohort of students, the educational environment of their program, the institutional culture, and the wider professional community. Community values and practices are instrumental for the development of faithful and virtuous clinicians who will flourish in their vocational lives.

In this final chapter, we consider how graduate programs involved in the training of mental health professionals can offer something more to students through explicit attention to personal and character formation. We explore resources from positive psychology, character education, and professional training to identify institutional virtues that promote growth in character toward professional flourishing. We look at graduate mental health training in particular and identify spiritual formation practices of exemplary programs, offering practical suggestions for graduate programs to integrate personal formation goals into the program culture and curriculum. Finally, we consider the person of the supervisor and the enterprise of supervision as advanced discipleship.

PROFESSIONAL GREENHOUSES AND ENABLING INSTITUTIONS

What are the essential characteristics of communities and institutions that promote optimal growth and development? Skovholt and Trotter-Mathison (2011) offer the image of the "professional greenhouse" as the ideal setting for counselors to grow and flourish. Like a greenhouse that provides the optimal conditions of soil, regulation of temperature, nutrients, and protection from the elements, an organization should prioritize the creation of a healthy workplace environment that can provide counselors with the relational support and community atmosphere for professional flourishing.

Organizations that provide a professional greenhouse environment are characterized by four practices, according to Skovholt and Trotter-Mathison (2011). First, individuals in leadership positions in the organization actively encourage counselors to balance self-care as they engage in the other-focused profession of counseling. Second, healthy organizations place a high value on relationships, ensuring that counselors are able to access support from colleagues and from mentors. Third, facilitating organizations provide opportunities for counselors to "give back" through mentoring and supervising others, which encourages an atmosphere of growth and training. Fourth, fun and humor are encouraged, and positive emotions are infused throughout the organizational atmosphere. The authors encourage counselors to take responsibility for creating this greenhouse environment in the institutions they are a part of, and not simply rely on employers alone to facilitate a growth-producing environment. Ideally, the outcome of creating a healthy work environment includes personal and professional balance, well-being, and resilience.

Similarly, positive psychologists have proposed the term *positive institutions* (Seligman & Csikszentmihalyi, 2000) to describe organizations that support the development of character strengths. Peterson (2006) suggests that *enabling institutions* promote the growth, flourishing, and success of both individual and institutional goals. Enabling institutions possess "institutional level virtues" (Peterson, 2006, p.

280) that are characteristic of the institutional culture and also shared by the members of the organization. In addition, institutions that promote growth and flourishing have a vision of the moral and virtuous goals they wish to achieve, and these goals are explicit, with clear expectations and equitable rules. Enabling institutions offer fair access to institutional goods, treat members with dignity, and exhibit mutual care and concern for the safety and protection of members (Peterson, 2006).

The study of workplace spirituality is a growing field that represents an interdisciplinary collaboration between psychology and the field of organizational management (Hill, Jurkiewicz, Giacalone, & Fry, 2013; Hill & Dik, 2012). Workplace spirituality is defined as follows: "Aspects of the workplace, either in the individual, the group, or the organization, that promote individual feelings of satisfaction through transcendence" (Giacalone & Jurkiewicz, 2010, p. 13). Research, theory, and interventions in this field seek to foster improved individual and corporate health and productivity through greater attention to spiritual issues. For example, incorporating spiritual and religious issues in the workplace can lead to a greater sense of meaning and purpose for employees. Hill and Dik (2012) write: "People bring their whole beings to work. The spiritually oriented individual is likely to imbue certain relevant workplace experiences with sacred significance. When allowed to flourish, this spiritual schema provides a coherent, central, and organizing framework for navigating workplace experiences that is recognized and respected" (p. 11). This area of research holds much promise for the development of organizational cultures, including educational institutions, that foster spiritual flourishing.

Institutions that promote professional flourishing and formation provide an atmosphere of supportive relationships, shared values and virtues across organizational levels, and opportunities for growth and development that are accessible to all. Let us examine resources from the educational literature on character-forming institutions.

EDUCATION AS FORMATION

Character education has grown in popularity over the past twenty years as principles of positive psychology have been integrated into curriculum, teaching methods, and extra-curricular emphases in elementary and secondary education (White, 2016). In higher education, the Christian liberal arts tradition has historically prioritized the goal of developing the moral and intellectual character of students toward producing good citizens who bring a broad-based liberal education into their personal, community, and vocational engagements (Holmes, 1987; Newman, Garland, Castro-Klarén, Landow, & Marsden, 1996). Faith-based institutions approach the formation of character from a Christian worldview, which provides the *telos* for mature character: to grow in Christlikeness to serve Christ's kingdom.

In a recent article published in *CCCU Advance* magazine, David Brooks commends faith-based institutions on their potential to form character:

> You guys [Christian colleges] are the avant-garde of 21st century culture. You have what everybody else is desperate to have: a way of talking about and educating the human person in a way that integrates faith, emotion and intellect. You have a recipe to nurture human beings who have a devoted heart, a courageous mind and a purposeful soul. Almost no other set of institutions in American society has that, and everyone wants it. From my point of view, you're ahead of everybody else and have the potential to influence American culture in a way that could be magnificent. (Brooks, 2016)

Brooks's words are certainly an encouragement and challenge to educators and supervisors working in faith-based settings. A Christian vision for character formation provides a roadmap for becoming the kind of people that can build Christ's kingdom. The Christian educational context provides the *telos* for character formation that is missing from positive psychology approaches. Grounded in faith, motivated by hope, and compelled by love, we seek to grow in Christian maturity and Christlikeness, our character shaped for service to Christ's kingdom.

Smith and Smith (2011) trace the history of "faith and learning" in Christian institutions and suggest that although the creation of uniquely Christian scholarship has proliferated, it has been at the neglect of developing uniquely Christian pedagogies that guide the learning process in the classroom. They write, "It seems fair to observe that our commitment to Christian scholarship has been significantly more articulate than our commitment to Christian pedagogy" (p. 3). Smith and Smith propose a reconsideration of historic Christian practices that can be integrated into the classroom and educational environment to promote the formation of students and faculty. For example, the authors question what the impact would be on learning and formation to ask students to practice the discipline of fasting before a lecture on poverty, or to engage in a *lectio divina* practice during a class on how to approach literature. The authors make the following observation:

> On the one hand, we are convinced that Christian education must be formative in just the sense that MacIntyre emphasizes. If Christian higher education is going to take seriously its responsibility for education in virtue, then it also needs to attend to matters of practice and formation. On the other hand, we are convinced that implicit in the inherited practices of the Christian tradition is a kind of pedagogical wisdom on which we can draw for Christian teaching more broadly. (pp. 16-17)

Smith and Smith challenge Christian educators to reconsider current pedagogical practices for faith and learning to incorporate individual and community spiritual practices. Graduate and professional training programs are particularly suited for Christian practices because of the applied, experiential emphases of most programs.

FORMATION IN GRADUATE AND PROFESSIONAL EDUCATION

Surprisingly, the formation of virtuous character in graduate and professional education has received minimal attention. This is unfortunate, as the development of characteristic habits of thought and action during the graduate school years as one is learning their professional craft will likely form the bedrock for vocational life.

One notable exception can be observed in medical school education, where there has been a renewed interest in the benefits of virtue education in the training of physicians. Growing concerns that medical training was producing physicians who were technically skilled and knowledgeable but vulnerable to mistreatment of patients and staff have prompted a rethinking of medical education to include attention to character formation and virtues such as empathy, collaboration, wisdom, and integrity (Seoane, Tompkins, De Conciliis, & Boysen, 2016). Educating physicians-in-training in character virtue has become a more prevalent approach to preventing loss of empathy and professional burnout and improving ethical decision making.

Seoane, Tompkins, De Conciliis, and Boysen (2016) describe one such program involving a virtues course taught to fourth-year medical students by physicians identified to be exemplars in character virtues. Students are introduced to six virtues identified as foundational to medical practice, including wisdom, justice, temperance, courage, humanity, and transcendence, based on Peterson and Seligman's (2004) classification. In five three-hour sessions, students are taught about each virtue, and faculty share personal narrative examples of the virtue and resulting impact on their professional work. Hypothetical case narratives are utilized to facilitate application of virtue to medical practice. Personal reflection is encouraged to identify the virtue in one's own life, and students are asked to look for examples of each virtue in action during the week and journal about what they have seen. Post-training assessments revealed high rates of student satisfaction at 97%. The authors conclude: "Virtues are the scaffolding of professional formation. They provide a foundation for us to maintain our humanism as we navigate the increasing complexity of medical practice. When physicians are distanced from themselves and from virtues such as honesty and altruism, patient safety may suffer" (Seoane et al., 2016, p. 53).

There is recognition among mental health professionals that the educational environment itself has an impact on ethical practice. Keller, Murray, and Hargrove (2012) advocate for "positive ethical cultures" that demonstrate and model the highest ethical behaviors and practices at all levels of the institution:

> The notion of a positive ethical culture assumes that teaching, learning, and the development of student character take place across the entire life of the institution, both in the formal contexts of the classroom and in other informal or cocurricular contexts of the overall college experience. Whether or not the formal mission of an institution recognizes its role in the development of student character, we would observe that character is shaped, for better or worse, as a function of the modeling that takes place as students scrutinize the behaviors of their faculty, advisors, university and student leaders, and other members of the campus community. (p. 239)

Virtue education in the training of mental health professionals has been proposed by Fowers (2005), who advocates for character considerations as an explicit focus in all aspects of graduate education, including admissions decisions, staff and faculty hiring, honors awards, and the educational and curricular goals. Fowers writes, "We can enhance our appreciation of character in ourselves and our trainees by making it an explicit part of our vocabulary and our activities" (p. 218). Urofsky and Engels (2003) have made a strong case for incorporating a more philosophically and morally sophisticated understanding of ethics into counselor education and training due to the importance of the person of the counselor. One novel suggested approach is to adopt a team-teaching model for ethics courses with a philosopher and counselor educator. Tying ethics discussions in graduate education closer to the humanities undergirds ethical thinking with important moral and philosophical teaching on goodness, humanity, and morality that can benefit counselors and ultimately clients (Urofsky & Engels, 2003).

MFT educators have also called for explicit attention to the development of "moral competence" as an identified MFT competency in faith-based programs:

> Moral character must be identified and developed in a Christian moral community. This moral community and its resulting character provide a foundation and stability to be courageous and challenge one to be ethically responsible. To foster this sense of moral character, therapists should be exposed to Christian moral and ethical philosophy. This moral education provides a context and language base to begin thinking morally about situations. Also, therapists should be encouraged to engage in religious and spiritual communities that have fostered and "supervised" the morality of their practitioners for centuries. Moral education and participation in moral community encourage Christian virtues such as faith, hope, and love. (Frederick & Steele, 2010, pp. 5-6)

From these examples, a case can be made for the value of introducing graduate students to the rich history of virtue ethics and moral formation as part of their graduate education. Integrating character formation goals into graduate education demonstrates promise for improving professional relationships and empathy and increasing ethical understanding—especially *why* we do what we do in ethical practice.

EXAMPLES AND EXEMPLARS

Faith-based graduate programs face the dual challenge of meeting professional accreditation standards and maintaining their commitment to faith-and-learning integration goals. It is tempting to relegate personal and spiritual formation goals to extracurricular activities and church involvement (Fleischer, 2012). However, facilitating growth in Christian maturity and formation needs to be an explicit goal of graduate programs that are serious about the long-term flourishing of their students.

A special issue of the *Journal of Psychology and Christianity* (2013) asked faculty from APA-accredited Christian doctoral programs to describe their approach to student spiritual formation. It is inspiring to read the creativity and commitment that various programs bring to this task. We consider the various programs and their spiritual formation approach here by way of example:

- Azusa Pacific University integrates spiritual formation goals throughout the curriculum and community practices. The program defines spiritual formation broadly as "the search for the sacred." Priority is given to one-on-one and small group mentoring in recognition of the importance of personal and professional formation during graduate years (Tisdale et al., 2013).

- Fuller Theological Seminary draws from James Smith's encouragement for communities to offer "cultural liturgies" for personal and spiritual formation and creates opportunities for spiritual growth through mentoring, pedagogy, and experiential practices. Fuller's MFT program identifies four specific virtues of focus in student spiritual formation: humility, hope, compassion, and sabbath. Fuller views all faculty as "spiritual agents" but emphasizes that the Holy Spirit is the "primary agent" of spiritual formation (Strawn & Hammer, 2013, p. 304).

- George Fox University demonstrates a high regard for students' actual experiences of spiritual formation efforts through their assessment practices, and models the importance of a courageous and honest examination of students' actual experience (versus faculty intentions only) (McMinn et al., 2013).

- Regent University emphasizes diversity in their spiritual formation aims and incorporates an understanding of diverse student faith and cultural experiences (Ripley et al., 2013).

- Rosemead School of Professional Psychology prioritizes the development of the person of the therapist in community through requiring 50 hours of individual therapy (36 can be spiritual direction or systemic therapy). In addition, Rosemead describes its chapel program as central to community spiritual formation for students and faculty (McMartin, Dodgen-Magee, Geevarughese, Gioielli, & Sklar, 2013).

- Wheaton College's approach to spiritual formation of students is closely tied to their mission of preparing students to work with underserved populations; thus an emphasis on developing biblical justice sensibilities is part of the formation of service-oriented practitioner-scholars (Flanagan et al., 2013).

Faith-based graduate programs in counseling, psychology, and MFT can be purposeful about incorporating character formation goals throughout the structure of the program, including mission statement, curriculum, learning outcomes, and assessment measures. Programs can identify specific virtues that are integral to their mission—for example, Fuller's MFT program's emphasis on relational virtues, Wheaton's PsyD program's focus on the virtue of justice, or Rosemead's focus on self-awareness. Personal and spiritual formation practices can be incorporated into coursework and assignments considering students' developmental needs and challenges. Opportunities for community practices such as worship, Scripture reading, hospitality, and service can become a regular and valued component of the educational process as seen at Rosemead and Azusa.

We can also make our program environments "enabling institutions" and "professional greenhouses" by prioritizing relationships, encouraging Sabbath-keeping toward work-life balance, and fostering shared values and virtues across institutions and programs. And we must not forget to have fun. After all, "sense of humor" was one of the faculty characteristics found to facilitate student integration in Sorenson's (1997) landmark study.

CONCLUDING THOUGHTS: THE PERSON OF THE SUPERVISOR IN THE EDUCATIONAL PROCESS

I hope that as you've considered the supervision approach proposed in this book, you've been thinking about what a graduate community might look like that prioritizes the character formation of faculty, students, and staff. It is an exciting and hopeful prospect to dream about what it could look like to build for the kingdom in our training programs and institutions through developing clinicians of character who are known by their faithfulness, hopefulness, and love, and who engage in their clinical work with wisdom, justice, temperance, and courage. We can be encouraged by exemplary programs that are already doing this well. Ideally, the education and training of mental health professionals who are prepared to uphold the public trust should occur in an educational environment where administrators, faculty, staff, and students are committed to the development of virtuous character and practice this with humility, generous grace for mistakes, humor, and collegiality.

In this text, we have explored how a Christian integrative approach to clinical supervision provides something more by explicitly focusing on the formation of character and personal/professional habits that promote long-term competency, effectiveness, and flourishing. These pages have provided a framework for clinical supervision that integrates Christian character formation with professional ethics and values and proposes specific supervision models, Christian integrative approaches, and spiritual discipline practices that aid in the development of classic Christian virtues. Each chapter has offered a theological and psychological understanding of a classic character virtue and the corresponding professional value, followed by supervision models and spiritual formation practices to cultivate this character strength in supervision. In sum, our guiding virtues as clinical supervisors should include the following:

- prioritizing the establishment of a secure, trusting supervision alliance marked by faithfulness, consistency, and fidelity

- fostering in our supervisees a hopeful vision for clinical work as kingdom service

- embodying love and an attitude that conveys "How good that you exist!" in the context of a safe, boundaried relationship

- pursuing our own wisdom vigorously through a commitment to lifelong learning, and encouraging our supervisees to do the same

- fanning the spark of biblical justice in our supervisees into a flame that can energize their vocational priorities

- modeling and encouraging reflective practice

- instilling courage through fostering resilience and well-being

Clinical supervision is in many ways a form of advanced discipleship. We provide professional, personal, and spiritual guidance and mentoring for students as they engage in professional practice and experience the inevitable and necessary disillusionment that real-world clinical work is not as they anticipated it would be. Supervision as advanced discipleship requires a roadmap, and the rich traditions of Christian virtue ethics, moral theology, and spiritual formation have provided this for us. But more important, supervision that is truly formative requires supervisors to be fully committed to inviting God's formation of our own souls, to pursue ongoing self-reflection, to be "supervisors of character" who do our best to model what we preach and are transparent and confessional when we inevitably fail. As we know from the research on cognitive neuroscience and virtue development, models and

mentors play an invaluable role in the development of moral character. Perhaps our most important supervision tool is our own moral and spiritual formation.

I have especially appreciated the writings of Fr. Ron Rolheiser on Christian maturity and advanced discipleship. In his book *Sacred Fire* (2014), he explores what it means to become increasingly generative and to give our lives away to others as we mature as Christ-followers. Rolheiser traces three phases of Christian maturity and discipleship based on the writings of Saint John of the Cross. First is the stage of "essential discipleship," where we find a calling and set out on the path of following Christ. Second, we enter into a stage of "mature discipleship" where we gradually learn to give our lives away in service to others. Finally, Rolheiser suggests that "radical discipleship" involves giving our death away by seeking to bless others in our death and dying. Giving our lives away as clinical supervisors requires blessing others generously and helping them grow in Christ, as we allow God's sacred fire to continually burn away the sins of pride, the need to be important, harmful competitiveness, envy, and slander. Rolheiser's words of wisdom are very relevant for the work of spiritually formative supervision as a form of advanced discipleship. As supervisors, we seek to give our knowledge and skills away by blessing, enabling, and building up the next generation of clinicians of character who will accomplish wonderful things for God's kingdom that we haven't yet dreamed of.

In the final estimation, then, the development of faithful clinicians of character through the process of clinical supervision depends largely on the character of the supervisor as a tool for God's formational work in love. If we are not willing to enroll ourselves in the "school of character" as a lifelong commitment, our efforts to cultivate virtuous habits of heart, mind, and practice in our supervisees will ring false. We have a responsibility—both to the profession and more importantly to our Creator—to continue to cultivate graceful habits that form us in his likeness as preparation for the kingdom to come. We do not need to be perfect, for sure, but we are called to continue to be formed in the likeness of Christ, humbly acknowledging our faults and failures, demonstrating faith, hope, and love in relation to our Creator and his larger plan for our lives and vocations.

There is no doubt that we need the formative experience of clinical supervision as much for our own sake as for the sake of our supervisees. This next generation of mental health professionals certainly inspires, challenges, and motivates us to run the race with endurance. Their curiosity, optimism, hope, and courage are an inspiration and a motivation for us. Supervision is a gift for the supervisor, and we can take great joy in this important professional role.

We end with a quotation from Teresa of Ávila (as cited in Rolheiser, 2014, p. ix), who captures the essence of supervision as advanced discipleship: "When one reaches the highest degree of human maturity, one has only one question left: How can I be helpful?"

SAMPLE SUPERVISION CONTRACT FOR GROUP SUPERVISION IN AN EDUCATIONAL CONTEXT

Supervision Contract

The purpose of this contract is to review important information relevant to our supervision work together, as I will serve as your faculty individual and group supervisor for your practicum experience this semester. This information is an addendum to your Practicum Seminar Syllabus and Clinical Training Handbook, which detail the learning outcomes, course requirements, and evaluation procedures for your practicum experience. This statement will provide an overview of my training and supervision credentials and supervision approach as part of informed consent, and will also identify evaluation procedures, limits of confidentiality, emergency contact information, and the supervision goals that will guide our work together.

About My Qualifications

For the past 30 years, I have had the professional joy and honor to supervise students and licensed professionals from a variety of mental health backgrounds including clinical psychology, professional counseling, and marriage and family therapy. My interest in clinical supervision led me to pursue the Approved Supervisor designation through advanced coursework in clinical supervision and one year of "supervision of supervision," receiving the AAMFT Approved Supervisor designation in 2000. Additionally, I pursued and received board certification in clinical psychology through the American Board of Professional Psychology in 2008. Most recently, I received the Approved Clinical Supervisor designation from the Center for Credentialing and Education, which is a professional counseling credential. Although I maintain my professional license as a clinical psychologist, I seek to utilize the best clinical and supervision resources from the professional counseling, clinical psychology, and marriage and family therapy literature and have enjoyed teaching our department's MA programs since their inception. As a generalist, my specialty areas include individual, couple, and family therapy with general mental health difficulties related to mood disorders, behavioral problems, interpersonal difficulties, life adjustment issues, career problems, and spiritual and religious concerns. Additional areas of competence include psychological assessment, clinical supervision, and consultation. I conduct my clinical work and supervision in adherence to the ACA, ACS, APA, and AAMFT ethical codes of professional conduct:

- ACA—www.counseling.org/resources/aca-code-of-ethics.pdf

- ACS—www.cce-global.org/Assets/Ethics/ACScodeofethics.pdf

- APA—www.apa.org/ethics/code/principles.pdf

- AAMFT—www.aamft.org/iMIS15/AAMFT/Content/legal_ethics/code_of_ethics.aspx

Key Values and Assumptions About Supervision

I place a strong value on collaboration and mutuality in supervisory relationships. I encourage supervisees to be proactive in setting goals for their professional/personal development, and at the same time I will focus on the development of basic MFT skills and key competencies during our supervision time. Significant emphasis is placed on developing the supervision relationship as a confidential, safe, supportive, and growth-producing environment where supervisees are free to explore strengths and areas of needed growth. I seek to promote "self-supervision" by encouraging the supervisee's own critical thinking about the process and content of their clinical work. For example, I will ask you to review your own tapes of sessions first and offer a critique of strengths and areas for growth before we review the tapes together in our supervision sessions.

A second key value involves the importance of helping supervisees pay attention to their affective, cognitive, and experiential reactions to clinical situations. Consistent with experiential approaches to treatment, I believe that exploration of automatic reactions to situations can lead to more effective treatment, as supervisees explore the fears, biases, and anxieties that block them from effective intervention. I believe it is important as a supervisor to continually practice this as well as I explore my reactions to interactions in the supervisory relationship.

A third key value involves the critical task of increasing the supervisee's awareness of contextual issues and use of that awareness to enhance therapeutic sensitivity and effectiveness. This includes exploration of issues of gender, sexuality, race, culture, religion, socioeconomic status, and ability. I hope to model curiosity, respect, and awareness of the impact of these issues in the supervisory relationship and, by doing so, to increase the supervisee's comfort and interest in considering context as an integral component of their work with individuals and families. This also involves attention to contextual issues for the supervisee, including their graduate program and place of employment or internship.

Finally, I place a strong value on identifying and exploring the supervisee's unique strengths and competencies. I seek to make the supervision experience one that is strength-based rather than deficit-oriented. I believe it is important to highlight experiences of success early on in the supervisee relationship to promote the supervisee's sense of confidence and hope in their ability to be an effective clinician.

Supervision Models and Methods

My approach to supervision utilizes humanistic-experiential and existential approaches to MFT and supervision, is developmentally oriented, and adapts to the needs of each supervisee. I use a variety of modalities to facilitate the supervision process, including use of raw data (video, audio, live), role-playing, modeling, teaching, skill development, expanding experiential awareness, and examination of person-of-the-therapist issues. Supervision involves comfortably moving between various modalities, keeping in mind the supervisee's presenting concerns. The two goals of promotion of client welfare and the professional and skill development of the student are kept as priorities at all times. Supervision moves between various modalities with an emphasis on seeking supervisee areas of strength and skill as a way of competency shaping. Expanding the supervisee's awareness of contextual issues such as culture and gender is a key component of supervision and is accomplished through a combination of education and increasing the supervisee's awareness of their own biases and assumptions about individuals and groups.

I also value the opportunity to integrate Christian faith and spiritual formation practices into the clinical supervision process. It has become increasingly clear to me over the years that excellent counselors develop through a combination of knowledge, skills, and character values that prepare them to counsel effectively and maintain professional vibrancy and integrity through the challenges of long-term mental health practice. In supervision, I look for opportunities to invite supervisees to consider spiritual formation practices that can enhance their love of God and neighbor with the goal of developing character virtues integral to effective and spiritually sensitive clinical practice. As students hear in our programs, our work as counselors is as much, if not more, about our character as the knowledge and techniques we develop.

Supervision Purpose, Practices, and Evaluation Procedures

The purpose of this group supervision experience is to provide opportunities for your clinical, professional, personal, and spiritual development as a clinician in training. Your on-site supervisor is considered your primary supervisor, as your clinical work occurs under their professional license. My input as your faculty supervisor will focus particularly on your clinical, professional, and personal development, while your on-site supervisor also safeguards the welfare of your clients. Any clinical recommendations made by me or members of your supervision group should be checked out with your primary supervisor before implementing.

As your faculty supervisor, I will provide face-to-face group supervision weekly during your practicum experience this semester. This will occur in addition to the on-site supervision you will receive. We will meet one hour each week for group supervision during your practicum experience. I encourage you to videotape all of your counseling sessions, and we will review the tapes during our group supervision meetings. Of course, you will need to obtain informed consent from your clients to tape sessions and can use the consent forms we have available in the department or use your site's consent forms.

In our group supervision time, you will have the opportunity to learn from the feedback and counseling experiences of your peers as we discuss cases, practice case formulation and diagnosis, and role-play clinical scenarios. As described in the course syllabus, you will be responsible for presenting two cases during the group supervision time.

In terms of evaluation procedures, you will receive regular feedback on your strengths and areas for growth during the group supervision time. Your feedback on the supervision process and your perceptions of your own progress are very important to me as well. I will raise any serious concerns about your progress or competence as soon as possible with you. If you have any substantive concerns about the supervision process or your practicum experience, I invite you to discuss them with me directly or with the clinical training director for your program. During the semester, I may also have contact with your site supervisor for coordination of our supervision efforts. I will be completing an evaluation on your progress this semester in December using the Practicum Evaluation Form that is available for review in your Clinical Training Handbook.

Your Responsibilities

Part of your professional development this semester involves attention to the details of professional practice. At your training site, this will likely include keeping session notes and other client paperwork. Your responsibilities as a member of our supervision group this semester include the following:

- weekly attendance and active participation
- submitting proof of your liability insurance before you begin your practicum
- tracking your practicum direct and indirect service hours and submitting this to me once per month, signed by your supervisor
- obtaining the necessary consent forms for taping sessions for supervision
- presenting two cases this semester
- completing the end of semester evaluation on your on-site and faculty supervisor

Confidentiality

The information you share in supervision about yourself and your clients will be kept confidential, with the following exceptions:

1. Information directly relevant to your progress and development as a student in the program, to be shared only with program faculty and staff

2. Situations where there is a risk of harm to self or others, including concerns about abuse or neglect of vulnerable persons including children

3. When required by a court order

Emergency Contact Information

In a clinical emergency, please feel free to contact me directly at my cell phone number: _____. If I am out of town during the semester, I will inform you of coverage arrangements with one of the other faculty members.

Supervision Goals

Early in our work together, we will collaboratively identify goals that you will be working on during our supervision sessions. We will keep these goals in mind as we discuss your cases and consider professional development issues. Goals can be adjusted and changed as supervision progresses.

_____

_____

_____

_____

_____

I look forward to our supervision work together.

_____   _____   _____   _____

Supervisee   Date   Supervisor   Date

SUPERVISION DOCUMENTATION FORM

Record of Supervision	
Date:	**Length of time:**
Supervisee:	**Supervisor:**
Supervision modality: ❑ Individual ❑ Triadic ❑ Group ❑ Other (_____)	
Supervision format: ❑ Review of recorded session ❑ Case consultation ❑ Live observation ❑ Other (_____)	
Supervision goals addressed:	
Cases discussed:	
Supervision themes:	
Homework assigned:	
Any risk management concerns? ❑ Yes ❑ No	
If yes, plan of action?	
Signature of supervisee	**Date**
Signature of supervisor	**Date**

COLLABORATIVE PROFESSIONAL DEVELOPMENT PLAN

Name of supervisee:	Date:

Informed consent for religious/spiritual issues in supervision: ☐ yes ☐ no ☐ haven't discussed

Collaborative assessment (religious/spiritual history and current practices, sense of vocation and calling):

Collaborative assessment of character strengths and areas for identified growth:

Goals for supervision (religious/spiritual competencies, professional/personal formation, vocational):

Religious/spiritual themes in supervision:

Invited spiritual practices (in supervision or recommended homework):

Signature of supervisee	Date
Signature of supervisor	Date

REFERENCES

Adichie, C. N. (2009). *The danger of a single story* [Video]. Available from http://www.ted.com/talks/chimamanda_adichie_the_danger_of_a_single_story

Ainsworth, M. D. S., Blehar, M. C., Waters, E., & Wall, S. (1978). *Patterns of attachment: A psychological study of the strange situation.* Hillsdale, NJ: Erlbaum.

Alexander, F. G., & French, T. M. (1946). *Psychoanalytic therapy: Principles and applications.* New York: Ronald.

Allen, D. E., Donham, R. S., & Bernhardt, S. A. (2011). Problem-based learning. *New Directions for Teaching and Learning, 128,* 21-29. doi:10.1002/tl.465

Allport, G. W. (1950). *The individual and his religion.* New York, NY: Macmillan.

Allport, G. W., & Ross, J. M. (1967). Personal religious orientation and prejudice. *Journal of Personality and Social Psychology, 5*(4), 432-43. doi:10.1037/0022-3514.5.4.432

Almeida, R., Hernandez-Wolfe, P., & Tubbs, C. (2011). Cultural equity: Bridging the complexity of social identities with therapeutic practices. *International Journal of Narrative Therapy and Community Work, 3,* 43-56. Available from: http://search.informit.com.au/documentSummary;dn=711681632630835;res=IELHEA.

American Association of Christian Counselors. (2014). *AACC code of ethics.* Retrieved from http://aacc.net/files/AACC%20Code%20of%20Ethics%20-%20Master%20Document.pdf

American Association of Pastoral Counselors. (2012). *Code of ethics.* Retrieved from www.aapc.org/page/Ethics

American Association for Marriage and Family Therapy. (2004). *Marriage and family therapy core competencies.* Retrieved from https://www.aamft.org/imis15/Documents/MFT_Core_Competencie.pdf

American Association for Marriage and Family Therapy. (2014). *Approved Supervision designation: Standards handbook.* Retrieved from https://dx5br1z4f6n0k.cloudfront.net/imis15/Documents/AS-Handbook.pdf

American Association for Marriage and Family Therapy. (2015). *Code of ethics.* Retrieved from http://www.aamft.org/iMIS15/AAMFT/Content/legal_ethics/code_of_ethics.aspx

American Counseling Association. (2014). *ACA code of ethics.* Retrieved from https://www.counseling.org/resources/aca-code-of-ethics.pdf

American Psychological Association. (2003). Guidelines on multicultural education, training, research, practice, and organizational change for psychologists. *American Psychologist, 58,* 377-402. doi:10.1037/0003-066X.58.5.37

American Psychological Association. (2005). *Policy statement on evidence-based practice in psychology.* Retrieved from http://www.apa.org/practice/guidelines/evidence-based-statement.aspx

American Psychological Association. (2008). *Report of the APA Task Force on the implementation of the Multicultural Guidelines.* Washington, DC: Author. Retrieved from http://www.apa.org/pi/

American Psychological Association. (2010). *Ethical principles of psychologists and code of conduct.* Retrieved from https://www.apa.org/ethics/code/principles.pdf

American Psychological Association. (2011). *Revised competency benchmarks for professional psychology.* Retrieved from http://www.apa.org/ed/graduate/competency.aspx

American Psychological Association. (2014). *Guidelines for clinical supervision in health service psychology.* Retrieved from http://apa.org/about/policy/guidelines-supervision.pdf

American Psychological Association. (2016). *Standards of accreditation for health service psychology.* Retrieved from http://www.apa.org/ed/accreditation/accreditation-roadmap.aspx

Anderson, H. (2012). Editorial—Section 1: Classic virtues considered. *Reflective Practice, 32,* 6-9. Retrieved from http://journals.sfu.ca/rpfs/index.php/rpfs/article/view/55/54

Annan, K. (2016). *Slow kingdom coming: Practices for doing justice, loving mercy, and walking humbly in the world.* Downers Grove, IL: InterVarsity Press.

Annas, J., Narvaez D., & Snow N. (Eds.) (2016). *Developing the virtues: Integrating perspectives.* New York, NY: Oxford University Press.

Ano, G. G., & Vasconcelles, E. B. (2005). Religious coping and psychological adjustment to stress: A meta-analysis. *Journal of Clinical Psychology, 61*(4), 461-80. doi:10.1002/jclp.20049

Aponte, H. J., & Carlsen, J. C. (2009). An instrument for person-of-the-therapist supervision. *Journal of Marital and Family Therapy, 35,* 395-405. doi:10.1111/j.1752-0606.2009.00127.x

Aponte, H. J., Powell, F. D., Brooks, S., Watson, M. F., Litzke, C., Lawless, J., & Johnson, E. (2009). Training the person of the therapist in an academic setting. *Journal of Marital and Family Therapy, 35,* 381-94. doi:10.1111/j.1752-0606.2009.00123.x

Aquinas, Thomas. *Summa Theologica.* (Fathers of the English Dominican Province, Trans; Benziger Bros., Ed.). Westminster, MD: Christian Classics, 1947. Online: http://www.ccel.org/ccel/aquinas/summa.html

Association for Counselor Education and Supervision. (2011). *Best practices in clinical supervision: ACES task force report.* Retrieved from http://www.saces.org/resources/documents/aces_best_practices.doc

Association for Spiritual, Ethical and Religious Values in Counseling. (2016). *Competencies for addressing spiritual and religious issues in counseling.* Retrieved from http://www.aservic.org/resources/spiritual-competencies/

Association of State and Provincial Psychology Boards. (2015). *Supervision guidelines for education and training leading to licensure as a health service provider.* Retrieved from http://c.ymcdn.com/sites/www.asppb.net/resource/resmgr/Guidelines/Final_Supervision_Guidelines.pdf

Aten, J. D., Boyer, M. C., & Tucker, B. (2007). Christian integration in clinical supervision: A conceptual framework. *Journal of Psychology and Christianity, 26*(4), 313-20.

Aten, J. D., & Hernandez, B. C. (2004). Addressing religion in clinical supervision: A model. *Psychotherapy: Theory, Research, Practice, Training, 41*(2), 152-60. doi:10.1037/0033-3204.41.2.152

Aten, J. D., & Leach, M. M. (Eds.). (2009). *Spirituality and the therapeutic process: A comprehensive resource from intake to termination.* Washington, DC: American Psychological Association.

Aten, J. D., McMinn, M., & Worthington, E. (Eds.). (2011). *Spiritually-oriented interventions for counseling and psychotherapy.* Washington, DC: American Psychological Association.

Atkinson, B. (1997). What is the difference between personal therapy and person-of-the-therapist supervision? In C. L. Storm & T. Todd (Eds.), *The reasonably complete systemic supervisor resource guide* (pp. 152-54). Boston, MA: Allyn and Bacon.

Austin, M. (2015). Christian humility as a social virtue. In C. B. Miller, R. M. Furr, A. Knobel, & W. Fleeson (Eds.), *Character: New directions from philosophy, psychology, and theology* (pp. 333-50). New York, NY: Oxford University Press.

Baillie, J. (1949). *A diary of private prayer.* New York, NY: Charles Scribner's Sons.

Balswick, J. O., & Balswick, J. K. (2006). *A model for marriage: Covenant, grace, empowerment and intimacy.* Downers Grove, IL: IVP Academic.

Balswick, J. O., & Balswick, J. K. (2007). *The family: A Christian perspective on the contemporary home.* Grand Rapids, MI: Baker Academic.

Barnett, J. E., Baker, E. K., Elman, N. S., & Schoener, G. R. (2007). In pursuit of wellness: The self-care imperative. *Professional Psychology: Research & Practice, 38*(6), 603-7. doi:10.1037/0735-7028.38.6.603

Barnett, L. (2009). The supervisory relationship. In E. Van Deurzen & S. Young (Eds.), *Existential perspectives on supervision widening the horizon of psychotherapy and counselling* (pp. 56-67). London, UK: Palgrave and Macmillan.

Barrett, J. L. (2011). Cognitive science of religion: Looking back, looking forward. *Journal for the Scientific Study of Religion, 50*, 229-39. doi:10.1111/j.1468-5906.2011.01564.x

Barrett, J. L., & Burdett, E. R. (2011). The cognitive science of religion. *The Psychologist, 42*, 252-55. Retrieved from https://thepsychologist.bps.org.uk/volume-24/edition-4/cognitive-science-religion

Bartels, D. M., Bauman, C. W., Cushman, F. A., Pizarro, D. A., & McGraw, A. P. (2015). Moral judgment and decision making. In G. Keren and G. Wu (Eds.), *The Wiley Blackwell handbook of judgment and decision making* (pp. 478-539). Chichester, UK: John Wiley & Sons. doi:10.1002/9781118468333.ch17

Bartlett, S. J. (1990). Acedia: The etiology of work-engendered depression. *New Ideas in Psychology, 8*(3), 389-96. doi:10.1016/0732-118x(94)90026-4

Barton, R. H. (2006). *Sacred rhythms: Arranging our lives for spiritual transformation.* Downers Grove, IL: InterVarsity Press.

Barton, R. H. (2008). *Strengthening the soul of your leadership: Seeking God in the crucible of ministry.* Downers Grove, IL: InterVarsity Press.

Batson, C. D. (1976). Religion as prosocial: Agent or double agent. *Journal for the Scientific Study of Religion, 15*(1), 29-45. doi:10.2307/1384312

Batson, C. D., Schoenrade, P., & Ventis, W. L. (1993). *Religion and the individual: A social-psychological perspective.* New York, NY: Oxford University Press.

Baumeister, R. F. (1991). *Meanings of life.* New York, NY: Guilford Press.

Baumeister, R. F., & Exline, J. (1999). Virtue, personality, and social relations: Self-control as the moral muscle. *Journal of Personality, 67*, 1165-94. doi:10.1111/1467-6494.00086

Baumeister, R. F., Vohs, K., & Tice, D. (2007). The strength model of self-control. *Current Directions in Psychological Science, 16*(6), 351-55. doi:10.1111/j.1467-8721.2007.00534.x

Baumeister, R. F., & Zell, A. L. (2013). How religion can support self-control and moral behavior. In R. F. Paloutzian & C. L. Park (Eds.), *Handbook of the psychology of religion and spirituality* (2nd ed., pp. 498-516). New York, NY: Guilford Press.

Beinart, H. (2014). Building and sustaining the supervision relationship. In C. E. Watkins & D. L. Milne (Eds.), *The Wiley International Handbook of Clinical Supervision*, 257-81. Hoboken, NJ: Wiley-Blackwell.

Bell, T., Dixon, A., & Kolts, R. (2016). Developing a compassionate internal supervisor: Compassion-focused therapy for trainee therapists. *Clinical Psychology & Psychotherapy.* doi:10.1002/cpp.2031

Benner, D. G. (2007). The incarnation as a metaphor for psychotherapy. In D. H. Stevenson, B. E. Eck, & P. C. Hill (Eds.), *Psychology & Christianity integration: Seminal works that shaped the movement* (pp. 244-49). Batavia, IL: Christian Association for Psychological Studies.

Bennett, C. (2008). Attachment-informed supervision for social work field education. *Clinical Social Work Journal, 36*, 97-107. doi:10.1007/s10615-007-0135-z

Bennett-Levy, J., Thwaites, R., Chaddock, A., & Davis, M. (2009). Reflective practice in cognitive behavioural therapy: The engine of lifelong learning. In J. Stedmon & R. Dallos (Eds.) *Reflective practice in psychotherapy and counselling* (pp. 115-35). Maidenhead, UK: Open University Press. doi:10.13140/2.1.1111.9040

Berger, R., & Quiros, L. (2014). Supervision for trauma-informed practice. *Traumatology, 20*(4), 296-301. doi:10.1037/h0099835

Bernard, J. M. (1997). The discrimination model. In C. E. Watkins (Ed.), *Handbook of psychotherapy supervision* (pp. 310-27). New York, NY: Wiley and Sons.

Bernard, J. M., & Goodyear, R. K. (2014). *Fundamentals of Clinical Supervision* (5th ed.). Boston, MA: Pearson.

Bersoff, D. N. (1996). The virtue of principle ethics. *Counseling Psychologist, 24*(1), 86-91. doi:10.1177/0011000096241004

Berthold, A., Ruch, W., Von Hecker, U., & Rosenberg, P. (2014). Satisfaction with life and character strengths of non-religious and religious people: It's practicing one's religion that makes the difference. *Frontiers in Psychology, 5*, 876. doi:10.3389/fpsyg.2014.00876

Bienenfeld, D., & Yager, J. (2007). Issues of spirituality and religion in psychotherapy supervision. *Israel Journal of Psychiatry and Related Sciences, 44*(3), 178-86.

Bland, E. (2008). An appraisal of psychological and religious perspectives of self-control. *Journal of Religion and Health, 47*(1), 4-16. doi:10.1007/s 10943-007-9 135-0

Bollinger, R. A., & Hill, P. C. (2012). Humility. In T. Plante (Ed.), *Religion, spirituality, and positive psychology: Understanding the psychological fruits of faith* (pp. 31-47). Santa Barbara, CA: Praeger.

Bonhoeffer, D. (2004). *Dietrich Bonhoeffer Works: Vol. 5. Life together and Prayerbook of the Bible* (G. B. Kelly, Ed.; D. W. Bloesch & J. H. Burtness, Trans.). Minneapolis, MN: Fortress Press.

Borders, L. D., Glosoff, H. L., Welfare, L. E., Hays, D. G., DeKruyf, L., Fernando, D. M., & Borders, B. P. (2014). Best practices in clinical supervision: Evolution of a counseling specialty. *The Clinical Supervisor, 33*(1), 26-44. doi:10.1080/07325223.2014.905225

Boszormenyi-Nagy, I., Grunebaum, J., & Ulrich, D. (1991). Contextual therapy. In A. S. Gurman & D. Kniskern (Eds.), *Handbook of family therapy* (Vol. 2, pp. 200-238). New York, NY: Brunner/Mazel.

Bouma-Prediger, S. (2007). The task of integration: A modest proposal. In D .H. Stevenson, B. E. Eck, & P. C. Hill (Eds.), *Psychology & Christianity integration: Seminal works that shaped the movement* (pp. 187-195). Batavia, IL: Christian Association for Psychological Studies.

Bowlby, J. (1969). *Attachment and loss.* New York, NY: Basic Books.

Bowlby, J. (1988). *A Secure Base.* New York, NY: Basic Books.

Boyatzis, C. (2012). Spiritual development during childhood and adolescence. In L. J. Miller (Ed.), *The Oxford handbook of psychology and spirituality* (pp. 151-64). New York, NY: Oxford University Press.

Breunlin, D. C., Lebow, J. L., & Buckley, C. K. (2014). Using evidence in systemic supervision. In T. C. Todd & C. L. Storm (Eds.), *The complete systemic supervisor: Context, philosophy, and pragmatics* (2nd ed., pp. 274-94). Hoboken, NJ: Wiley-Blackwell.

Brooks, D. (2015). *The road to character*. New York, NY: Random House.

Brooks, D. (2016). The cultural value of Christian higher education. *CCCU Advance, 7*(1). Retrieved from https://www.cccu.org/magazine/cultural-value-christian-higher-education/

Brooks, S., & Roberto-Forman, L. (2014). The transgenerational supervision models. In T. C. Todd & C. L. Storm (Eds.), *The complete systemic supervisor: Context, philosophy, and pragmatics* (2nd ed., pp. 186-207). Hoboken, NJ: Wiley-Blackwell.

Brunner, E. (1956). *Faith, hope, and love*. Philadelphia, PA: Westminster Press.

Buechner, F. (1973). *Wishful thinking: A theological ABC*. New York, NY: Harper & Row.

Bufford, R. (2007). Philosophical foundations for clinical supervision within a Christian worldview. *Journal of Psychology and Christianity, 26*(4), 293-97.

Burke, P., & Hohman, M. (2014). Encouraging self-reflection in the reflective listening process. In R. A. Bean, S. D. Davis, & M. P. Davey (Eds.), *Clinical Supervision activities for increasing competence and self-awareness* (pp. 33-40). Hoboken, NJ: Wiley.

Butman, R. E., & Kruse, S. J. (2007). On creating a healthy supervisory environment: A Christian relational and developmental perspective. *Journal of Psychology and Christianity, 26*(4), 307-12.

Calhoun, A. A. (2015). *Spiritual disciplines handbook: Practices that transform us* (2nd ed.). Downers Grove, IL: InterVarsity Press.

Cameron, C. D., & Rapier, K. (2017). Compassion is a motivated choice. In W. Sinnott-Armstrong & C. B. Miller (Eds.), *Moral Psychology: Vol. 5. Virtue and character* (pp. 373-408). Cambridge, MA: MIT Press.

Campbell, C. D. (2007). Integrating Christianity across the supervision process. *Journal of Psychology and Christianity, 26*(4), 321-27.

Canadian Psychological Association. (2009). *Ethical guidelines for supervision in psychology: Teaching, research, practice and administration*. Retrieved from http://www.cpa.ca/docs/File/Ethics/Ethical GuidelinesSupervisionPsychologyMar2012.pdf

Canning, S. S., Pozzi, C. F., McNeil, J. D., & McMinn, M. R. (2000). Integration as service: Implications of faith-praxis integration for training. *Journal of Psychology and Theology, 28*(3), 201-11.

Carlo, G., & Davis, A. N. (2016). Benevolence in a justice-based world: The power of sentiments (and reasoning) in predicting prosocial behaviors. In J. Annas, D. Narvaez, & N. Snow (Eds.), *Developing the virtues: Integrating perspectives* (pp. 255-72). New York, NY: Oxford University Press.

Carver, C. S., & Scheier, M. E. (2011). Self-regulation of action and affect. In K. D. Vohs & R. Baumeister (Eds.), *Handbook of self-regulation: Research, theory, and applications* (2nd ed., pp. 3-21). New York, NY: Guilford Press.

Cashwell, C. S., & Watts, R. E. (2010). The new ASERVIC competencies for addressing spiritual and religious issues in counseling. *Counseling and Values, 55*(1), 2-5. doi:10.1002/j.2161-007X.2010 .tb00018.x/epdf

Casler, K., & Kelemen, D. (2007). Reasoning about artifacts at 24 months: The developing teleo-functional stance. *Cognition, 103*(1), 120-30. doi:10.1016/j.cognition.2006.02.006

Catechism of the Catholic Church. (2003). Article 7, The Virtues. Vatican City: Libreria Editrice Vaticana. Retrieved from http://www.vatican.va/archive/ccc_css/archive/catechism/p3s1c1a7.htm

Center for Credentialing and Education. (2015). *Requirements for Approved Clinical Supervisor*. Retrieved from http://www.cce-global.org/Credentialing/ACS/Requirements

Chang, C. Y., Hays, D. G., & Milliken, T. F. (2009). Addressing social justice issues in supervision: A call for client and professional advocacy. *The Clinical Supervisor, 28*(1), 20-35. doi:10.1080/07325220902855144

Charry, E. T. (1997*). By the renewing of your minds: The pastoral function of Christian doctrine*. New York, NY: Oxford University Press.

Charry, E. T. (2010). *God and the art of happiness*. Grand Rapids, MI: Eerdmans.

Charry, E. T. (2011). Positive theology: An exploration in theological psychology and positive psychology. *Journal of Psychology and Christianity, 30*(4), 284-93.

Chase, D. P. (1847). *The ethics of Aristotle (The Nicomachean ethics, Chase's translation, newly revised)*. London, UK: Walter Scott.

Cheavens, J. S., Feldman, D. B., Gum, A., Michael, S. T., & Snyder, C. R. (2006). Hope therapy in a community sample: A pilot investigation. *Social Indicators Research, 77*, 61-78. doi:10.1007/s11205-005-5553-0

Christian Association for Psychological Studies. (2005). *Ethics statement of the Christian Association for Psychological Studies*. Retrieved from http://caps.net/about-us/statement-of-ethical-guidelines

Clohessy, S. (2008). *Supervisors' perspectives on their supervisory relationships: A qualitative study* (Unpublished doctoral thesis). University of Hull, UK.

Cochran, L. (1997). *Career counseling: A narrative approach*. Thousand Oaks, CA: Sage.

Coe, J. H., & Hall, T. W. (2010). *Psychology in the Spirit: Contours of a transformational psychology*. Downers Grove, IL: IVP Academic.

Colin, V. L. (1996). *Human attachment*. New York, NY: McGraw-Hill.

Constantine, M., & Sue, D. W. (2007). Perceptions of racial microaggressions among black supervisees in cross-racial dyads. *Journal of Counseling Psychology, 54*, 142-53. doi:10.1037/0022-0167.54.2.142

Constantino, M. J., Glass, C. R., Arnkoff, D. B., Ametrano, R. M., & Smith, J. Z. (2011). Expectations. In J. C. Norcross (Ed.), *Psychotherapy relationships that work: Evidence-based responsiveness* (2nd ed., pp. 354-76). New York, NY: Oxford University Press.

Cook, J. L., & Cook, G. (2009). *Child development: Principles and perspectives* (2nd ed.). New York, NY: Pearson.

Cook, K. V., Kimball, C. N., Leonard, K. C. & Boyatzis, C. J. (2014). The complexity of quest in emerging adults' religiosity, well-being, and identity. *Journal for the Scientific Study of Religion, 53*, 73-89. doi:10.1111/jssr.12086

Cottone, R. R. (2012). Ethical decision making in mental health contexts: Representative models and an organizational framework. In S. J. Knapp, M. C. Gottlieb, M. M. Handelsman, & L. D. VandeCreek (Eds.), *APA Handbook of Ethics in Psychology: Vol. 1. Moral foundations and common themes* (pp. 99-121). Washington, DC: American Psychological Association. doi:10.1037/13271-004

Council for Accreditation of Counseling and Related Educational Programs. (2016). *2016 CACREP standards*. Retrieved from http://www.cacrep.org/for-programs/2016-cacrep-standards/

Csikszentmihalyi, M. (1990). *Flow: The psychology of optimal experience* (1st ed.). New York, NY: Harper & Row.

Curtis, D. F., Elkins, S. R., Duran, P., & Venta, A. C. (2016). Promoting a climate of reflective practice and clinician self-efficacy in vertical supervision. *Training and Education in Professional Psychology, 10*(3), 133-40. doi:10.1037/tep0000121

Davis, D. E., & Hayes, J. A. (2011). What are the benefits of mindfulness? A practice review of psycho-therapy-related research. *Psychotherapy, 48*(2), 198-208. http://dx.doi.org/10.1037/a0022062

Davis, D. E., Worthington, E. L., Jr., Hook, J. N., & Hill, P. C. (2013). Research on religion/spirituality and forgiveness: A meta-analytic review. *Psychology of Religion and Spirituality*, *5*(4), 233-41. doi:10.1037/a0033637

Davis, D. E., Worthington, E. L., Jr., Hook, J. N., Emmons, R. A., Hill, P. C., Bollinger, R. A., & Van Tongeren, D. R. (2013). Humility and the development and repair of social bonds: Two longitudinal studies. *Self and Identity, 12*(1), 58-77. doi:10.1080/15298868.2011.636509

Davis, D. H., Hook, J. N., Worthington, E. L., Jr., Van Tongeren, D. R., Gartner, A. L., Jennings, D. J., II, & Emmons, R. A. (2011). Relational humility: Conceptualizing and measuring humility as a person-ality judgment. *Journal of Personality Assessment, 93*(3), 225-34. doi:10.1080/00223891.2011.558871

Diamond, G. S., Diamond, G. M., & Levy, S. A. (2014). *Attachment-based family therapy for depressed adolescents*. Washington, DC: American Psychological Association.

Dreher, D. E. (2012). Vocation: Finding joy and meaning in our work. In T. Plante (Ed.), *Religion, spirituality, and positive psychology: Understanding the psychological fruits of faith* (pp. 127-42). Santa Barbara, CA: Praeger.

Dreher, D., Holloway, K., & Schoenfelder, E. (2007). The vocation identity questionnaire: Measuring the sense of calling. *Research in the Social Scientific Study of Religion, 18*, 99-120. doi:10.1163/ej.9789004158511.i-301.42

Dressel, J. L., Consoli, A. J., Kim, B. S. K., & Atkinson, D. R. (2007). Successful and unsuccessful mul-ticultural supervisory behaviors: A Delphi poll. *Journal of Multicultural Counseling and Development, 35*, 51-64. doi:10.1002/j.2161-1912.2007.tb00049.x

Druher, D. E. (2012). Vocation: Finding joy and meaning in our work. In T. G. Plante (Ed.). *Religion, spirituality, and positive psychology* (pp. 127-42). Santa Barbara, CA: Praeger.

Duffy, K. A., & Chartrand, T. L. (2017). From mimicry to morality: The role of prosociality. In W. Sinnott-Armstrong & C. Miller (Eds.), *Moral Psychology: Vol. 5. Virtue and character* (pp. 439-64). Cambridge, MA: MIT Press.

Dwiwardani, C., & Waters, A. (2015). Cultural humility in Christian clinical psychology programs. *Society for the Psychology of Religion and Spirituality Newsletter*, Division 36, American Psycho-logical Association. Retrieved from http://www.apadivisions.org/division-36/publications/news letters/religion/2015/04/cultural-humility.aspx

Eck, B. E. (2002). An exploration of the therapeutic use of spiritual disciplines in clinical practice. *Journal of Psychology and Christianity, 21*(3), 266-80.

Edman, L. R. O. (2015). Applying the science of faith: The cognitive science of religion and Christian practice. *Journal of Psychology and Christianity, 34*(3), 240-51.

Edwards, K. (2015). When word meets flesh: A neuroscience perspective on embodied spiritual for-mation. *Journal of Psychology and Christianity, 34*(3), 228-39.

Eisenberg, N., Fabes, R. A., & Spinrad, T. L. (2006). Prosocial development. In W. Damon, R. M. Lerner (Series Eds.), & N. Eisenberg (Vol. Ed.), *Handbook of Child Psychology: Vol. 3. Social, emotional, and personality development* (6th ed., pp. 646-718). Hoboken, NJ: Wiley.

Ellis, M. V. (2010). Bridging the science and practice of clinical supervision: Some discoveries, some misconceptions. *The Clinical Supervisor, 29*(1), 95-116. doi:10.1080/07325221003741910

Emmons, R., & Kneezel, T. (2005). Giving thanks: Spiritual and religious correlates of gratitude. *Journal of Psychology and Christianity, 24*(2), 140-48.

Emmons, R. A., & Mishra, A. (2012). Gratitude. In T. Plante (Ed.), *Religion, spirituality, and positive psychology: Understanding the psychological fruits of faith* (pp. 9-29). Santa Barbara, CA: Praeger.

Erickson, E. H. (1963). *Childhood and Society.* New York, NY: W. W. Norton.

Eriksson, C. B., & Abernethy, A. D. (2014). Integration in multicultural competence and diversity training: Engaging difference and grace. *Journal of Psychology and Theology, 42*(2), 174-87.

Epstein, R. M., & Hundert, E. M. (2002). Defining and assessing professional competence. *Journal of the American Medical Association, 287*, 226-35. doi:10.1001/jama.287.2.226

Evagrius, P. (1971). *The praktikos: Chapters on prayer.* Spencer, MA: Cistercian Press.

Eyberg, S. M., Funderburk, B. W., HembreeKigin, T. L., McNeil, C. B., Querido, J. G., & Hood, K. (2001). Parent-child interaction therapy with behavior problem children: One and two year maintenance of treatment effects in the family. *Child & Family Behavior Therapy, 23*, 1-20. doi:10.1300/j019v23n04_01

Falender, C. A., & Shafranske, E. P. (2004). *Clinical supervision: A competency-based approach.* Washington, DC: American Psychological Association.

Falender, C. A., Shafranske, E. P., & Falicov, C. J. (2014). Diversity and multiculturalism in supervision. In C. A. Falender, E. P. Shafranske, & C. J. Falicov (Eds.), *Multiculturalism and diversity in clinical supervision: A competency-based approach* (pp. 3-28). Washington, DC: American Psychological Association.

Farber, E. W. (2014). Supervising humanistic and existential psychotherapies. In C. E. Watkins & D. L. Milne (Eds.), *The Wiley international handbook of clinical supervision* (pp. 530-51). Hoboken, NJ: Wiley-Blackwell.

Farley, B. W. (1995). *In praise of virtue: An exploration of the biblical virtues in a Christian context.* Grand Rapids, MI: Eerdmans.

Fave, A., Brdar, I., Vella-Brodrick, D., & Wissing, M. (2013). Well-being and cultures: Perspectives from positive psychology. In Chu Kim-Prieto (Ed.)., *Religion, spirituality, and well-being across nations: The eudaemonic and hedonic happiness investigation* (pp. 117-34). Dordrecht, Netherlands: Springer. doi:10.1007/978-94-007-4611-4_8

Fehr, G., Gelfand, M. J., & Nag, M. (2010). The road to forgiveness: A meta-analytic synthesis of its situational and dispositional correlates. *Psychological Bulletin, 136*(5), 894-914. doi:10.1037/a0019993

Feldman, D. B., & Kubota, M. (2012). Hope: Psychological perspectives on a spiritual virtue. In T. G. Plante (Ed.), *Religion, spirituality, and positive psychology: understanding the psychological fruits of faith* (pp. 49-62). Westport, CT: Praeger/Greenwood.

Figley, C. R. (1995). *Compassion fatigue: Coping with secondary traumatic stress disorder in those who treat the traumatized.* New York, NY: Brunner-Routledge.

Fiscalini, J. (1997). On supervisory parataxis and dialogue. In M. H. Rock (Ed.), *Psychodynamic Supervision* (pp. 29-58). Northvale, NJ: Aronson.

Fisk, L. K., Flores, M. H., McMinn, M. R., Aten, J. D., Hill, P. C., Tisdale, T. C., . . . Gathercoal, K. (2013). Spiritual formation among doctoral students in explicitly Christian programs. *Journal of Psychology and Christianity, 32*(4), 279-90.

Flanagan, K. S., Pressley, J. D., Davis, E. B., Aten, J. D., Sanders, M., Carter, J. C., . . . Kent, J. (2013). Spiritual formation training in the Wheaton College PsyD Program: Nurturing the growth of servant-oriented practitioner-scholars. *Journal of Psychology and Christianity, 32*(4), 340-51.

Fleischer, B. (2012). Virtues and praxis in ministry education. *Reflective Practice, 32*, 172-83. Retrieved from http://journals.sfu.ca/rpfs/index.php/rpfs/article/view/69/68

Forsyth, P. T. (2002). *The soul of prayer*. Vancouver, BC: Regent College Publishing.

Foster, R. J. (1988). *Celebration of discipline: The path to spiritual growth*. New York, NY: HarperCollins.

Foster, R. J. (1992). *Prayer: Finding the heart's true home*. San Francisco, CA: HarperSanFrancisco.

Foster, R. J. (2011). *Sanctuary of the soul: Journey into meditative prayer*. Downers Grove, IL: InterVarsity Press.

Fowers, B. J. (2001). The limits of a technical concept of a good marriage: Examining the role of virtues in communication skills. *Journal of Marital and Family Therapy, 27*, 327-40. doi:10.1111/j.1752-0606.2001.tb00328.x

Fowers, B. J. (2005). *Virtue and psychology: Pursuing excellence in ordinary practices*. Washington, DC: American Psychological Association.

Fowers, B. J., & Davidov, B. J. (2006). The virtue of multiculturalism: Personal transformation, character, and openness to the other. *American Psychologist, 61*, 581-94. doi:10.1037/0003-066x.61.6.581

Fowers, B. J., & Winakur, E. (2014). Key virtues of the psychotherapist: A eudaimonic view. In S. van Hooft & N. Saunders (Eds.), *The handbook of virtue ethics* (pp. 386-96). Durham, UK: Acumen.

Fowler, J. W. (1981). *Stages of faith: The psychology of human development and the quest for meaning*. San Francisco, CA: Harper & Row.

Frawley-O'Dea, M. G. (2003). Supervision is a relationship too: A contemporary approach to psychoanalytic supervision. *Psychoanalytic Dialogues, 13*(3), 355-66. doi:10.1080/10481881309348739

Frawley-O'Dea, M. G., & Sarnat, J. E. (2001). *The supervisory relationship: A contemporary psychodynamic approach*. New York, NY: Guilford Press.

Frederick, T. V., & Steele, L. L. (2010). Core competencies and Christian education: An integrative approach to education in marriage and family therapy programs. *ICCTE Journal, 11*(1). Retrieved from http://icctejournal.org/issues/v5i2/v5i2-frederick-steele/

Fredrickson, B. L., & Losada, M. F. (2005). Positive affect and the complex dynamics of human flourishing. *American Psychologist, 60*(7), 678-86. doi:10.1037/0003-066X.60.7.678

Freud, S., Strachey, J., & Gay, P. (1989). *The future of an illusion*. New York, NY: Norton.

Frost, K. (2004). *A longitudinal exploration of the supervisory relationship: A qualitative study* (Unpublished doctoral dissertation). University of Oxford, UK.

Fullam, L. (2014). Humility and magnanimity in spiritual guidance. *Reflective Practice*, 32. Retrieved from http://journals.sfu.ca/rpfs/index.php/rpfs/article/view/69/68

Gallagher, T. M. (2006). *The examen prayer: Ignatian wisdom for our lives today*. New York, NY: Crossroad.

Garcia, M., Kosutic, I., McDowell, T., & Anderson, S. A. (2009). Raising critical consciousness in family therapy supervision. *Journal of Feminist Family Therapy, 21*(1), 18-38. doi.org/10.1080/08952830802683673

Gardner, H. (2012). Harvard's cheating scandal as a play in four acts. Retrieved from http://cognoscenti.wbur.org/2012/10/02/harvards-cheating-scandal-as-a-play-in-four-acts

Garner, C. M., Webb, L. K., Chaffin, C., & Byars, A. (2017). The Soul of supervision: Counselor spirituality. *Counseling and Values, 62*, 24-36. doi:10.1002/cvj.12047

Germer, C. K., & Siegel, R. D. (Eds). (2012). *Wisdom and compassion in psychotherapy: Deepening mindfulness in clinical practice*. New York, NY: Guilford Press.

Giacalone, R. A., & Jurkiewicz, C. L. (2010). The science of workplace spirituality. In R. A. Giacalone & C. L. Jurkiewicz (Eds.), *Handbook of workplace spirituality and organizational performance* (pp. 3-26). Armonk, NY: Sharpe.

Gilligan, C. (1982). *In a different voice.* Cambridge, MA: Harvard University Press.

Gingrich, F., & Worthington, E. L. (2007). Supervision and the integration of faith into clinical practice: Research considerations. *Journal of Psychology and Christianity, 26*(4), 342-55.

Gingrich, H. D., & Gingrich, F. C. (Eds.) (2017). *Treating trauma in Christian counseling.* Downers Grove, IL: IVP Academic.

Glück J., & Bluck, S. (2013). MORE wisdom: A developmental theory of personal wisdom. In M. Ferrari & N. Weststrate (Eds.), *The scientific study of personal wisdom* (pp. 75-98). New York, NY: Springer.

Goetz, J. L., Keltner, D., & Simon-Thomas, E. (2010). Compassion: An evolutionary analysis and empirical review. *Psychological Bulletin, 136*(3), 351-74. doi:10.1037/a0018807

Gonsalvez, C. J., Bushnell, J., Blackman, R., Deane, F., Bliokas, V., Nicholson-Perry, K., . . . Knight, R. (2013). Assessment of psychology competencies in field placements: Standardized vignettes reduce rater bias. *Training and Education in Professional Psychology, 7*(2), 99-111. doi:10.1037/a0031617

Goodyear, R. K., & Nelson, M. L. (1997). The major formats of psychotherapy supervision. In C. E. Watkins Jr. (Ed.), *Handbook of psychotherapy supervision* (pp. 328-44). New York, NY: Wiley Press.

Goodyear, R. K., & Rodolfa, E. (2012). Negotiating the complex ethical terrain of clinical supervision. In S. J. Knapp, M. C. Gottlieb, M. M. Handelsman, & L. D. VandeCreek (Eds.), *APA handbook of ethics in psychology*, Vol. 2: *Practice, teaching, and research* (pp. 261-75). Washington, DC: American Psychological Association. doi:10.1037/13272-013

Granqvist, P. (1998). Religiousness and perceived childhood attachment: On the question of compensation or correspondence. *Journal for the Scientific Study of Religion, 37*(2), 350-67. doi:10.2307/1387533

Graziano, W. C., & Tobin, R. M. (2009). Agreeableness. In M. R. Leary & R. H. Hoyle (Eds.), *Handbook of individual differences in social behavior* (pp. 46-61). New York, NY: Guilford Press.

Green, E. J., McCollum, V. C., & Hays, D. G. (2008). Teaching advocacy counseling within a social justice framework: Implications for school counselors and educators. *Journal for Social Action in Counseling and Psychology, 1*(2), 14-30. Retrieved from http://www.psysr.org/jsacp/editorial-board.htm

Greene, J. D. (2014). Beyond point-and-shoot morality: Why cognitive (neuro)science matters for ethics. *Ethics, 124*(4), 695-726. doi:10.1086/675875

Greene, J. D., Morelli, S. A., Lowenberg, K., Nystrom, L. E., & Cohen, J. D. (2008). Cognitive load selectively interferes with utilitarian moral judgment. *Cognition, 107*(3), 1144-54. doi:10.1016/j.cognition.2007.11.004

Greene, J. D., Sommerville, R. B., Nystrom, L. E., Darley, J. M., & Cohen, J. D. (2001). An fMRI investigation of emotional engagement in moral judgment. *Science, 293*(5537), 2105-8. doi:10.1126/science.1062872

Grenz, S. J. (1997). *The moral quest: Foundations of Christian ethics.* Downers Grove, IL: InterVarsity Press.

Grus, C. L., & Kaslow, N. J. (2014). Professionalism: Professional values and attitudes in psychology. In W. B. Johnson & N. J. Kaslow (Eds.), *Oxford handbook of education and training in professional psychology* (pp. 491-509). New York, NY: Oxford University Press.

Gushee, D. P., & Stassen, G. H. (2016). *Kingdom ethics: Following Jesus in contemporary context* (2nd ed). Grand Rapids, MI: Eerdmans.

Hackney, C.H. (2007). Possibilities for a Christian positive psychology. *Journal of Psychology and Theology, 35*(3), 211-21.

Hall, M. E. L., Langer, R. C., & McMartin, J. (2010). The role of suffering in human flourishing: contributions from positive psychology, theology, and philosophy. *Journal of Psychology and Theology, 38*(2), 111-21.

Hall, S. S. (2010). *Wisdom: From philosophy to neuroscience.* New York, NY: Alfred A. Knopf.

Hannah, S. T., Sweeney, P. J., & Lester, P. B. (2010). The courageous mind-set: A dynamic personality system approach to courage. In C. L. S. Pury & S. J. Lopez (Eds.), *The psychology of courage: Modern research on an ancient virtue* (pp. 125-48). Washington, DC: American Psychological Association.

Hardy, K., & Laszloffy, T. (1995). The cultural genogram: A key to training culturally competent family therapists. *Journal of Marital and Family Therapy, 21*, 227-37. doi:10.1111/j.1752-0606.1995.tb00158.x

Harris, J. I., Erbes, C. R., Engdahl, B. E., Olson, R. A., Winskowski, A. M., & McMahill, J. (2008). Christian religious functioning and trauma outcomes. *Journal of Clinical Psychology, 64*(1), 17-29. doi:10.1002/jclp.20427

Hathaway, W. L. (2011). Ethical guidelines for using spiritually oriented interventions. In J. Aten, M. McMinn, & E. Worthington (Eds.). *Spiritually-oriented interventions for counseling and psychotherapy* (pp. 65-81). Washington, DC: American Psychological Association.

Hathaway, W. L., & Ripley, J. S. (2009). Ethical concerns around religion and spirituality in clinical practice. In J. Aten & M. Leach (Eds.), *Spirituality and the therapeutic process: A comprehensive resource from intake to termination* (pp. 25-52). Washington, DC: American Psychological Association.

Hauerwas, S., & Wells, S. (2011a). Christian ethics as informed prayer. In S. Hauerwas & S. Wells (Eds.), *The Blackwell companion to Christian ethics* (2nd ed., pp. 3-11). Oxford, UK: Blackwell. doi:10.1002/9781444396683.ch1

Hauerwas, S., & Wells, S. (2011b). The gift of the church and how God gives it. In S. Hauerwas & S. Wells (Eds.), *The Blackwell companion to Christian ethics* (2nd ed., pp. 13-27). Oxford, UK: Blackwell. doi:10.1002/9781444396683.ch2

Haug, I. E., & Storm, C. L. (2014). Developing ethical decision-making in systemic supervision. In T. C. Todd & C. L. Storm (Eds.), *The complete systemic supervisor*, supplementary online resources. Retrieved from http://www.wiley.com//legacy/wileychi/todd/supp/Supervisory/Transitioning/sec 01d.pdf?type=SupplementaryMaterial

Hays, P. A. (2001). *Addressing cultural complexities in practice: A framework for clinicians and counselors.* Washington, DC: American Psychological Association.

Heatherton, T. F. (2011). Neuroscience of self and self-regulation. *Annual Review of Psychology, 62*, 363-90. http://doi.org/10.1146/annurev.psych.121208.131616

Heidegger, M. (1962). *Being and time* (John Macquarrie and Edward Robinson, Trans.). New York, NY: Harper & Row.

Herdt, J. A. (2011). The virtue of the liturgy. In S. Hauerwas & S. Wells (Eds.), *The Blackwell companion to Christian ethics* (2nd ed., pp. 535-46). Oxford, UK: Blackwell. doi:10.1002/9781444396683.ch40

Hernández, P., & McDowell, T. (2010). Intersectionality, power, and relational safety in context: Key concepts in clinical supervision. *Training and Education in Professional Psychology, 4*(1), 29-35. doi:10.1037/a0017064

Hernandez-Wolfe, P., & McDowell, T. (2014). Bridging complex identities with cultural equity and humility in systemic supervision. In T. C. Todd & C. L. Storm (Eds.), *The complete systemic supervisor: Context, philosophy, and pragmatics* (2nd ed., pp. 43-61). Hoboken, NJ: Wiley-Blackwell.

Heschel, A. J. (2003). *The Sabbath: Its meaning for modern man.* Boston, MA: Shambhala.

Hill, C. E. (2014a). *Helping skills: Facilitating exploration, insight, and action* (4th ed.) Washington, DC: American Psychological Association.

Hill, C. E. (2014b). Helping skills training. In C. E. Watkins & D. L. Milne (Eds.), *The Wiley international handbook of clinical supervision* (pp. 329-41). Hoboken, NJ: Wiley-Blackwell.

Hill, P. C., Jurkiewicz, C. L., Giacalone, R. A., & Fry, L. W. (2013). From concept to science: Continuing steps in workplace spirituality research. In R. F. Paloutzian & C. L. Park (Eds.), *Handbook of the psychology of religion and spirituality* (2nd ed., pp. 617-31). New York, NY: Guilford Press.

Hill, P. C., & Dik, B. J. (2012). Toward a science of workplace spirituality: Contributions from the psychology of religion and spirituality. In P. C. Hill & B. J. Dik (Eds.), *Psychology of religion and workplace spirituality* (pp. 3-24). Charlotte, NC: Information Age.

Hoang, B. H. (2012). *Deepening the soul for justice.* Downers Grove, IL: InterVarsity Press.

Holmes, A. F. (1987). *The idea of a Christian college* (Rev. ed.). Grand Rapids, MI: Eerdmans.

Hood, R. W., Hill, P. C., & Spilka, B. (2009). *The psychology of religion: An empirical approach.* New York, NY: Guilford Press.

Hook, J. N., & Davis, D. E. (2012). Integration, multicultural counseling, and social justice. *Journal of Psychology and Theology, 40*(2), 102-6.

Hook, J. N., Davis, D. E., Owen, J., Worthington, Jr., E. L., & Utsey, S. O. (2013). Cultural humility: Measuring openness to culturally diverse clients. *Journal of Counseling Psychology, 60*, 353-66. doi:10.1037/a0032595

Howard, F. (2008). Managing stress or enhancing wellbeing? Positive psychology's contributions to clinical supervision. *Australian Psychologist, 43*, 105-13. doi:10.1080/00050060801978647

Hull, C. E., Suarez, E. C., & Hartman, D. (2016). Developing spiritual competencies in counseling: A guide for supervisors. *Counseling and Values, 61*, 111-26. doi:10.1002/cvj.12029

Inman, A. G., Hutman, H., Pendse, A., Devdas, L., Luu, L., & Ellis, M.V. (2014). Current trends concerning supervisors, supervisees, and clients in clinical supervision. In C. E. Watkins & D. L. Milne (Eds.), *The Wiley international handbook of clinical supervision* (pp. 61-102). Hoboken, NJ: Wiley-Blackwell.

Ivey, A. E., Ivey, M. B., & Zalaquett, C. P. (2014). *Intentional interviewing and counseling: Facilitating client development in a multicultural society* (8th ed.). Belmont, CA: Brooks/Cole, Cengage Learning.

James, W., & Marty, M. E. (1982). *The varieties of religious experience: A study in human nature.* Harmondsworth, UK: Penguin Books.

Jeffrey, D. L. (2009). Sharing wisdom as an act of love. Where wisdom is found [Issue]. *Christian Reflection: A Series in Faith and Ethics*, 66-73.

Jennings, L., Sovereign, A., Renninger, S., Goh, M., Skovholt, T., Lakhan, S., & Hessel, H. (2016). Bringing it all together: A qualitative meta-analysis of seven master therapists studies from around the world. In L. Jennings & T. Skovholt (Eds.), *Expertise in counseling and psychotherapy: Master therapist studies from around the world.* New York, NY: Oxford University Press. Retrieved from http://www.oxfordclinicalpsych.com/view/10.1093/med:psych/9780190222505.001.0001/med-9780190222505-chapter-8

Johnson, E. L. (Ed). (2010). *Psychology and Christianity: Five views.* Downers Grove, IL: IVP Academic.

Johnson, S. M. (2004). *The practice of emotionally focused couple therapy: Creating connection.* New York, NY: Brunner-Routledge.

Jones, D. C. (1994). *Biblical Christian ethics*. Grand Rapids, MI: Baker Books.

Jones, S. L., & Butman, R. E. (2011). *Modern psychotherapies: A comprehensive Christian appraisal* (2nd. ed.). Downers Grove, IL: IVP Academic.

Jordan, A. E., & Meara, N. M. (1990). Ethics and the professional practice of psychologists: The role of virtues and principles. *Professional Psychology: Research and Practice, 21*(2), 107-14. doi:10.1037/0735 -7028.21.2.107

Julian of Norwich. (1901). *Revelations of Divine Love* (Grace Warrack, Trans.). Retrieved from https:// www.ccel.org/ccel/julian/revelations.xiv.i.html

Jung, C. G. (1933). *Modern man in search of a soul*. New York, NY: Harcourt, Brace & World.

Kaczor, C. R. (2008). *Thomas Aquinas on faith, hope, and love: Edited and explained for everyone*. Ave Maria, FL: Sapientia Press of Ave Maria University.

Kaczor, C. R. (2015). Aristotle, Aquinas, and Seligman on happiness. *Journal of Psychology and Christianity, 34*(3), 196-204.

Kaczor, C., & Sherman, T. (2009). *Thomas Aquinas on the cardinal virtues: Edited and explained for Everyone*. Ave Maria, FL: Sapientia Press of Ave Maria University.

Kagan, N. (1984). Interpersonal process recall: Basic methods and recent research. In D. Larson (Ed.), *Teaching psychological skills* (pp. 229-44). Monterey, CA: Brooks/Cole.

Kelemen, D. (2004). Are children 'intuitive theists'? Reasoning about purpose and design in nature. *Psychological Science, 15*(5), 295-301. doi:10.1111/j.0956-7976.2004.00672.x

Keller, P. A., Murray, J. D., & Hargrove, D. S. (2012). Creating ethical academic cultures within psychology. In S. J. Knapp, M. C. Gottlieb, M. M. Handelsman, & L. D. VandeCreek (Eds.). *APA Handbook of Ethics in Psychology: Vol. 2. Practice, teaching, and research.* (pp. 219-68). Washington, DC: American Psychological Association.

Keller, T. (2010). *Generous justice: How God's grace makes us just*. New York, NY: Dutton, Penguin Group USA.

Kirkpatrick, L. A. (2005). *Attachment, evolution, and the psychology of religion*. New York, NY: Guilford Press.

Kirkpatrick, L., & Shaver, P. (1990). Attachment theory and religion: Childhood attachments, religious beliefs, and conversion. *Journal for the Scientific Study of Religion, 29*(3), 315-34. doi:10.2307/1386461

Kish-Gephart, J. J., Harrison, D. A., & Treviño, L. K. (2010). Bad apples, bad cases, and bad barrels: Meta-analytic evidence about sources of unethical decisions at work. *Journal of Applied Psychology, 95*(1), 1-31. doi:10.1037/a0017103

Kitchener, R. F., & Kitchener, K. S. (2012). Ethical foundations of psychology. In S. J. Knapp, M. C. Gottlieb, M. M. Handelsman, & L. D. VandeCreek (Eds.), *APA Handbook of Ethics in Psychology, Vol 1: Moral foundations and common themes* (pp. 3-42). Washington, DC: American Psychological Association. doi:10.1037/13271-001

Knapp, S. J., VandeCreek, L. D., & Fingerhut, R. (2017). *Practical ethics for psychologists: A positive approach* (3rd ed.). Washington, DC: APA Press. http://dx.doi.org/10.1037/0000036-001

Knobel, A. (2015). A different kind of wisdom. In C. Miller, R. Furr, A. Knobel, & W. Fleeson (Eds.), *Character: New directions from philosophy, psychology, and theology*. Oxford, UK: Oxford University Press.

Kocet, M. M., & Herlihy, B. J. (2014). Addressing value-based conflicts within the counseling relationship: A decision-making model. *Journal of Counseling & Development, 92*, 180-86. doi:10.1002/ j.1556-6676.2014.00146.x

Koenig, H. G. (2012). Religion, spirituality, and health: The research and clinical implications. *ISRN Psychiatry, 2012*, Article ID 278730. doi:10.5402/2012/278730

Kohlberg, L. (1984). *The psychology of moral development.* San Francisco, CA: Harper & Row.

Krause, N., & Hayward, R. (2015). Virtues, practical wisdom and psychological well-being: A Christian perspective. *Social Indicators Research, 122*(3), 735-55. doi:10.1007/s11205-014-0709-4

Kwon, S.-Y. (2012). Empathy in pastoral counseling: Cultivating a clinical virtue of Christian incarnation. *Reflective Practice, 32,* 118-31. Retrieved from http://journals.sfu.ca/rpfs/index.php/rpfs/article/view/64/63

Ladany, N., Hill, C., Corbett, M., & Nutt, E. (1996). Nature, extent, and importance of what psychotherapy trainees do not disclose to their supervisors. *Journal of Counseling Psychology, 43*(1), 10-24. doi:10.1037/0022-0167.43.1.10

Ladany, N., Inman, A. G., Constantine, M. G., & Hofheinz, E. W. (1997). Supervisee multicultural case conceptualization ability and self-reported multicultural competence as functions of supervisee racial identity and supervisor focus. *Journal of Counseling Psychology, 44*(3), 284-93. doi:10.1037/0022-0167.44.3.284

Ladany, N., Mori, M., & Mehr, K. (2013). Effective and ineffective supervision. *Counseling Psychologist, 41*(1), 28-47. doi:10.1177/0011000012442648

Lampropoulos, G. K. (2002). A common factors view of counseling supervision process. *The Clinical Supervisor, 21*(1), 77-95. doi:10.1300/j001v21n01_06

Landauer, T., McNamara, S., Dennis, S., & Kintsch, W. (2007). *Handbook of latent semantic analysis.* Mahwah, NJ: Lawrence Erlbaum Associates.

Lee, M. M., & Vennum, A. V. (2010). Using critical incident journaling to encourage cultural awareness in doctoral marriage and family therapy students. *Journal of Family Psychotherapy, 21,* 238-52. doi:10.1080/08975353.2010.529008

Lehrman-Waterman, D., & Ladany, N. (2001). Development and validation of the evaluation process within supervision inventory. *Journal of Counseling Psychology, 48,* 168-77. doi:10.1037/0022-0167.48.2.168

Lenz, A. S., Sangganjanavanich, V. F., Balkin, R. S., Oliver, M., & Smith, R. L. (2012). Wellness model of supervision: A comparative analysis. *Counselor Education and Supervision, 51,* 207-21. doi:10.1002/j.1556-6978.2012.00015.x

Lenz, A. S., & Smith, R. L. (2010). Integrating wellness concepts within a clinical supervision model. *The Clinical Supervisor, 29*(2), 228-45. doi:10.1080/07325223.2010.518511

Lester, P. B., Vogelgesang, G. R., Hannah, S. T., & Kimmey, T. (2010). Developing courage in followers: Theoretical and applied perspectives. In C. L. S. Pury & S. J. Lopez (Eds.), *The psychology of courage: Modern research on an ancient virtue.* Washington, DC: American Psychological Association.

Lewis-Fernández, R., Aggarwal, N. K., Hinton, L., Hinton, D. E., & Kirmayer, L. J. (2015). *DSM-5 Handbook on the Cultural Formulation Interview.* Washington, DC: American Psychiatric Publishing.

Lewis, C. S. (1977). *The Screwtape letters.* New York, NY: MacMillan.

Liese, B. S., & Beck, J. S. (1997). Cognitive therapy supervision. In C. E. Watkins (Ed.), *Handbook of psychotherapy supervision.* New York, NY: Wiley Press.

Livni, D., Crowe, T. P., & Gonsalvez, C. J. (2012). Effects of supervision modality and intensity on alliance and outcomes for the supervisee. *Rehabilitation Psychology, 57*(2), 178-86. doi:10.1037/a0027452

Macaro, A. (2009). Virtue in supervision. In E. van Deurzen & S. Young (Eds.), *Existential perspectives on supervision: Widening the horizon of psychotherapy and counselling.* London, UK: Palgrave Macmillan.

MacIntyre, A. C. (1984). *After virtue: A study in moral theory.* Notre Dame, IN: University of Notre Dame Press.

Mackey, H. B. (1997). *Treatise on the love of God by Frances de Sales.* Rockford, IL: Tan Book and Publishers.

Mangione, L., & Nadkarni, L. C. (2010). The relationship competency: Broadening and deepening. In M. B. Kenkel & R. L. Peterson (Eds.), *Competency-based education for professional psychology* (pp. 69-86). Washington, DC: American Psychological Association.

Manney, J. (2011). *A simple, life-changing prayer: Discovering the power of St. Ignatius Loyola's examen.* Chicago, IL: Loyola Press.

Martz, E., & Kaplan, D. (2014). New responsibilities when making referrals. *Counseling Today, 57*(4), 24-25. Retrieved from https://www.counseling.org

Maxwell, M. J., & Henriksen, R. C., Jr. (2011). *Teaching social justice through service learning. Vistas,* article 32. Retrieved from https://www.counseling.org

McCann, L. I., & Pearlman, L. A. (1990). Vicarious traumatization: A framework for understanding the psychological effects of working with victims. *Journal of Traumatic Stress, 3,* 131-49. doi:10.1002/jts.2490030110

McCollum, E. E., and Gehart, D. R. (2010). Using mindfulness meditation to teach beginning therapists therapeutic presence: A qualitative study. *Journal of Marital and Family Therapy, 36,* 347-60. doi:10.1111/j.1752-0606.2010.00214.x

McConnell, K. M., Pargament, K. I., Ellison, C. G., & Flannelly, K. J. (2006). Examining the links between spiritual struggles and symptoms of psychopathology in a national sample. *Journal of Clinical Psychology, 62*(12), 1469-84. doi:10.1002/jclp.20325

McCullough, M. E., & Tsang, J. (2004). Parent of the virtues: The prosocial contours of gratitude. In R. Emmons & M. E. McCullough (Eds), *The psychology of gratitude* (pp. 123-41). New York, NY: Oxford University Press.

McCullough, M. E., & Willoughby, B. B. (2009). Religion, self-regulation, and self-control: Associations, explanations, and implications. *Psychological Bulletin, 135*(1), 69-93. doi:10.1037/a0014213

McInerny, D. (2014). Fortitude and the conflict of frameworks. In C. A. Boyd & K. Timpe (Eds.), *Virtues and their vices* (pp. 75-92). Oxford, UK: Oxford University Press.

McKay, A. M. (2004). *The infused and acquired virtues in Aquinas' moral philosophy* (Doctoral dissertation, University of Notre Dame). Retrieved from: https://curate.nd.edu/show/73666397v1r.

McMartin, J. (2015). The work of the Holy Spirit in natural psychological growth. *Journal of Psychology and Christianity, 34*(3), 216-27.

McMartin, J., Dodgen-Magee, D., Geevarughese, M. C., Gioielli, S., & Sklar, Q. T. (2013). Spiritual formation training at Rosemead School of Psychology. *Journal of Psychology and Christianity, 32*(4), 329-39.

McMinn, M. R., & Campbell, C. D. (2007). *Integrative psychotherapy: Toward a comprehensive Christian approach.* Downers Grove, IL: InterVarsity Press.

McMinn, M. R., Goodworth, M. C., Borrelli, J., Goetsch, B., Lee, J. L., & Uhder, J. (2013). Spiritual formation training in the George Fox University Graduate Department of Clinical Psychology. *Journal of Psychology and Christianity, 32*(4), 313-19.

McMinn, M. R., Vogel, M. J., Hall, M. E. L., Abernethy, A. D., Birch, R., Galuza, T., . . . Putman, K. (2015). Religious and spiritual diversity training in clinical psychology doctoral programs: Do explicitly Christian programs differ from other programs? *Journal of Psychology and Theology, 43*(3), 155-64.

McRay, B. W., Yarhouse, M. A., & Butman, R. E. (2016). *Modern psychopathologies: A comprehensive Christian appraisal* (2nd ed.). Downers Grove, IL: IVP Academic.

Mehr, K., Ladany, N., & Caskie, G. (2010). Trainee nondisclosure in supervision: What are they not telling you? *Counselling and Psychotherapy Research, 10*(2), 103-13. doi:10.1080/14733141003712301

Miller, M. M., & Ivey, D. C. (2006). Spirituality, gender, and supervisory style in supervision. *Contemporary Family Therapy: An International Journal, 28*(3), 323-37. doi:10.1007/s10591-006-9012-0

Miller, M. M., Korinek, A. W., & Ivey, D. C. (2006). Integrating spirituality into training: The spiritual issues in supervision scale. *American Journal of Family Therapy, 34*(4), 355-72. doi:10.1080 /01926180600553811

Milne, D. (2009). *Evidence-based clinical supervision: Principles and practice.* Hoboken, NJ: Wiley-Blackwell.

Moja-Strasser, L. (2009). Deliberations on supervision. In E. van Deurzen & S. Young (Eds.), *Existential perspectives on supervision: Widening the horizon of psychotherapy and counselling* (pp. 31-42). London, UK: Palgrave Macmillan.

Moltmann, J. (1967). *Theology of Hope: On the ground and the implications of a Christian eschatology.* New York, NY: Harper & Row.

Morgan, M. M., & Sprenkle, D. H. (2007). Toward a common-factors approach to supervision. *Journal of Marital and Family Therapy, 33*(1), 1-17. doi:10.1111/j.1752-0606.2007.00001.x

Mother Teresa. (1996). *The joy in loving: A guide to daily living.* New York, New York: Penguin Compass.

Myers, J. E., & Sweeney, T. J. (2005). *Counseling for wellness: Theory, research and practice.* Alexandria, VA: American Counseling Association.

Myers, J. E., Sweeney, T. J., & Witmer, J. M. (2000). The wheel of wellness counseling for wellness: A holistic model for treatment planning. *Journal of Counseling & Development, 78*(3), 251-66. doi:10.1002/j.1556-6676.2000.tb01906.x

Nadelhoffer, T., & Wright, J. C. (2017). The twin dimensions of the virtue of humility: Low self-focus and high other focus. In W. Sinnott-Armstrong & C. Miller (Eds.), *Moral Psychology: Vol. 5. Virtue and character* (pp. 309-42). Cambridge, MA: MIT Press.

Narvaez, D. (2014). *Neurobiology and the development of human morality: Evolution, culture, and wisdom.* New York, NY: W. W. Norton.

Neff, K. D. (2003). The development and validation of a scale to measure self-compassion. *Self and Identity, 2,* 223-50. doi:10.1080/15298860390209035

Nelson, J. M. (2009). *Psychology, religion, and spirituality.* New York, NY: Springer.

Newman, J., Garland, M., Castro-Klarén, S., Landow, G., & Marsden, G. (1996). *The idea of a university* (F. Turner, Ed.). New Haven, CT: Yale University Press.

Niemiec, R. M. (2013). VIA character strengths: Research and practice (the first 10 years). In H. H. Knoop and A. Delle Fave (Eds.), *Cross-Cultural Advancements in Positive Psychology: Vol. 3. Well-being and cultures: Perspectives from positive psychology* (pp. 11-29). Dordrecht, Netherlands: Springer. doi:10.1007/978-94-007-4611-4_2

Ng, H. K. (2013). Spiritual, personal, and cultural values in counseling ethics. In C. M. Jungers & J. Gregoire (Eds.), *Counseling ethics: Philosophical and professional foundations* (pp. 73-92). New York, NY: Springer.

Norcross, J. C. (Ed.) (2011). *Psychotherapy relationships that work: Evidence-based responsiveness* (2nd ed.) New York, NY: Oxford University Press.

Nouwen, H. J. M. (1981). *The way of the heart: Desert spirituality and contemporary ministry.* New York, NY: Seabury Press.

Nouwen, H. J. M. (1989). *In the Name of Jesus: Reflections on Christian leadership.* New York, NY: Crossroad.

Nystrom, D. (1997). *NIV Application Commentary: James.* Grand Rapids, MI: Zondervan.

Ortberg, J. (1997). *The life you've always wanted: Spiritual disciplines for ordinary people.* Grand Rapids, MI: Zondervan.

Owen, J., & Lindley, L. (2010). Therapists' cognitive complexity: Review of theoretical models and development of an integrated approach for training. *Training and Education in Psychology, 4*(2), 128-37. doi:10.1037/a0017697

Paine, D. R., Sandage, S. J., Rupert, D., Devor, N. G., & Bronstein, M. (2015). Humility as a psychotherapeutic virtue: Spiritual, philosophical, and psychological foundations. *Journal of Spirituality in Mental Health, 17*(1), 3-25. doi:10.1080/19349637.2015.957611

Palmer, P. J. (2007). *The courage to teach* (10th anniversary ed.). San Francisco, CA: John Wiley and Sons.

Palmer, P. J., Zajonc, A., & Scribner, M. (2010). *The heart of higher education: A call to renewal.* San Francisco, CA: Jossey-Bass.

Pargament, K. I. (1997). *The psychology of religion and coping: Theory, research, practice.* New York, NY: Guilford Press.

Pargament, K. I., Falb, M. D., Ano, G. G., & Wachholtz, A. B. (2013). The religious dimensions of coping: Advances in theory, research, and practice. In R. F Paloutzian & C. L. Park (Eds.), *Handbook of the psychology of religion and spirituality* (2nd ed., pp. 560-79). New York, NY: Guilford Press.

Pargament, K., Kennell, J., Hathaway, W., Grevengoed, N., Newman, J., & Jones, W. (1988). Religion and the problem-solving process: Three styles of coping. *Journal for the Scientific Study of Religion, 27*(1), 90-104. doi: 10.2307/1387404

Pargament, K. I., Magyar-Russell, G. M., & Murray-Swank, N. A. (2005). The sacred and the search for significance: Religion as a unique process. *Journal of Social Issues, 61*(4), 665-87. doi:10.1111/j.1540-4560.2005.00426.x

Park, C. L. (2005). Religion as a meaning-making framework in coping with life stress. *Journal of Social Issues, 61*(4), 707-29. doi:10.1111/j.1540-4560.2005.00428.x

Park, C. L. (2009). Overview of theoretical perspectives. In C. L. Park (Ed.), *Medical Illness and Positive Life Change: Can crisis lead to personal transformation?* (pp. 11-30). Washington, DC: American Psychological Association.

Park, C. L. (2013). Religion and meaning. In R. F. Paloutzian, & C. L. Park (Eds.), *Handbook of the psychology of religion and spirituality* (2nd ed., pp. 357-79). New York, NY: Guilford Press. Retrieved from http://ebookcentral.proquest.com

Park, N., Peterson, C., & Seligman, M. E. P. (2004). Strengths of character and well-being. *Journal of Social and Clinical Psychology, 23*(5), 603-19. doi:10.1521/jscp.23.5.603.50748

Parker, T. S., & Blackburn, K. M. (2014). The empathy game. In R. A. Bean, S. D. Davis, & M. P. Davey (Eds.), *Clinical supervision activities for increasing competence and self-awareness* (pp. 15-20). Hoboken, NJ: Wiley.

Patsiopoulos, A. T., & and Buchanan, M. J. (2011). The practice of self-compassion in counseling: A narrative inquiry. *Professional Psychology: Research and Practice, 42*(4), 301-7. doi:10.1037/a0024482

Patton, M. J., & Kivlighan, D. M. J. (1997). Relevance of the supervisory alliance to the counseling alliance and to treatment adherence in counselor training. *Journal of Counseling Psychology, 44*(1), 108-15. http://dx.doi.org/10.1037/0022-0167.44.1.108

Pearce, N., Beinart, H., Clohessy, S., & Cooper, M. (2013). Development and validation of the supervisory relationship measure: A self-report questionnaire for use with supervisors. *British Journal of Clinical Psychology, 52*(3), 249-68. doi:10.1111/bjc.12012

Peterson, C. (2006). *A primer in positive psychology.* Oxford, UK: Oxford University Press.

Peterson, C., & Seligman, M. (2004). *Character strengths and virtues.* Washington, DC: American Psychological Association.

Piaget, J. (1948). *The moral judgment of the child.* Glencoe, IL: Free Press.

Pieper, J. (1966). *The four cardinal virtues.* Notre Dame, IN: University of Notre Dame Press.

Pieper, J. (1997). *Faith, hope, love.* San Francisco, CA: Ignatius Press.

Pistole, M. C., & Watkins, C. E. J. (1995). Attachment theory, counseling process, and supervision. *Counseling Psychologist, 23*(3), 457-78. doi:10.1177/0011000095233004

Plante, T. G. (2009). *Spiritual practices in psychotherapy: Thirteen tools for enhancing psychological health.* Washington, DC: American Psychological Association. doi:10.1037/11872-000

Pohl, C. D. (1999). *Making room: Recovering hospitality as a Christian tradition.* Grand Rapids, MI: Eerdmans.

Pohl, C. D. (2007). Building a place for hospitality. Hospitality [Issue]. *Christian Reflection: A Series in Faith and Ethics,* 27-36.

Polanski, P. J. (2003). Spirituality in supervision. *Counseling & Values, 47*(2), 131. doi:10.1002/j.2161-007x .2003.tb00230.x

Polansky, R. (2014). Introduction: Ethics as practical science. In R. Polansky (Ed.), *The Cambridge companion to Aristotle's Nichomachean ethics* (pp. 1-13). New York, NY: Cambridge University Press.

Pomerantz, A. M. (2012). Informed consent to psychotherapy (empowered collaboration). In S. J. Knapp, M. C. Gottlieb, M. M. Handelsman, & L. D. VandeCreek (Eds.), *APA Handbook of Ethics in Psychology: Vol. 1. Moral foundations and common themes* (pp. 311-32). Washington, DC: American Psychological Association. doi:10.1037/13271-012

Pope, K. S., Tabachnick, B. G., & Keith-Spiegal, P. (1987). Ethics of practice: The beliefs and behaviors of psychologists as therapists. *American Psychologist, 42,* 993-1006. doi.org/10.1037/0003 -066X.42.11.993

Pretorius, W. (2006). Cognitive behavioural therapy supervision. *Behavioural and Cognitive Psychotherapy, 34,* 413-420. doi:10.1017/s1352465806002876

Ratts, M. J. (2009). Social justice counseling: Toward the development of a fifth force among counseling paradigms. *The Journal of Humanistic Counseling, Education and Development, 48:* 160-72. doi:10.1002/j.2161-1939.2009.tb00076.x.

Ratts, M. J., & Hutchins, A. M. (2009). ACA advocacy competencies: Social justice advocacy at the client/ student level. *Journal of Counseling & Development,* 87: 269-75. doi:10.1002/j.1556-6678.2009.tb00106.x

Ratts, M. J., Singh, A. A., Nassar-McMillan, S., Butler, S. K., & McCullough, J. R. (2016). Multicultural and social justice counseling competencies: Guidelines for the counseling profession. *Journal of Multicultural Counseling and Development, 44*, 28-48. doi:10.1002/jmcd.12035

Ratts, M. J., Toporek, R., & Lewis, J. (Eds.). (2010). *ACA advocacy competencies: A social justice framework for counselors.* Alexandria, VA: American Counseling Association.

Reiner, P. (2014). Systemic psychodynamic supervision. In T. C. Todd & C. L. Storm (Eds.), *The Complete systemic supervisor: Context, philosophy, and pragmatics* (2nd ed.) (pp. 166-85). Hoboken, NJ: Wiley-Blackwell.

Richards, P. S., & Bergin, A. E. (2005). *A spiritual strategy for counseling and psychotherapy* (2nd ed.). Washington, DC: American Psychological Association. doi:10.1037/11214-000

Ripley, J. S., Bekker, C. J., Yarhouse, M. A., Jackson, L. D., Kays, J., & Lane, C. R. (2013). Spiritual formation training at Regent University's psychology doctoral program. *Journal of Psychology and Christianity, 32*(4), 320-28.

Ripley, J. S., Garzon, F. L., Hall, M. E. L., Mangis, M. W., & Murphy, C. J. (2009). Pilgrims' progress: Faculty and university factors in graduate student integration of faith and profession. *Journal of Psychology and Theology, 37*, 5-14.

Ripley, J. S., Jackson, L. D., Tatum, R. L., & Davis, E. B. (2007). A developmental model of supervisee religious and spiritual development. *Journal of Psychology and Christianity, 26*(4), 298-306.

Ripley, J. S., & Worthington, E. L. (2014). *Couple therapy: A new hope-focused approach.* Downers Grove, IL: InterVarsity Press.

Robinson, M. (2004). *Gilead.* New York, NY: Farrar, Straus and Giroux.

Rock, M. H. (1997). *Psychodynamic supervision.* Northvale, NJ: Aronson.

Rolheiser, R. (2001). Anxiety as the opposite of faith. Retrieved from http://ronrolheiser.com/anxiety-as-the-opposite-of-faith/#.V7CoX5grI2w

Rolheiser, R. (2004). *The shattered lantern: Rediscovering a felt presence of God.* New York, NY: Crossroad.

Rolheiser, R. (2014). *Sacred fire: A vision for a deeper human and Christian maturity.* New York, NY: Random House.

Rogers, C. R. (1957). The necessary and sufficient conditions of therapeutic personality change. *Journal of Consulting Psychology, 21*(2), 95-103. doi:10.1037/h0045357

Rose, E. D., & Exline, J. J. (2012). Personality, spirituality, and religion. In L. J. Miller (Ed.), *The Oxford handbook of psychology and spirituality* (pp. 85-103). New York, NY: Oxford University Press.

Ross, D. K., Suprina, J. S., & Brack, G. (2013). The spirituality in supervision model (SACRED): An emerging model from a meta-synthesis of the literature. *The Practitioner Scholar: Journal of Counseling and Professional Psychology, 68*(2), 68-83.

Ruch, W., Huber, A., Beermann, U., & Proyer, R. T. (2007). Character strengths as predictors of the "good life" in Austria, Germany and Switzerland. In Romanian Academy, "George Barit" Institute of History, Department of Social Research (Ed.), *Studies and researches in social sciences* (Vol. 16, pp. 123-31). Cluj-Napoca, Romania: Argonaut Press.

Sadler-Gerhardt, C. J., & Stevenson, D. L. (2011). When it all hits the fan: Helping counselors build resilience and avoid burnout. *Ideas and Research You Can Use: VISTAS 2012, 1*, 1-8. Retrieved from: https://www.counseling.org/resources/library/vistas/vistas12/Article_24.pdf

Safran, J. D., Muran, J. C., Stevens, C., & Rothman, M. (2008). A relational approach to supervision: Addressing ruptures in the alliance. In C. A. Falender and E. P. Shafranske (Eds.), *Casebook for Clinical Supervision: A competency-based approach* (pp. 137-57). Washington, DC: American Psychological Association.

Saint Teresa of Ávila (2008). *Interior castle: The soul's spiritual journey to union with God*. Alachua, FL: Bridge Logos Publishers.

Sandage, S. J., & Harden, M. G. (2011). Relational spirituality, differentiation of self, and virtue as predictors of intercultural development. *Mental Health, Religion & Culture, 14*(8), 819-38. doi:10.1080/13674676.2010.527932

Sanders, R. K. (2013). *Christian counseling ethics: A handbook for psychologists, therapists and pastors* (2nd ed). Downers Grove, IL: IVP Academic.

Sarnat, J. (2010). Key competencies of the psychodynamic psychotherapist and how to teach them in supervision. *Psychotherapy: Theory, research, practice, training, 47*, 20-27. doi:10.1037/a0018846

Sarnat, J. (2012). Supervising psychoanalytic psychotherapy: Present knowledge, pressing needs, future possibilities. *Journal of Contemporary Psychotherapy, 42*, 151-60. doi:10.1007/s10879-011-9201-5

Saroglou, V. (2013). Religion, spirituality, and altruism. In K. I. Pargament, J. Exline, & J. Jones, (Eds.), *APA Handbook of Psychology, Religion, and Spirituality: Vol. 1. Context, theory, and research* (pp. 439-57). Washington, DC: American Psychological Association. doi:10.1037/14045-024

Schön, D. A. (1987). *Educating the reflective practitioner*. San Francisco, CA: Jossey-Bass.

Schwartz, B., & Sharpe, K. (2006). Practical wisdom: Aristotle meets positive psychology. *Journal of happiness studies, 7*(3), 377-95. doi:10.1007/s10902-005-3651-y

Seligman, M. E. P. (1991). *Learned optimism*. New York, NY: A. A. Knopf.

Seligman, M. E. P. (2011). *Flourish: A visionary new understanding of happiness and well-being*. New York, NY: Free Press.

Seligman, M. E. P., & Csikszentmihalyi, M. (2000). Positive psychology: An introduction. *American Psychologist, 55*(1), 5-14. doi:10.1037/0003-066x.55.1.5

Sells, J. N., & Hagedorn, W. B. (2016). CACREP accreditation, ethics, and the affirmation of both religious and sexual identities: A response to Smith and Okech. *Journal of Counseling & Development, 94*, 265-79. doi:10.1002/jcad.12083

Seoane, L., Tompkins, L. M., De Conciliis, A., & Boysen, P. G. (2016). Virtues education in medical school: The foundation for professional formation. *Ochsner Journal, 16*(1), 50-55. Retrieved from https://www.ncbi.nlm.nih.gov/pmc/articles/PMC4795502/pdf/i1524-5012-16-1-50.pdf

Shafranske, E. P. (2014). Addressing religiousness and spirituality as clinically relevant cultural features in supervision. In C. A. Falender, E. P. Shafranske, & C. Falicov (Eds.), *Multiculturalism and diversity in clinical supervision: A competency-based approach*. Washington, DC: American Psychological Association.

Shafranske, E. P., & Falender, C. A. (2008). Supervision addressing personal factors and countertransference. In E. P. Shafranske & C. A. Falender (Eds.), *Casebook for clinical supervision* (pp. 97-120). Washington, DC: American Psychological Association.

Sherman, A. L. (2011). *Kingdom calling: Vocational stewardship for the common good*. Downers Grove, IL: InterVarsity Press.

Sherman, M. D. (1996). Distress and professional impairment due to mental health problems among psychotherapists. *Clinical Psychology Review, 16*, 299-315. doi:10.1016/0272-7358(96)00016-5

Sileo, F. J., & Kopala, M. (1993). An A-B-C-D-E worksheet for promoting beneficence when considering ethical issues. *Counseling & Values, 37*(2), 89. doi:10.1002/j.2161-007X.1993.tb00800.x

Skovholt, T. M., & Trotter-Mathison, M. (2011). *The resilient practitioner: Burnout prevention and self-care strategies for counselors, therapists, teachers, and health professionals* (2nd ed.). New York, NY: Taylor and Frances.

Smith, B. W., Ortiz, A., Wiggins, K. T., Berhard, J. F., & Dalen, J. (2012). Spirituality, resilience, and positive emotions. In L. J. Miller (Ed.). *The Oxford handbook of psychology and spirituality.* (pp. 437-54). New York, NY: Oxford University Press.

Smith, L. C., & Okech, J. E. A. (2016). Ethical issues raised by CACREP accreditation of programs within institutions that disaffirm or disallow diverse sexual orientations. *Journal of Counseling & Development, 94*, 252-64. doi:10.1002/jcad.12082

Smith, D. I., & Smith, J. K. A. (Eds.). (2011). *Teaching and Christian practices: Reshaping faith and learning.* Grand Rapids, MI: Eerdmans.

Snyder, C. R. (1994). *The psychology of hope: You can get there from here.* New York, NY: Free Press.

Snyder, C. R., Sigmon, D., & Feldman, D. B. (2003). Hope for the sacred and vice versa: Positive goal-directed thinking and religion. *Psychological Inquiry, 13*, 201-38.

Sobell, L. C., Manor, H., Sobell, M. B., & Dum, M. (2008). Self-critiques of audiotaped therapy sessions: A motivational procedure for facilitating feedback during supervision. *Training and Education in Professional Psychology, 2*(3), 151-55. doi:10.1037/1931-3918.2.3.151

Sorenson, R. L. (1997). Doctoral students' integration of psychology and Christianity: Perspectives via attachment theory and multidimensional scaling. *Journal for the Scientific Study of Religion, 36*(4), 530-648. doi:10.2307/1387688

Sorenson, R. L., Derflinger, K. R., Bufford, R. K., & McMinn, M.R. (2004). National collaborative research on how students learn integration: Final report. *Journal of Psychology and Christianity, 23*, 355-65.

Sparks, J. A., Kisler, T. S., Adams, J. F., & Blumen, D. G. (2011). Teaching accountability: Using client feedback to train effective family therapists. *Journal of Marital and Family Therapy, 37*, 452-67. doi:10.1111/j.1752-0606.2011.00224.x

Sperry, L., & Sperry, J. J. (2012). Psychotherapy and virtue: Positive psychology and spiritual well-being. In T. Plante (Ed.), *Religion, spirituality, and positive psychology: Understanding the psychological fruits of faith* (pp. 145-58). Santa Barbara, CA: Praeger.

Staudinger, U., & Glück, J. (2011). Psychological wisdom research: Commonalities and differences in a growing field. *Annual Reviews of Psychology, 62*, 215-41. doi:10.1146/annurev.psych.121208.131659

Stoltenberg, C. D., Bailey, K. C., Cruzan, C. B., Hart, J. T., & Ukuku, U. (2014). The integrative developmental model of supervision. In C. E. Watkins & D. L. Milne (Eds.), *The Wiley international handbook of clinical supervision* (pp. 576-97). Hoboken, NJ: Wiley-Blackwell.

Stoltenberg, C. D., McNeill, B. W., & Delworth, U. (1998). *IDM: An integrated developmental model for supervising counselors and therapists.* San Francisco, CA: Jossey-Bass.

Stoltenberg, C. D., & McNeill, B. W. (2010). *IDM supervision: An integrative developmental model for supervising counselors and therapists* (3rd ed.). New York, NY: Brunner-Routledge.

Storm, C. L. (1997). Positive self-monitoring: Positive images lead to positive actions. In C. L. Storm & T. C. Todd (Eds.), *The reasonably complete systemic supervisor resource guide* (pp. 181-82). Needham Heights, MA: Allyn & Bacon.

Storm, C. L., & Todd, T. (2014a). Core premises and a framework for systemic/relational supervision. In T. C. Todd & C. L. Storm (Eds.), *The complete systemic supervisor: Context, philosophy, and pragmatics* (2nd ed., pp. 1-16). Hoboken, NJ: Wiley-Blackwell.

Storm, C. L., & Todd, T. (2014b). Developing contextually informed best practices in systemic supervision. In T. C. Todd & C. L. Storm (Eds.), *The complete systemic supervisor: Context, philosophy, and pragmatics* (2nd ed., pp. 337-56). Hoboken, NJ: Wiley-Blackwell.

Strawn, B. D., & Hammer, M. Y. (2013). Spiritual formation through direction at Fuller Theological Seminary School of Psychology. *Journal of Psychology and Christianity, 32*(4), 304-12.

Substance Abuse and Mental Health Services Administration. (2014). Improving Cultural Competence. Treatment Improvement Protocol (TIP) Series No. 59. HHS Publication No. (SMA) 14-4849. Rockville, MD: Substance Abuse and Mental Health Services Administration. Retrieved from: https://www.ncbi.nlm.nih.gov/books/NBK248428/

Tan, S.-Y. (1999). Holy Spirit: Role in counseling. In D. G. Benner and P. Hill (Eds.), *Baker encyclopedia of psychology and counseling* (2nd ed., pp. 568-69). Grand Rapids: Baker.

Tan, S.-Y. (2006). Applied positive psychology: Putting positive psychology into practice. *Journal of Psychology and Christianity, 25*, 68-73.

Tan, S.-Y. (2007). Using spiritual disciplines in clinical supervision. *Journal of Psychology and Christianity, 26*(4), 328-35.

Tan, S.-Y. (2009). Developing integration skills: The role of clinical supervision. *Journal of Psychology and Theology, 37*(1), 54-61.

Tan, S.-Y. (2011a). Mindfulness and acceptance-based cognitive behavioral therapies: Empirical evidence and clinical applications from a Christian perspective. *Journal of Psychology and Christianity, 30*(3), 243-49.

Tan, S.-Y. (2011b). *Counseling and psychotherapy: A Christian perspective.* Grand Rapids, MI: Baker Academic.

Tangney, J. P. (2000). Humility: Theoretical perspectives, empirical findings and directions for future research. *Journal of Social and Clinical Psychology, 19*(1), 70-82. doi:10.1521/jscp.2000.19.1.70

Tangney, J. P., Baumeister, R. F., & Boone, A. L. (2004). High self-control predicts good adjustment, less pathology, better grades, and interpersonal success. *Journal of Personality, 72*(2), 271-324. doi:10.1111/j.0022-3506.2004.00263.x

Thomas, J. T. (2007). Informed consent through contracting for supervision: Minimizing risks, enhancing benefits. *Professional Psychology, Research and Practice, 38*(3), 221-31. doi:10.1037/0735-7028.38.3.221

Thomas, J. T. (2014). International ethics for psychotherapy supervisors. In C. E. Watkins & D. L. Milne (Eds.), *The Wiley international handbook of clinical supervision* (pp. 129-54). Hoboken, NJ: Wiley-Blackwell.

Tillich, P. (1952). *The courage to be.* New Haven, CT: Yale University Press.

Tillich, P. (1975). *Systematic theology* (Vol. 2). Chicago, IL: University of Chicago Press.

Tisdale, T. C., Ziesel, J., Ying, A., Shier, K., Powell, E., Park, E., . . . Klein, M. (2013). Holding both unity and diversity: Spiritual formation at Azusa Pacific University Department of Graduate Psychology. *Journal of Psychology and Christianity, 32*(4), 291-303.

Titus, C. S. (2006). *Resilience and the virtue of fortitude.* Washington, DC: Catholic University of America Press.

Todd, T. C. (2014). Self-supervision as a universal supervision goal. In T. C. Todd & C. L. Storm (Eds.), *The complete systemic supervisor: Context, philosophy, and pragmatics* (2nd ed., pp. 17-25). Hoboken, NJ: Wiley-Blackwell.

Todd, T. C., & Storm, C. L. (Eds.). (2014). *The complete systemic supervisor: Context, philosophy, and pragmatics* (2nd ed). Hoboken, NJ: Wiley-Blackwell.

Toussaint, L., Worthington, E., & Williams, D. (2015). Introduction: Context, overview, and guiding questions. In L. Toussaint, E. L. Worthington, Jr., & D. R. Williams (Eds.), *Forgiveness and health: Scientific evidence and theories relating forgiveness to better health* (pp. 1-9). Dordrecht, Netherlands: Springer. doi:10.1007/978-94-017-9993-5_1

Urofsky, R. I., & Engels, D. W. (2003). Issues and insights: Philosophy, moral philosophy, and counseling ethics: Not an abstraction. *Counseling and Values, 47*, 118-30. doi:10.1002/j.2161-007X.2003.tb00229.x

van Deurzen, E., & Young, S. (Eds.). (2009). *Existential perspectives on supervision widening the horizon of psychotherapy and counselling.* London, UK: Palgrave and Macmillan.

Van Slyke, J. A. (2015). Understanding the moral dimension of spirituality: Insights from virtue ethics and moral exemplars. *Journal of Psychology and Christianity, 34*(3), 205-15.

Vieten C., Scammell S., Pilato R., Ammondson I., Pargament, K. I., & Lukoff, D. (2013). Spiritual and religious competencies for psychologists. *Psychology of Religion and Spirituality, 5*(3), 129-44. doi:10.1037/a0032699

Waddams, H. M. (1964). A new introduction to moral theology. London, UK: SCM Press.

Wade, J. C., & Jones, J. E. (2015). *Strength-based clinical supervision: A positive psychology approach to clinical training.* New York, NY: Springer.

Walker, D. F., & Hathaway, W. L. (Eds.). (2013). *Spiritual interventions in child and adolescent psychotherapy.* Washington, DC: American Psychological Association.

Walker, D. F., Courtois, C. A., & Aten, J. D. (Eds.). (2015). *Spiritually oriented psychotherapy for trauma.* Washington, DC: American Psychological Association. doi:10.1037/14500-000

Wang, D. C., Strosky, D., & Fletes, A. (2014). Secondary and vicarious trauma: Implications for faith and clinical practice. *Journal of Psychology and Christianity, 33*(3), 281-86.

Watkins Jr., C. E. (2014a). The supervisory alliance as quintessential integrative variable. *Journal of Contemporary Psychotherapy: On the Cutting Edge of Modern Developments in Psychotherapy, 44*(3), 151-61. doi:10.1007/s10879-013-9252-x

Watkins Jr., C. E. (2014b). The supervisory alliance: A half century of theory, practice, and research in critical perspective. *American Journal of Psychotherapy, 68*(1), 19-55. https://doi.org/10.1007/s10879-013-9252-x

Watkins, C. E., Hook, J. N., Ramaeker, J., & Ramos, M. J. (2016) Repairing the ruptured supervisory alliance: Humility as a foundational virtue in clinical supervision. *The Clinical Supervisor, 35*(1), 22-41. doi:10.1080/07325223.2015.1127190

Watkins, C. E., & Milne, D. L. (Eds.). *The Wiley international handbook of clinical supervision.* Hoboken, NJ: Wiley-Blackwell.

Watson, T. S., & Eveleigh, E. (2014). Teaching psychological theories: Integration tasks and teaching strategies. *Journal of Psychology and Theology, 42*(2), 100-110.

Watterson, K., & Giesler, R. B. (2012). Religiosity and self-control: When the going gets tough, the religious get self-regulating. *Psychology of Religion and Spirituality, 4*(3), 193-205. http://dx.doi.org/10.1037/a0027644

Webb, A., & Wheeler, S. (1998). How honest do counsellors dare to be in the supervisory relationship? An exploratory study. *British Journal of Guidance and Counselling, 26*(4), 509-24. doi:10.1080/03069889808253860

Weis, R., & Speridakos, E. C. (2011). A meta-analysis of hope enhancement strategies in clinical and community settings. *Psychology of Well-Being: Theory, Research and Practice, 1*(1), 5. doi:10.1186/2211-1522-1-5

Westberg, D. A. (2015). *Renewing moral theology: Christian ethics as action, character and grace.* Downers Grove, IL: IVP Academic.

White, M. A. (2016). Why won't it stick? Positive psychology and positive education. *Psychology of Well-Being, 6*(2). doi.org/10.1186/s13612-016-0039-1

Willard, D. (1988). *The spirit of the disciplines: Understanding how God changes lives.* New York, NY: HarperCollins.

Willard, D. (1998). Spiritual disciplines, spiritual formation and the restoration of the soul. *Journal of Psychology and Theology, 26*(1), 101-9.

Wise, E. H., Bieschke, K. J., Forrest, L., Cohen-Filipic, J., Hathaway, W. L., & Douce, L. A. (2015). Psychology's proactive approach to conscience clause court cases and legislation. *Training and Education in Professional Psychology, 9*(4), 259-68. doi:10.1037/tep0000092

Wong, K., Baker, B., & Franz, R. (2015). Reimagining business education as character formation. *Christian Scholars Review, 45*(1), 5-24.

Worthington, E. L., Jr. (2005). *Hope-focused marriage counseling: A guide to brief therapy* (Rev. ed.). Downers Grove, IL: InterVarsity Press.

Worthington, E. L., Jr., Davis, D. E., Hook, J. N., Webb, J. R., Toussaint, L., Sandage, S. J. . . . VanTongeren, D. R. (2012). Forgiveness. In T. G. Plante (Ed.), *Religion, spirituality, and positive psychology: Understanding the psychological fruits of faith* (pp. 63-78). Santa Barbara, CA: Praeger.

Worthington, E. L., Jr., Johnson, E. L., Hook, J. N., & Aten, J. D. (Eds.). (2013). *Evidence-based Practices for Christian counseling and psychotherapy.* Downers Grove, IL: IVP Academic.

Worthington, E. L., Jr., Kurusu, T. A., McCollough, M. E., & Sandage, S. J. (1996). Empirical research on religion and psychotherapeutic processes and outcomes: A 10-year review and research prospectus. *Psychological Bulletin, 119*(3), 448-87. doi:10.1037/0033-2909.119.3.448

Wright, N. T. (2006). *Simply Christian: Why Christianity makes sense.* San Francisco, CA: HarperSanFrancisco.

Wright, N. T. (2008). *Surprised by hope: Rethinking heaven, the resurrection, and the mission of the church.* New York, NY: HarperOne.

Wright, N. T. (2010). *After you believe: Why Christian character matters.* New York, NY: HarperOne.

Yalom, I. D. (1980). *Existential psychotherapy.* New York, NY: Basic Books.

Youssef, C. M., & Luthans, F. (2007). Positive organizational behavior in the workplace: The impact of hope, optimism, and resilience. *Journal of Management, 33*(5), 774-800. doi:10.1177/0149206307305562

AUTHOR INDEX

SUBJECT INDEX

SCRIPTURE INDEX

CAPS
INTERNATIONAL

An Association for Christian Psychologists,
Therapists, Counselors and Academicians

CAPS is a vibrant Christian organization with a rich tradition. Founded in 1956 by a small group of Christian mental health professionals, chaplains and pastors, CAPS has grown to more than 2,100 members in the U.S., Canada and more than 25 other countries.

CAPS encourages in-depth consideration of therapeutic, research, theoretical and theological issues. The association is a forum for creative new ideas. In fact, their publications and conferences are the birthplace for many of the formative concepts in our field today.

CAPS members represent a variety of denominations, professional groups and theoretical orientations; yet all are united in their commitment to Christ and to professional excellence.

CAPS is a non-profit, member-supported organization. It is led by a fully functioning board of directors, and the membership has a voice in the direction of CAPS.

CAPS is more than a professional association. It is a fellowship, and in addition to national and international activities, the organization strongly encourages regional, local and area activities which provide networking and fellowship opportunities as well as professional enrichment.

To learn more about CAPS, visit www.caps.net.

CAPS BOOKS
from IVP Academic

The joint publishing venture between IVP Academic and CAPS aims to promote the understanding of the relationship between Christianity and the behavioral sciences at both the clinical/counseling and the theoretical/research levels. These books will be of particular value for students and practitioners, teachers and researchers.

For more information about CAPS Books, visit InterVarsity Press's website at www.ivpress.com/christian-association-for-psychological-studies-books-set.

Finding the Textbook You Need

The IVP Academic Textbook Selector
is an online tool for instantly finding the IVP books
suitable for over 250 courses across 24 disciplines.

ivpacademic.com